EXPOSED

Living with scandal, rumour, and gossip

LUND
UNIVERSITY
PRESS

Exposed

Living with scandal, rumour, and gossip

MIA-MARIE HAMMARLIN

Translation: Lena Olsson

Lund University Press

Copyright © Mia-Marie Hammarlin 2019

The right of Mia-Marie Hammarlin to be identified as the author of this work has been asserted by her in accordance with the Copyright, Designs and Patents Act 1988.

Lund University Press

The Joint Faculties of Humanities and Theology

LUND
UNIVERSITY
PRESS

P.O. Box 117
SE-221 00 LUND
Sweden
http://lunduniversitypress.lu.se

Lund University Press books are published in collaboration with Manchester University Press.

British Library Cataloguing-in-Publication Data
A catalogue record for this book is available from the British Library

An earlier version of this book appeared in Swedish, published by Hammarlin Bokförlag in 2015 as *I stormens öga*
ISBN   978-91-9793-812-9

ISBN   978-91-983768-3-8   hardback
ISBN   978-91-983768-4-5   open access

First published 2019

An electronic version of this book is also available under a Creative Commons (CC-BY-NC-ND) licence, thanks to the support of Lund University, which permits non-commercial use, distribution and reproduction provided the author(s) and Manchester University Press are fully cited and no modifications or adaptations are made. Details of the licence can be viewed at https://creativecommons.org/licenses/by-nc-nd/4.0/

The publisher has no responsibility for the persistence or accuracy of URLs for any external or third-party internet websites referred to in this book, and does not guarantee that any content on such websites is, or will remain, accurate or appropriate.

> Lund University Press gratefully acknowledges publication assistance from the Thora Ohlsson Foundation (*Thora Ohlssons Stiftelse*)

Typeset
by Toppan Best-set Premedia Limited

Contents

Introduction		*page* 1
	The project and purpose of this book	4
	Previous research and theoretical points of departure	5
	Affects, emotions, feelings	8
	The lifeworld	12
	Swedish scandals in an international perspective	15
	The low level of corruption and the high level of trust in Sweden	17
	The meaning of the concepts	21
	Bricolage as a method	23
	A methodological experiment	25
	Flashback Forum	26
	The interviews	27
1	**In the middle of the media storm**	31
	The food-and-sleep clock	31
	The paradox of visibility and loneliness	35
	The branding and the escape	40
	Shame, self-contempt, and laughter	48
	Lies and damned lies	58
	Family, love, caring	63
	Fellowship-of-the-hounded letters	68
	How things change	72
	Concluding comment	75
2	**Gossip, rumour, and scandals**	77
	Mediated orality	77
	Chronique scandaleuse	81
	Gossip and scandals in today's media system	85
	Digital town squares	87

	The rumour about Under-Secretary of State Ingmar Ohlsson	89
	Hot topics	96
	The spatial and the social dimension	101
	The role as an *exemplum*	104
	Concluding comment	105
3	**Floorball Dad**	**107**
	Confusion	110
	Anxiety, fear, and community	115
	A child's sense of vulnerability	118
	The police interrogations	119
	The pale cast of thought	120
	News legends	123
	Passing-down and narrative contagion	126
	Fake news as folklore	128
	Concluding comment	129
4	**The journalists and the rabbits**	**131**
	The objectivity talisman	132
	Scepticism – media scandals, do they exist?	136
	Undignified behaviour and a lack of independence	139
	The art of justifying one's actions	143
	Honour, fame, and rabbits	149
	Feeling empathy	154
	Concluding comment	163

Concluding words   **165**

Appendix   169
Bibliography   182
Index   197

Introduction

At long last, twenty-seven-year-old housekeeper Katharina Blum has had enough. She raises her gun and kills reporter Werner Tötges with multiple shots. The murder takes place on a Sunday around lunchtime in Miss Blum's previously so neat and tidy flat, which is now a study in disorder. Tötges had come there to interview her. He worked for 'die ZEITUNG' – in capital letters ('the *News*' in the English translation) – which had for several days dragged Blum through the dirt, had indeed ruined her entire life. And not just her life, but also the lives of members of her family.

This brutal murder of a journalist opens Nobel Prize laureate Heinrich Böll's novel *The Lost Honour of Katharina Blum*, which sold well and occasioned debate in West Germany when it was published in 1974. The reader follows the repercussions of the cynical headlines in everyday life, described in a documentary style characterised by ironic distance. Scenes depict the concealed and open loathing to which Miss Blum is subjected. Neighbours whisper, gossip, and spread malicious rumours about her, she who was previously, before the scandalous articles, known as a loyal, proud, and correct woman. Now they stare at her and no longer want to ride in the lift with her. They avoid or attack her. Friends desert her. Acquaintances make statements about her being a shady character. Anonymous men call her at night and breathe heavily into the receiver. The newspaper's obsession with the crime Blum has supposedly committed – before the murder, that is; throughout the novel, she is accused of harbouring a fugitive from justice – gives rise to inventive interpretations of the statements made by the people around her. When Blum's aged mother exclaims in despair, 'Why did it have to end like this, why did it have to come to this?', Tötges translates this into 'It was bound to come to this, it was bound to end like this.' The justification for the change is that he, as a reporter, is used to 'helping simple people to express themselves more clearly'.[1]

Heinrich Böll himself regarded the story of Katharina Blum as a pamphlet in the sense of a polemical piece of writing which describes a person who is subjected to the most profound public humiliation through a relentless campaign of demonisation. This is a form of violation, the writer claimed, that leads to Blum losing her sense of belonging in society and being exiled into a barren landscape of loneliness. In this context, the subtitle of the book makes sense: 'How violence develops and where it can lead'. The murder of the journalist can be seen as a grim metaphor for Miss Blum's defencelessness against the mudslinging and the prying into the smallest details of her life that characterise this kind of journalism. Böll wrote in anger and claimed that even the headlining done at a newspaper's editorial office can be defined as a form of violation. His wrath against what he called the *Boulevardpresse* (gutter press), and especially the tabloid *Bild-Zeitung,* did not abate over time. Ten years after the original publication of the novel, he wrote the following in a postscript: 'It would be a task for criminology some day to investigate the problems newspapers can cause in all their bestial "innocence"' (Böll 2011:153). His powerful feelings were not only expressed in statements like this one but also in the book itself, where the characters are torn between hope and despair, a desire for revenge and shame, fury and powerlessness. While Böll's story arose from a peculiarly charged political background, it nevertheless provides insights into the possible social consequences of scandal journalism, and here I do not mean the dramatic act of vengeance carried out by Miss Blum.

Four decades after the publication of Böll's controversial book came the release of an award-winning documentary about the much-criticised American congressman Anthony Weiner. Like *The Lost Honour of Katharina Blum,* the film, which is simply called *Weiner,* supplies insights into the contagious effects that lurk in every scandal: the scandal does not simply revolve around the main figure but also pulls in the people in the immediate vicinity of the scandalised person. By way of the invasive camera, it is Huma Abedin, Anthony Weiner's wife, who is made to symbolise this fact. Her naked,

---

[1] All three quotations may be found in Heinrich Böll, *The Lost Honor of Katharina Blum, or: How,* [sic] *Violence Develops and Where It Can Lead,* trans. Leila Vennewitz (New York: Penguin, 1975), p. 105.

shifting facial expressions stay with the viewer: she is sometimes determined, sometimes vulnerable, sometimes angry, sometimes in despair. The look she occasionally gives her husband, in connection with the exposure of his frequent sex-chatting with young women, is heavy with venom. As his electoral support plummets, she seems to hate him while at the same time, almost reluctantly, loving his increasingly broken figure. Her vulnerability is beyond question, and it appears to be on a par with that of her husband, or perhaps even greater than his. The whole thing is excruciating to watch. And very entertaining.

It should, by way of introduction, be said that media landscapes differ a great deal from one country to another. Scandals in Sweden cannot be directly compared to scandals in the United States, or to scandals in other parts of the world for that matter. At the same time, scandals are connected across the borders of countries and across continents, not only through the universal, emotional experiences undergone by the main figures of these scandals and their families, but also through a kind of resilience over time that characterises the phenomenon in question. This is one of the things that the present book will demonstrate.

What is unique about the stories of the fictive character Katharina Blum and the real-life Anthony Weiner is that they succeed in illuminating dimensions of media scandals that have escaped the attention of many people, not least scholars: the scandals in no way play out in the media only; they find their sustenance, their breath of life, outside the media, in regular everyday conversations and interactions between people. Ultimately this deficiency has to do with a limited interpretation of *media* in the term *media scandal*, where it is assumed that scholars agree on what this word means. There are, of course, those who recognise and are interested in the complexity of the phenomenon; in the present publication I refer to several of these researchers, and like them I want to investigate media scandals as social and cultural phenomena. The scandals neither begin nor end in the newsrooms but branch out into people's everyday lives and take shape through a number of different, interconnected forms of communication. Media scandals say something essential about how we get along with one another. After having sat face to face with several people who have been at the centre of this type of reporting, and journalists who have contributed to it in one way or another, listening to their stories, I am convinced that this is true. But let us begin at the beginning.

The project and purpose of this book

This book was written within the framework of a multidisciplinary research project financed by the Joint Faculties of Humanities and Theology at Lund University. The project, which is called 'Mediedrevets mekanismer och aktörer' ('Media houndings – mechanisms and actors'), should, according to its description, include perspectives from media and communication studies as well as from ethnology applied to the phenomenon of mediated scandals. It is directed by myself, an ethnologist, former journalist, and Senior Lecturer of Media and Communication Studies, and by Gunilla Jarlbro, Professor of Media and Communication Studies. Both of us are active at the Department of Communication and Media at Lund University. In previous project publications we have combined quantitative and qualitative data, for instance in a detailed study of the so-called 'Toblerone affair' – with the then Deputy Prime Minister of Sweden, Mona Sahlin, in the leading role (Hammarlin & Jarlbro 2012) – and in the book *Kvinnor och män i offentlighetens ljus* ('Women and men in the public eye'; Hammarlin & Jarlbro 2014). In another study we foreground perspectives from cultural history on public scandals, where the view of these as a typical present-day phenomenon is problematised (Hammarlin 2013a). The historical perspectives provide the focus of yet another ongoing research project, which is a kind of extension of the one mentioned above and funded by the foundation Ridderstads Stiftelse (Hammarlin & Jönsson 2017:93–115).

The orientation of the present book is ethnological and phenomenological. I want to bring out more or less forgotten universal human existential aspects of media scandals, among other things by paying attention to the emotions of the affected parties. They feel what most of us would have experienced if we had ended up at the centre of a scandal, that is, anything from shame and self-contempt to grief, anxiety, fear, anger, and the desire for revenge. Because emotions – which are of course relational in nature – bind us together as people and help us enter into one another's lifeworlds, this is what I have chosen as my analytical point of departure. By giving space to people – and their families – who have experienced media scandals from within in their roles as protagonists, I hope to be able to increase the understanding of what a media scandal does to the life of an individual, but also of what these people do with the media scandal, considered as an experience.

Introduction

The purpose is dual, but intertwined: my intention is partly to explore the emotional experience of being the main figure of a media scandal, partly to study the complex media circuits that create the scandal. The following questions accompany this study: What does the scandal feel like for the person who is affected by it, and what can these emotions teach us about both people and media? How is the scandal as a phenomenon possible, i.e., through which media and which journalistic genres, in a wide sense, is it created? And in relation to this: how is the scandal created and re-created through gossip and rumour?

The last question underlines my special interest in the relationship between oral, interpersonal, face-to-face communication and communication via traditional and digital media, where I find folkloristic perspectives on news particularly useful. I will also investigate the relationship between the persons who are written about and the reporters who stir up and add fuel to media scandals. The reporters also experience and live through the scandals via the practice of their profession. I wished to establish a dialogue between people at opposing ends of the drama after the scandal has died down. They do not encounter one another in reality; but they meet here, in the text, through language. For this reason attention is paid not only to research about media scandals, but also to a number of published texts written by Swedish journalists who deal with the phenomenon critically and with curiosity. Such a reflective text was written by the internationally well-respected Swedish publicist and author Göran Rosenberg (2000). He describes journalists who, like beaters and hounds, hunt 'rabbits', i.e., the central figures of the scandals – an allegory to which I keep returning.

Perhaps the purpose of a study can also be expressed in a negation. If so, it would sound like this: the purpose is not to persuade the reader to feel sorry for the affected individuals. Instead, the accounts of experiences should be considered as an indispensable source for understanding media scandals better – how they arise, how they develop, how they gain energy, and how they are experienced.

Previous research and theoretical points of departure

One of the reasons for this emotion-orientated introduction to the topic is that such a perspective is missing in social-science-influenced media research, where emotions are often conspicuous by their absence. This may seem surprising because the field in fact quivers with emotion, dealing as it does with a topic described by Norwegian media researchers Anders Todal Jenssen and Audun Fladmoe as exhibiting a special kind of aura which is largely occasioned by indignation. A person who comments on a scandal can show his or her anger without reservations through the choice of words and facial expressions. They write that words such as 'shocking', 'scandalous', and 'reprehensible' in combination with raised eyebrows and an indignant tone of voice are typical of media scandals (Jenssen & Fladmoe 2012:64). However, these authors do not conduct an in-depth analysis of the emotional expressions themselves in relation to the scandal. There is a gap to be filled here. In order to understand the scandal as a phenomenon, we need to understand the emotions it engenders.

Research on media scandals gathered momentum during the beginning of the twenty-first century, not least in the Nordic countries, where two anthologies were published (Allern & Pollack 2009, 2012c). The fact that media scandals are more and more often the object of scientific analysis appears logical because public scandals are increasing in number, keeping pace with the expansion of the media industry. In a comparison among the Nordic countries, some researchers maintain that there has been a significant increase in the number of scandals during the most recent decades, where Sweden is in the lead with an almost fivefold increase during the period from 1980 to 2010 (Allern et al. 2012; see also Thompson 2008:106–18 for a discussion of the general increase in the West). Scholarly descriptions of the reasons for the increase in frequency are part of a picture of the industry with which we are nowadays quite familiar, where an increased number of actors and intensified competition – as well as convergence – among different media in an increasingly digitalised and competitive media market lead to a type of journalism that to an ever greater extent rests on a commercial rather than an ideological basis, sales figures coming before altruistic ideals (Deuze 2005:443–65, Allern & Pollack 2009:193–207, Deuze 2014:119–30).[2]

A scholarly convention seems to have come into existence regarding how media scandals are to be studied. In line with that convention, several researchers have – besides counting scandals – to a great extent been busy defining what media scandals, particularly political scandals, *are* on the basis of an almost essentialist interest. This is done by determining the temporal and dramaturgical development of

---

[2] I will return to this discussion in greater detail in Chapter 4.

scandals, creating typologies of media scandals, dividing scandals into genres, evaluating various currently popular terms and, in addition, introducing new names for them (see Sabato 1993, Lull & Hinerman 1997, Wien & Elmelund-Præstekær 2007, 2009, Ekström & Johansson 2008, Allern et al. 2012, Boydstun et al. 2014, Jenssen & Fladmoe 2012).[3] Often this has to do with content studies, which means that the scholar in question examines media production in itself and its publications, often press materials. The project in which I am myself active has also conducted investigations of this type, and on the whole these provide valuable knowledge.

When I use the term *media scandal* I lean on this research, but at the same time I regard it with circumspection. While following in the footsteps of these earlier studies, my ambition is to move beyond them. I want to argue that the human aspect is lost in this type of investigation. To be sure, these studies teach us more about the functions of the media – that is, after all, their express purpose – but rather little about the ways in which human beings function. Instead, I see the present book as a contribution to the few anthropologically influenced studies of mediated scandals (Bird 1997, 2003), as well as to those with a historical perspective (Thompson 2008, Darnton 1997, 2000, 2004, 2005, 2010) and those influenced by social psychology (Wästerfors 2005, 2008).

As a natural consequence of my interest in the cultural dimension of media scandals, I am also interested in another type of communication, namely that which takes place during interpersonal meetings. I want to explore how this kind of communication relates to communication conveyed through the media. Daniel Dayan and Elihu Katz's now classic analyses of the public sphere as an interaction between the media and the audience where mediated communication encounters interpersonal communication, such as conversations, actions, and the creation of public opinion, have influenced my understanding of the cultural dimension of media scandals and how

---

3 Such labels include *political scandal*, which is subdivided into *sex scandal*, *financial scandal*, and *power scandal* (Thompson 2008); closely related is the *mediated political scandal* (Midtbø 2007, Todal Jenssen 2014); the *talk scandal*, with its subcategories *first-order talk scandal* and *second-order talk scandal* (Ekström and Johansson, 2008); the *moral scandal* (Djerf-Pierre et al. 2013); the *SMS scandal* (Laine 2010); *political wave-making* (Wolfsfeld and Schaefer 2006); *media hype* (Elmelund-Præstekær & Wien 2008, 2009); and the *media storm* or *media waves*, with the subgenres *wave storm*, *spike storm*, and *non-storm* (Boydstun et al. 2014).

different forms of communication interact (see Dayan & Katz 1992). I have also been inspired by media researcher David Morley's call for a kind of analytic decentralisation. He writes: 'we need to "decentre" the media, in our analytical framework, so as to better understand the ways in which media processes and everyday life are interwoven with each other' (Morley 2007:200).

Like all ethnologists, I take everyday life as my point of departure. It is through a focus on everyday life that the function and significance of the media, and their importance in people's lives, can be made visible. Hence, decentring the media does not mean that they are relegated to the background. Rather, I wish to show how deeply integrated they are into our culture and our everyday lives.

Affects, emotions, feelings

Should one, on the basis of the above, assume that studying emotions is not in favour within media studies? Not at all. A research survey lists over 400 studies within the media field where emotions (or, more correctly, affects) are foregrounded (Wirth & Schramm 2005). From the 1960s until the early twenty-first century traditional research on effects dominated the field, with a focus on emotional reactions to media consumption or media stimuli. Through experiments scholars have, for instance, studied facial expressions and other physical signals in order to connect reactions to certain types of media stimuli, or to map these reactions by way of interview answers.[4] The now heavily criticised tradition within media and communication studies of effects research – research built on stimulus–response models that were problematised as early as the 1970s (Gerbner & Gross 1976) – lives on, not least within the area of emotions. In summary, the interpretations of emotions within psychology, medicine, and cognitive science may be said to have had quite an

---

4 The belief in the possibility of measuring short- or long-term emotional effects resulting from people's media use is not so easily dislodged. An impressively voluminous anthology with the title *The Routledge Handbook of Emotions and Mass Media* (Döveling et al. 2011) presents a number of studies on emotional expressions awakened as a result of mass-media consumption, with keywords such as *measurement, gratification, response, control, influence, reactivity, persuasion*, and *coping*. The majority of the writers focus on psychological effects and on the reactions of individuals as a consequence of media use, i.e., how these effects and reactions arise and are expressed within individuals.

impact on multidisciplinarily orientated media and communication studies, where emotions are often treated as phenomena that can be classified, categorised, and measured, and that are assumed to be important for a person's inner life rather than for what is happening outside the individual human being.

It is time to take this knowledge on board and venture to move towards a more context-orientated view of emotions, as sociologist Jack Katz argued almost two decades ago with the following exhortation: 'A next challenge is to develop empirically grounded explanations of emotions as they rise and decline in the vibrant flow of social life' (Katz 1999:3). It is fair to say that Katz's call was heeded. Alongside the production of psychologically focused studies, a newly awakened interest in perspectives on emotion in cultural analysis, sociology, and social psychology became apparent during the early twenty-first century and had an impact on a number of social-science disciplines as well as on society in general. As time went by, this development came to be known as *the affective turn*, foregrounding – among other things – an acute need for an academic rapprochement between different disciplines, such as psychology and sociology (see Clough & O'Malley Halley 2007). The key role of emotions in the elementary forms of social life had been neglected for a long time, certain theoreticians claimed, and that neglect had impeded a social-science-based understanding of the basic conditions of human beings here on earth. Since then, during the most recent decade, interdisciplinary studies of affects and emotions have spawned a veritable explosion of research and theory development within this area. In addition to supplying valuable knowledge, this has contributed vigorous discussions regarding the concepts being used, concepts which often mean different things to different scholars from various disciplines: *affect*, *emotion*, *feeling*, *sentiment*. Simply put, it may be said that *affect* is customarily used as an umbrella term which includes all the above-mentioned concepts, but it also denotes physical and internal experiences. Traditionally speaking, *emotion* has signified the social dimension of feelings, whereas the word *feelings* itself has mostly been used as a synonym for the two first-mentioned terms (see Frykman & Povrzanović Frykman 2016:9–28 for an exhaustive survey of the concepts). I personally agree with the idea that it can be hazardous to insist too strongly on the differences between these concepts, because this, too, risks becoming a simplified classification of the emotions (Frykman & Povrzanović Frykman 2016:15ff). It seems considerably more productive to focus on what emotions *do* rather than what they *are*. In this book, that view finds expression in an ethnological method whereby emotions are observed in everyday life through ethnographic studies (Ahmed 2004:14, Frykman & Povrzanović Frykman 2016:17ff). As ethnologists Jonas Frykman and Maja Povrzanović Frykman write: 'the focus on practice – what affect *does* – also tends to widen the scope for what it *is*' (Frykman & Povrzanović Frykman 2016:16). Criticism has also been levelled at the very idea of the affective turn – did it happen at all? – and at literature which, in sweeping terms, maintains that the affective turn had a liberating influence on studies that deal with people's lives. Therefore, I try to accept anthropologist Stef Jansen's challenge regarding the need for clarification when briefly explaining my own points of departure below (Jansen 2016:55–79; see also Gilje 2016:31–55).

At the beginning of the twenty-first century, in conjunction with the newly awakened interest in emotions in the social sciences, the study of emotions developed within Swedish ethnology as well, not least in Lund. As a result, this field of inquiry became more methodologically and theoretically useful than it had been before. Here, too, scholars dissociated themselves from the psychological and medical view of emotions while simultaneously using it as a point of departure. That view sometimes makes emotions appear as things held in a container within us, placed in what is usually, for lack of better words, called the soul, and this container may become full and overflow, making us ill if we do not empty it at regular intervals. The danger of such an instrumental view is that emotions are then only allowed to say something about our own internal existence and not about the world. Jean-Paul Sartre expresses his criticism of this view in explicit terms: 'La conscience émotionnelle est d'abord conscience du monde' (Sartre 2002:70) – 'the emotional consciousness is primarily consciousness of the world' (Sartre 2002:34). A point of departure for an ethnologist could thus be the use of empirical studies to try to understand how emotions make the world appear. Our interest should be directed at how my and other people's individual emotions correspond to the world, reflect it, affect it, and transform it. Emotions are individual and universal at the same time. They are relational 'interspatial phenomena' and always actualise a relationship to the Other (Frykman & Löfgren 2005:17; see also Ehn & Löfgren 2004). As we all know, emotional states such as dread, fear, and elation have a strange ability to spread within a group. In fact, language is rich in expressions for how moods are transposed and reproduced non-verbally, as in the following sentence: 'The atmosphere was so dense that one could cut it with a knife' (see Frykman 2012:23–36). Or, in the almost poetic words of communications scholar Gregory Seigworth and cultural researcher Melissa Gregg:

> [C]ast forward by its open-ended in-between-ness, affect is integral to a body's perpetual *becoming* (always becoming otherwise, however subtly, than what it already is), pulled beyond its seeming surface-boundedness by way of its relation to, indeed its composition through, the forces of encounter. With affect, a body is as much outside itself as in itself – webbed in its relations – until ultimately such firm distinctions cease to matter. (Gregg & Seigworth 2010:3; original emphasis)

It is this intervening space between subjects, and the space between an individual and society, that Gregg and Seigworth feel can offer new paths to an understanding not only of emotions themselves but of the context, culture, and time in which they operate. Thus it is not emotions in themselves that are the object of study here; the intention is to use them as a point of departure in order to be better able to understand the social,cultural, and historical anchoring and significance of media scandals. Stef Jansen calls this 'go[ing] beyond evocation', one of several options for ethnologists and anthropologists who study emotions (Jansen 2016:55–79). Their vagueness may entail analytical challenges, but that vagueness can also be considered an asset for the same reason; complex and ambiguous, emotions open up for the meeting between subject and object, instinct and fantasy, the conscious and the unconscious, body and thought, individual and collective. Emotions can function as indicators of inactivity, of something that is happening or is about to happen; a reiteration, a reinforcement, a change, a degradation (Frykman & Löfgren 2005:15). The fact that Swedish has a single word (*känsla*) for haptic experience, sensation, and mood can be confusing. For example, feeling grief can be indicated by the same word as touching something with one's hand, a sensory quality: *känna* (feel/touch), just as the mood in a room can be described with the noun of the same word: *känsla* (mood). Here the English language is more precise.[5]

---

[5] Gender scholar Melissa Autumn White has written about the affective turn in relation to her own field of study in different contexts. She concisely explains the respective significance of and the differences among the three concepts *emotion, feeling,* and *affect*: 'Where emotion might be thought of as a capture of affect – an "intensity owned and recognized" by the subject (Massumi 2002:28), and feeling closely linked to the perception and movement of sensation, Clough et al. draw on Deleuze (and ultimately Spinoza) to consider affect as intensity related to a capacity and potential to act. In a Spinozan sense, affect refers to the "power to act," the simultaneous power to affect the world and to be affected by it' (White 2007:183).

The point of departure in this book is, however, the word *feelings*, which is anchored in an everyday context to a greater extent than *affects* and *emotions*. Even so, I, too, am in need of synonyms when I write, which is why I also use other words.

Very little research has been done on the experiences of the central figure of a media scandal, but they are not completely absent in the literature on the subject (Brurås 2004, Johansson 2006, Kepplinger 2007, 2016, Bjerke 2012; see also Pihlblad 2010, Karlsen & Duckert 2018). These studies contain traces of what I want to foreground in this study, namely how the stories in the media reach beyond the media context itself and into everyday life; but as a rule, a reader learns rather little about what these people have experienced on an emotional and existential level. The feelings experienced in a Swedish context by the central figures of the scandals I examine may, of course, be different from how scandals affect people in other cultural contexts. In the words of Harvard Professor Robert A. LeVine: 'Rather than seeking to isolate the basic elements of universal building blocks of emotional experience, ethnographers seek to uncover and understand that experience *in all its complexity* in a particular setting' (LeVine 2007:398; emphasis added). At the same time, the emotions that are described in this book have a universal character, not least shame, which is carefully studied in certain sections of the book.

The lifeworld

On the basis of the phenomenological concept of the *lifeworld*, I thus wish to study how the life of an individual is affected by a media scandal and how the scandal is manifested as an experience, something that is related to the discussion above. 'Feelings connect people to the surrounding world – feelings situate people in a lifeworld', writes Frykman (2012:39). As has already been mentioned, I take my point of departure in the individual as an *experiencer*, an acting subject among other acting subjects, where the theoretical direction is taken from a phenomenological view of human beings as actors with a certain freedom of action. In their everyday lives they move, do things, plan, reflect on things, feel, sort, and organise their lives.

Phenomenologist Alfred Schutz's (1970, 1973, 1989) interpretation of the lifeworld plays a particularly important role in the present book. He describes the lifeworld as the reality in which we live and which we take for granted, a world that is immediately and directly experienced through the actions of the subject and his or her meetings with other subjects in everyday life. Schutz uses the expression 'the social, natural attitude' to denote the original relationship between subject and world, our daily lives that make up the often overlooked prerequisite for all actions, all social intercourse, all emotions, and all reflections (Schutz 1973:59). A curiosity about people as acting beings, experiencers, and creators of meaning rather than as recipients and interpreters of diverse messages is the central starting-point in the present book, irrespective of whether I study them online or offline; that curiosity also connects my work to that of researchers who have emphasised the importance of a phenomenological and existential attitude to communication and media. We create meaning through that which surrounds us. Here I find phenomenologist and media scholar Amanda Lagerkvist's studies inspiring. Her simple and beautiful phrase 'questions concerning digital technologies are ... questions about human existence' (Lagerkvist 2017:97) forms a kind of point of departure for my research as well. On the basis of Martin Heidegger's concept of *thrownness*, Lagerkvist poses the initial question: '*What does it mean to be a human being in the digital age?*' (Lagerkvist 2017:97; original emphasis). She believes that a new form of idiosyncratic, existential vulnerability has taken shape alongside the development towards what is called the 'culture of connectivity', a process which originates in digital technology and which to a great extent takes place through social media (Lagerkvist 2017). What surrounds us is also something we are forced to begin from and relate to. Focusing on everyday life, it becomes clear that encounters among people, things, and places are something we have to think about and deal with; those encounters form the 'ready-to-hand' that causes the results of our actions to mostly be something completely different from what we originally expected (Frykman 2012:21). Lagerkvist writes:

> Following Heidegger, our thrownness implies being faced with a world where we are precariously situated in a particular place, at a particular historical moment, and among a particular crowd with the inescapable task of tackling our world around us and making it meaningful. (Lagerkvist 2017:97)

The present book will, I hope, contribute curious, open questions, with the scandal as a phenomenon at the centre of attention. In my view, mediated scandals say something specific about what it means to be a human being among other human beings, or, if you will, a humane human being among other humane human beings, at a certain time and in a certain cultural context. We are human by nature, but we can only become humane human beings in a community (Kindeberg 2011:42f, 67f).

Communication theorist James W. Carey's theories (1992, 1998) are also of significance for this analysis. In his studies he foregrounds the importance of anthropology and phenomenology for understanding the relationship between communication and culture. Carey's innovative view (at the time of its introduction) of media technology as being both incorporated into culture – i.e., ultimately inseparable from it – and equipped with a unique capacity to affect and transform its development has given him a special position within that part of media and communication studies where cultural studies have been particularly influential. In the now classic book *Communication as Culture* (1992) Carey investigates, among other issues, how the introduction of the telegraph led to revolutionary transformations of entire societies and changed people's views on and relationship to basic phenomena such as place and time. Media development affects 'the habits of mind and structures of thought', he writes (Carey 1992:2). At bottom, this has to do with symbolic processes through which reality is produced, constructed, maintained, renegotiated, and transformed (Carey 1992:23, 30). According to Carey's view, culture is thus not expressed through mass-mediated communication because this communication is in fact a significant part of culture itself. The symbols and signs that are conveyed in this manner create and transform reality, laying the foundation for human existential conditions.

But what does Carey mean by 'culture' in this context? With reference to Peter L. Berger and Thomas Luckmann, he might be said to succeed in breathing some life into this well-worn word by seeing it as 'a set of practices, a mode of human activity, a process whereby reality is created, maintained, and transformed, however much it may subsequently become reified into a force independent of human action' (Carey 1992:65). However, there is reason to be sceptical regarding Carey's frequent use of the word 'symbolic'. The pervasive processes of the media are symbolic, he writes repeatedly in his book. In what way are they not also concrete and tangible in an everyday context? As a reader, one suspects the presence of a lingering idea of media as being *something else*, that is to say, something that merely conveys reality rather than forming a self-evident part of it, in spite of Carey's desire to settle accounts concerning precisely this idea.

On the basis of this framework I wish to argue that knowledge about media scandals, and about mediated stories in a wider sense, has been restricted by a sort of academic barrier where researchers in their analyses often distinguish stories in the media from other types of narrative forms, and mediated communication from other pathways of communication. Making such distinctions separates these stories from the human context out of which they spring. Here, the concept of culture can function as an opening, or, as anthropologist Elizabeth Bird writes: '[w]e really cannot isolate the role of the media in culture, because the media are firmly anchored into the web of culture' (Bird 2003:30). One could say the same about media scandals: they are not just embedded in culture; they also contribute to maintaining its boundaries.

Swedish scandals in an international perspective

'But how could this have become a scandal in the first place?? I don't get it!' Over the years, my colleague Annette Hill, Professor of Media and Communication Studies at Lund University, has never ceased to be amazed at my material on Swedish media scandals. In comparison to scandals in England, they occasionally appear quaint. In her eyes, they often have to do with trivial matters that are nowhere near to forming serious transgressions of norms. And yet the hounding begins, time after time. Swedish scandals may, from an outside perspective, have to do with insignificant issues; but the extent of the reporting is, conversely, surprising in the other direction – so much fuss for so little! On the one hand, Swedish scandals often come closer to what could be classified as 'rather inappropriate behaviour'[6] than is the case in many other countries. On the other hand, all the major media usually tag along when the ground starts shaking under a public figure, with the result that events that would elsewhere lead to insignificant local affairs become matters of national concern in Sweden. This is of course an advantage for a researcher of scandals – here one has many opportunities to study the phenomenon in question.

I have also become aware of these cultural differences when presenting my research results to colleagues at conferences, as a

---

6 With the exception of sexually related affairs, for which we seem to have greater forbearance in comparison to other countries. Thus far the myth of the sexually liberal Swedes seems to be correct, at least in part. On the other hand, two of the scandals studied in this book have sexual connotations.

few examples will illustrate. At an international conference on political scandals at Stockholm University, I presented a detailed analysis of the so-called 'Toblerone affair', one of the political scandals that have engraved themselves on the collective memory of the Swedish people (Hammarlin & Jarlbro 2012:113–33). At the centre of the scandal was Mona Sahlin, who was at that time, in 1995, the Deputy Prime Minister and presumptive new chair of the Social Democratic Party, and thus automatically the future Prime Minister. Her crime? To have bought a Toblerone chocolate bar and a pack of nappies, paying for them with her government credit card. I did not get further than this in my lecture before a British professor in the front row succumbed to an attack of the giggles. He tried to stop himself by holding his hand to his mouth. Rather concerned, I then wished to make it clear that Mona Sahlin had in fact borrowed some 50,000 Swedish crowns from the public purse, intending, it is true, to pay the money back, which she also did in several cases. This made the professor in question burst into a guffaw. Afterwards he apologised and said, highly amused, 'This is just *too* amazing! It's so incredibly funny!' And then he explained at length what all we nerdy scandal researchers already knew, namely that sentences were just then being passed on British Members of Parliament after a massive police investigation. The so-called MPs' Expenses Scandal shook up the entire British political system when it was unravelled in the news media in 2009. The *Daily Telegraph* had had the sense to make use of a reinforcement of the right of access, which led to stunning revelations on the astronomical expenses claimed by MPs for private purposes. For instance, an already wealthy politician demanded money for draining the moat to his thirteenth-century castle. Another claimed expenses for changing the plumbing at his tennis court. Some additional Members of Parliament employed their children in various advantageous positions within the administration. The calculated lack of transparency and liability caused strong public anger, where the parliamentary allowances routines were perceived to be the real offence (van Heerde-Hudson & Ward 2014:4–5). The scandal led to a number of MPs and ministers having to step down from their positions. Later came a dozen or so convictions, most of them for some form of corruption.

When I delivered a number of lectures about my research at the Department of Communication and Journalism at the University of Kerala, in southern India, there were similar reactions. Teachers and students did not laugh; but again and again they asked how much money the financial scandals actually involved, in order to ensure that they had heard aright. Could there really be a scandal over such a tiny amount? Was it really just a few hundred euros? Is it true that one minister was forced to throw in the towel after having neglected to pay their TV licence fee? The only way to describe the Indian political climate regarding the scandal phenomenon in a reasonably even-handed manner is to say that people have contracted *scandal fatigue* (Kumlin & Esaiasson 2012:263–82). In India, the scandals are so vast and occur so frequently that news reporting about them is incorporated in everyday media activities in a way that makes them, in spite of their magnitude, pass by comparatively unnoticed. Slowly but surely, the scandal phenomenon has depreciated in value.[7]

The low level of corruption and the high level of trust in Sweden

Even though this issue has been insufficiently investigated, it is obvious to every researcher in this narrow field of media studies that certain behaviour which can cause a scandal in one country will be overlooked in another. I would like to argue that Sweden is a particularly interesting country to study if you want to understand mediated scandals: why they arise, how they develop, and how they affect people. In Sweden the threshold seems to be exceptionally low, in particular with regard to financial irregularities, but also when it comes to other types of transgressive behaviour in public individuals. This claim occasions a brief historical excursion into Swedish culture.

Every now and then, more or less successful attempts are made by researchers to describe the essence of Swedishness. One such attempt that has received some international attention is a book by historians Henrik Berggren and Lars Trägårdh, *Är svensken människa? Gemenskap och oberoende i det moderna Sverige* ('Are Swedes human beings? Community and independence in modern Sweden') (Berggren & Trägårdh 2015).[8] In this book, just as in the classic

---

7 In 2016 India ended up in seventy-ninth place among 176 countries in the 'Corruption Perceptions Index 2016'. However, development seems tentatively to be going in the right direction. See *Transparency International*, http://www.transparency.org/news/feature/corruption_perceptions_index_2016 (accessed 7 March 2019).
8 The acclaimed documentary *The Swedish Theory of Love* from 2016, by director Erik Gandini, is based on this book.

ethnology book *Den kultiverade människan* (Frykman & Löfgren 1979, translated into English as *Culture Builders: A Historical Anthropology of Middle-Class Life*, 1987), certain crucial developments in Swedish society are described, including the radical transformation of society during the latter part of the nineteenth century from agriculture to urbanisation, from farm life to city life. During that century, a number of Swedish philosophers, authors, scientists, and politicians managed in a fascinating way to create direct connections between the Lutheran ideals of an agricultural society, characterised by strictness, conscientiousness, and duty, and a more universal egalitarian philosophy inspired by Enlightenment France. The Nordic version of the Enlightenment was not utopian but anchored in the pragmatic rationality of the agricultural community (Berggren & Trägårdh 2015:98). Applied to class structures that were made visible and questioned during the nineteenth century, this combination of ideals became a revolutionary force.

Out of these different movements sprang the rational Social Democracy that was to shape government politics in Sweden – and other Nordic countries – for almost a century. Its egalitarian Enlightenment ideology characterised the modern project throughout the twentieth century. There are many Swedish traits that are characteristic of this period; I would like to mention two well-known ones which are interrelated and may be linked to the subject of this study: *equality* and *social trust*. During the twentieth century Sweden, together with the other Nordic countries, stood out as evincing significantly smaller class differences than Southern and Central Europe. These differences reflect circumstances such as a higher level of employment and a narrower distribution of wages, as well as a redistributive welfare state. The class differences eroded on a long-term basis until the mid-1980s, after which the levelling stagnated for a period. Since the end of the 1990s class differences in Sweden have increased little by little as a consequence of liberal currents, increased unemployment, an increase in the income of high-salary groups, and changes in redistribution (Vogel 2003:43–79, Vogel & Råbäck 2003:81–101). Nevertheless, Sweden remains one of the world's most egalitarian countries, distinguishing itself by – relatively speaking – continued small class differences between the upper and lower strata of society as well as by equality between the sexes (Wilkinson & Pickett 2010).

In addition, there seem to be exciting connections between equality in the Nordic countries and the absence of corruption, something that seems to promote the formation of *social capital*. This concept can, in simple terms, be interpreted as a kind of lubrication for society, a lubrication composed of qualities and resources that facilitate collective actions and cooperation with ultimately beneficial effects on democracy and on civil morality, for instance trust between people, social networks of different kinds, and an experience of reciprocity (Putnam 1995:65–78, 2000).

Swedish political scientist Bo Rothstein has devoted a significant part of his professional life to studying social capital, in particular *social trust*, which is an aspect of his colleague Robert M. Putnam's original concept. The overarching question found in this theory formation is this: Which qualities in social relationships result in people's cooperation being based upon trust? In several studies, Rothstein's point of departure is his own native country – a country which is at the top of global statistics with respect to social capital and trust among people and which is, in addition, almost top of the class with respect to anti-corruption (Rothstein 2007).[9] In 2014, 64 per cent of Swedish citizens answered in the affirmative to the assertion that 'Most people can be trusted', a remarkably high figure, globally speaking, and one which has fluctuated only marginally over time.[10]

However, things have not always been this sunny with respect to trust in general. When Rothstein depicts Swedish society during the first decades of the nineteenth century, a dark and dirty picture emerges. Corruption and cliquishness were ubiquitous; in addition, contacts with the upper reaches of society determined which positions a person could attain within public administration and were generally more highly valued than hard work and a good education, even within the universities (Rothstein 2007). One and the same person within the top tier of the administration could, for instance, draw several full-time salaries simultaneously, in spite of unclear working duties. Top civil servants could also enjoy a number of other feudal-seeming privileges, such as income from land and housing which, as it were, 'came with the job' (Rothstein 2007).

During the latter part of the nineteenth century, however, there were gradual structural changes in the direction of more Weberian

---

9 In 2016 Sweden ended up in fourth place among 176 countries: 'Corruption Perceptions Index 2016', *Transparency International*, http://www.transparency.org/news/feature/corruption_perceptions_index_2016 (accessed 7 March 2019).

10 Cross-country surveys, *Our World in Data*, https://ourworldindata.org/trust (accessed 7 March 2019).

bureaucratic ideals. Rothstein maintains that the whole idea of what the profession of civil servant really implies, and should imply, slowly changed during this half-century, from a set of functions and roles that were acquired through nepotism and patronage and included special privileges to a full-time job which was attained through meritocratic examination on the basis of universal rules and laws, and which was remunerated at a fixed salary. Of course corruption remained in the system, but it was no longer seen as 'standard operating procedure' (Rothstein 2007). The people's trust in the civil service and its officials increased, little by little; and according to the theory of interpersonal trust, it is precisely this confidence in officials that is the directly decisive factor for the social capital of a society. Investigations show that the likelihood that people one does not know will behave honestly increases if public institutions function in the manner they are meant to. Expressed in terms of trust, one can say that if you trust the honesty of officials, you probably also trust people in general (Rothstein 2013:1009–32).

In a broader perspective, these circumstances illustrate the relationship of Swedish people to social institutions, such as the family and the state. Berggren and Trägårdh assert, by way of an ideal-typical classification of different kinds of welfare logic, that Sweden as a nation has developed an exceptionally strong connection between the state and the individual, at the expense of the relationship between the individual and the family. In this respect Sweden is similar to Germany, but the view of what constitutes the basic unit in society is different. In Sweden, the authors claim, the individual citizen is at the centre. It is toward him or her that measures and resources are directed, without going through the family or private organisations. 'In this way, the individual is protected from the risk of ending up in a position of dependency towards parents, spouses, or charity organisations', they write (Berggren & Trägårdh 2015:82). The thesis that the writers argue for is that Swedes have over time, because of strong ties to the state, been able to develop an individualism which is exceptional in an international comparison, with independence and self-realisation as bywords. This self-realisation is, however, culturally regulated insofar as it should preferably not happen at the expense of the happiness and success of other people, the idea of individual freedom acting alongside a strong egalitarian ideal. Berggren and Trägårdh again: 'Modern Sweden is less a collectivist project emerging from a warm solidarity and more a fusion of an individualistic view on human beings and a strong egalitarian tradition' (Berggren & Trägårdh 2015:167). In popular parlance in Sweden, this doubleness is called *Jantelagen* ('the Law of Jante'), in reference to a set of ironic maxims which declare that a person must not believe that he or she is in any way special, although there is no prohibition against attempting to attain that status (Daun 1996:52, 207).

All this – the consistently low level of corruption, the social trust, egalitarianism, and the Law of Jante – is more or less explicitly expressed in Swedish mediated scandals. Through these characteristics, corruption is held at bay, morality and a sense of duty are re-established, and the elite are taken down from their pedestals. The Swedish National Council for Crime Prevention (Brå), which is administered by the Ministry of Justice, writes in one of its reports:

> It could be that different revelations and scandals have led to an increased awareness of corruption, which has in its turn produced better routines, reviews of guidelines, and improved controls. One bold idea is that the problems with corruption might have been reduced, especially in forms that are visible and more apt to attract suspicion.[11]

By way of conclusion, I would like to emphasise that Swedish scandals appear odd only when they are placed at the cultural periphery. To Swedes, this scandal behaviour is what one would expect. In the eyes of a Swede, by contrast, the British MPs' expenses scandal appears horrendous and almost unbelievable in its seriousness and scope. As for the Indian scandals, they should not even be mentioned in this context; they come across as fiction more than anything else. Nor is it this or that particular scandal in this or that country which is at the focus of this study. Rather, I emphasise universal and general human aspects – that is to say, what it means for a human being to become publicly disgraced, as well as what the scandal as a phenomenon can teach us about both historical and contemporary media systems. I use the stories of individuals as points of departure, but my interest is ultimately directed at the scandal as a cultural phenomenon, with both a long history and special features in our time.

The meaning of the concepts

Words are important; through them, etymological clues are available. Consequently, I wish to briefly consider the basic concept, *scandal*,

---

11 Brå, report 2013:15, p. 8.

and investigate where it hails from. In the Anglo-Saxon part of the world it is, above all, the term *media scandal* that has gained ground, but *political scandal* is also used, as well as the variant *mediated political scandal*. The first two of these are the most common concepts, both in daily parlance and in international research. In Spanish, too, the word *scandal* is at the centre, as it is in France, where the expression *scandale médiatique* is used. The corresponding German terms are *Medienskandal* and *Skandalberichterstattung*. Words designating mediated scandals are thus internationally disseminated, which suggests that there is a linguistic need for being able to talk about this type of phenomenon.

The word *scandal* originally comes from ecclesiastical Latin *scandalum* and Greek *skándalon* and made its way into Early Middle English (*scandle, scha(u)ndle*) by way of the Old Northern French *escandle* (*OED* online, s.n. *scandal*; see also Allern & Pollack 2012b:11). Going even further back in time, the word was used metaphorically in early versions of the Old Testament in order to represent a trap or an obstacle on the way – such as a boulder or a stream that prevented or hindered passage – in order to test the faith of an enemy (Hellquist 1922:727). Eventually the religious meaning of the word weakened, and in time it was replaced by other connotations. For instance, in eleventh-century France the word *esclandre* appeared, a development from *scandalum*, which meant 'scandal', 'slander', and 'vicious gossip'. *Esclandre* has in its turn given rise to the English word *slander* (Harper 2012). The concepts *scandal* and *gossip* are thus connected, which the reader is encouraged to remember. This leads us into relationships between a number of interesting phenomena and further into an area that may be regarded as the social and cultural dimensions of scandals, all of which will be analysed in this book.

Yet another word should be explained in greater detail, namely the Swedish word *mediedrev* (herein rendered as *media hounding*). This widely disseminated metaphor symbolises the intense and organised hunt for prey by hunters and hunting dogs. It was used for the first time in Swedish in May 1990 by the well-known Swedish-American journalist Hans Bergström in *Dagens Nyheter*, one of the oldest, biggest, and most respected daily newspapers in Sweden. After a modest introduction, the concept has become established in earnest; indeed, in Swedish popular parlance it is far more common than the concept 'media scandal'. Different versions of this type of designation exist in other languages as well. For instance, it is reminiscent of Norwegian *klappejakt*, English *media hunt*, and German *Medienhetze*. Here the media themselves are at the centre of things, journalists being actors who urge on the hounding of the prey during the hunt. In comparison, *media scandal* refers to cause and content; the focus is on the scandal itself and the story about it. That focus becomes even more evident in the expression *political scandal*, where the media are not mentioned at all, the subject being politics, or, more often, a politician, and the story about him or her. In this book I try to stick to the term established in scholarship, *media scandal*, even though (as was pointed out above) writers are always in need of synonyms. In Chapter 4, I return to a problematisation of these concepts.

Bricolage as a method

The material I start out from may appear sprawling at a first glance. I have conducted many interviews and read even more journalistic texts, both news pieces and advocacy materials, in a number of newspapers. I have also read other people's interviews with persons who have been at the centre of media scandals. In addition, I have studied blogs, images, billboards, biographies, and interminable Flashback threads (described below). The choice of this extensive collection of materials was inspired by anthropologist George E. Marcus's method *multisited ethnography* (Marcus 1995). It has several points in common with cultural analysis in that it promotes mobility and openness in order to come closer to what is being studied. Follow the people, the stories, the metaphors, the objects, and the conflicts, says Marcus; follow wherever the topic leads you. Such an attitude makes it possible for a deeper understanding of the significance of a phenomenon to take shape, an understanding where stability and variability over time can be studied, where cultural bearings on different places and in different spaces are investigated, and where the importance of a phenomenon to different people in different contexts is made visible (Marcus 1995:95–116, Ehn & Löfgren 2012:157–63). It is characteristic of this method that the researcher takes what is irregular as a starting-point. The method is improvised, curious, and tentative rather than structured – an open, curiosity-driven process whose development is not determined beforehand (Willim 2010:36f). I thus study the smallest constituents of the media scandal by close-reading texts, and then lift my gaze to understand the totality through an observation of moods, feelings, movements, directions, and events. However, the in-depth interviews that will soon be presented are always in the foreground.

In addition, ethnological cultural analysis recommends drawing attention to what is so common and insignificant that it does not attract any particular interest – to what happens in what ethnologists Billy Ehn and Orvar Löfgren call 'the secret world of doing nothing' (Ehn & Löfgren 2010), i.e., things which are so taken for granted that one does not give them a second thought, but which are nevertheless crucial to our innate attempts to create order and meaning in the continuous everyday flows of small incidents and great events, sensuous experiences, and encounters with our fellow human beings. 'How, for example, should we write about pauses, gaps in time where nothing of any great importance seems to be going on?', they ask (2012:109). According to another argument of theirs, it can be difficult to perceive lasting values and social principles when small talk and eventlessness rule, although the regular progress of life is of interest to ethnologists. It is not easy to illuminate normality by way of something that is normal. Something has to happen if the deeply embedded mechanisms of one's own culture are to become apparent. It is in the wake of crises, conflicts, and deviations that ideas and agreements are put to the test, occasions when they have to be defended against internal or external threats. Boundaries that may normally be taken for granted are given contours in connection with revolutionary events. In these moments, we become aware of the element of culture. For the researcher, studying an everyday existence in free fall may, for instance, pave the way for discoveries of elusive things such as experiences of belonging or exclusion, ideas about normality and deviation, and typical and atypical behaviours.

This book directs attention to the complete opposite of the common run of everyday life. A scandal can be compared to a landslide that catches everything in its way and drags it along. It changes terrains, demolishes constructions, obliterates plans, makes relationships impossible. It represents a cultural occasion where everything happens, with an intensification of existence as a result. Like intoxication, a heightened emotional state travels through the body of the individual as well as through the social body. Paradoxically enough, though, the word 'pause' also fits this phenomenon. The life of the affected individual is temporarily put on hold, ideas about the future cease to be valid, and the routines of everyday life must give way to more inventive approaches.

A methodological experiment

As was pointed out above, I have a particular interest in the relationship between interpersonal communication which occurs face to face and mediated communication. A starting-point is that speech in the form of gossip and everyday, oral exchanges of information constitute – and have always constituted – a significant proportion of journalistic sources, even in respect of journalism of the more serious kind. Lars-Eric Jönsson, Professor of Ethnology at Lund University, and I have developed a method we call 'listening to talk in texts' (Hammarlin & Jönsson 2017:93–115). By way of this method, we want to draw attention to and investigate the relationship of gossip to journalism and its methodological foundations in a manner that is never encountered in journalism handbooks and extremely rarely in research on journalism and media studies. Science has, according to media researcher John Hartley, consciously or unconsciously adapted itself to the desire of journalism to be seen as a serious activity, a desire which has resulted in some unflattering journalism and less than rigorous journalistic methodology ending up under the radar (Hartley 2008:679–91). The informal Swedish word *snackis* (a hot topic doing the rounds whenever people gather and talk) is the closest one gets to transparency among journalists regarding this practical skill, i.e., listening in on and making journalism out of gossip; it is described as newsroom jargon for news that 'is not particularly important, but able to stir up discussions around coffee tables and on sofas in TV shows' (Häger 2014:112).[12]

In our research, we have been especially interested in how such hot topics move between speech and writing and are interwoven with other kinds of statements, as well as in how newspaper journalists use them in their work, not least when famous people are being discussed (Hammarlin & Jönsson 2017:93–115). We have been inspired by book historian Robert Darnton's many studies, not least by the method he uses when mapping the borderland between written and oral materials (Darnton 1997, 2000, 2004, 2005, 2010). Darnton has devoted a large part of his research to precisely this intractable borderland, starting out from the French media landscape of the mid-eighteenth century. How, then, does Darnton locate the remnants of talk in his material? In his book

---

12 The quoted book, which was originally published in 2009, is commonly used in Swedish journalism courses.

Poetry and the Police he notes, among other things, how written poems and songs were modified by the people who recorded them (Darnton 2010:75). There are comments on how such a writer, having heard a song, wrote it down from memory. Minor adjustments then create different versions of the same song or poem, as in a kind of whispering game. Darnton takes these changes as evidence for oral communication, extracting new knowledge about the media system of the time by means of listening (Darnton 2010:76ff). Following written-down versions of talk and dialogue, reproductions of gossip, and gaol sentences for spreading rumours and so-called 'bad talk' (*mauvais propos*), he is able to describe the murmur of all these voices that together formed the sound of the people and simultaneously made up the framework for the news distribution of the time.

My methodological point of departure in this book is that I also listen through reading, in the process of which I do not only use my eyesight but also hone my hearing – metaphorically speaking – in order to pay attention to linguistic constructions that testify to a kind of union between talk and text. I also pay attention to flows, transfers, tones of voice, and moods. This method is particularly apparent in Chapters 2 and 3 where I not only read texts, but also put my ear to them.

Flashback Forum

A Swedish digital community, Flashback Forum (henceforth Flashback), is repeatedly mentioned in this study and should be presented in some detail. The biggest online discussion forum in Sweden, with one million registered users and over fifty million posts at the beginning of 2016, it is partly comparable to open Internet forums such as 4chan and Reddit. Flashback's watchword is that they offer users a place for 'real freedom of speech!' The creators of the website defend it with arguments based on freedom of speech and freedom of expression, and have on several occasions avoided Swedish law by moving their activities abroad (Uhnoo & Ekbrand 2017:126–51). On this forum an impressively extensive exchange of prattle and information is conducted on absolutely anything, from the innocent to the serious; but generally it may be said that the users are very interested in discussing crime (Uhnoo & Ekbrand 2017:126–51). The business idea is to guarantee anonymity for those participating in the discussions, and so far the owners have not been forced to surrender the IP addresses of their users, which makes Flashback a more 'secure' forum than Facebook, Twitter, Google+, and Instagram for those who wish to publish without revealing their respective identity.

The interviews

At the centre of this book is a total of twenty qualitative interviews that can be divided into three categories: (a) twelve with people who have been exposed to media scandals (six women and six men), and who are the main informants of the book; (b) two with partners of these people (one man and one woman); and finally (c) six interviews with journalists (three women and three men).

The people affected were selected on the basis of scientifically established criteria regarding media scandals:

- all the interviewees, while no law-breakers, have committed what has in Swedish society been considered a violation of norms, or morally dubious and/or reprehensible actions (transgression);
- their actions have become widely known, subsequent to which the people in question have been exposed to very hard media scrutiny during one or several limited periods of at least a few consecutive days, but often longer (knowledge);
- the scandals around them have been national and have emerged from the interaction of the coverage by several media of the relevant events;
- they have all been front-page matter and have often been commented on by media actors and other agents, but also by the general public who have responded to the scandals (reaction);
- the speculation about the main figures has to do with the inherent unpredictability of the scandals, which is to say that no one knew in advance how they would end (Thompson 2008:11–118, Allern & Pollack 2012b:9–28, Bromander 2012:8ff, Hammarlin & Jarlbro 2014:81–119).

The taped interviews have been transcribed and comprise around 370 A4 pages of material, and during my work I have alternated between reading and listening to them. Several interviewees have worked within the top tier of politics or in the immediate vicinity of top politics, including six as politicians and one as a senior civil servant. However, it should be emphasised that I have chosen not to interview only politicians and former politicians. This is a deliberate choice on my part, and it has to do with an ambition to extend the view of media scandals, which are otherwise as a rule almost exclusively associated with the political sphere. Nevertheless, if we broaden the concept of politics it is possible to claim that all except one of the scandals that are taken up here have political connotations. For instance, one of the affected individuals works as a political journalist, one writes editorials, and one was previously the leader of an advocacy organisation. Writer Maja Lundgren also devoted herself to a political issue in her book *Myggor och tigrar* ('Mosquitoes and tigers', 2007), which exposes patriarchal structures within the Swedish cultural sector and the tabloid business, and caused much debate in Sweden.

What most clearly ties eleven of the twelve main informants together is that they may be considered people from the elite; they have or have had influential positions in society and/or have been successful within their respective areas. As was pointed out above, there will be no scandals without an element of moral transgression. The purpose of this investigation is not, however, to expose the specific causal background of any particular scandal, but rather to look for shared and comprehensive themes in the experience-based stories of the interviewees. Consequently, the question of guilt – that is, whether these people deserved the hard media scrutiny to which they were exposed – is not addressed because it is irrelevant in this particular context. An in-depth study of the events themselves would jeopardise the direction and goals of the study.

It would be appropriate to give a few examples of how the question of guilt has a tendency to control the discussions of scandals. As my work progressed, I regularly presented my results to other researchers, and on those occasions I chose to make all my informants anonymous, a choice which elicited strong opinions. During my seminars, several colleagues have exclaimed: 'But what have they done?! We've got to be told!' When I have asked why this is important, they explained that otherwise it is impossible to understand the scandal. If one does not know what the central figures have done, one cannot have an opinion concerning their guilt, and, by extension, concerning the reporting about them. During a project meeting early on at the Joint Faculties of Humanities and Theology at Lund University, my colleague and I mentioned in passing that we wanted to study the above-mentioned 'Toblerone affair' with Mona Sahlin in the leading role. The research director looked worried and then offered a personal opinion on the issue, saying that the minister made herself impossible because of unpaid nursery-school bills and parking tickets rather than because she was careless with her official credit card. 'If she can't control her own financial affairs, she can hardly be put in charge of the country's finances!' Suddenly we had left the research issue behind, the one we were supposed to talk about, and instead ended up in the guilt issue pertaining to a scandal that had taken place in the public sphere many years before. In contexts where I have mentioned any of the interviewees by their real names in informal conversations with individual colleagues, there have been exclamations such as: 'But he wasn't the victim of a media hounding, he's a criminal!' The same thing occasionally happens in my personal life. If my research topic comes up at dinner parties, speculations soon have the upper hand. Dead-certain condemnations of and emotional apologies for the scandalised people follow one after the other, even though the details of the event have often been forgotten.

I believe the question of defence, guilt, and punishment repays consideration on the basis of precisely this social aspect. For the stated reasons, I will not present the individual scandals in detail by way of introductions to my analyses, but instead refer the reader to the book's Appendix. However, two cases will be analysed at some length in Chapters 3 and 4, because they shed light on the complexity of the media circuits in particular ways. All except three of the affected people appear voluntarily under their own names in this study.

Interviewees who have been at the centre of media scandals are presented in alphabetical order:

Floorball Dad, private individual (fictitious name)
Håkan Juholt, former party chair (Swedish Social Democratic Party)
Peter Karlsson, former top politician (fictitious name)
Hanne Kjöller, well-known journalist and editorial writer, *Dagens Nyheter*
Sven Otto Littorin, former minister in the Swedish government (the Moderate Party, Sweden's 'Conservatives')
Maja Lundgren, award-winning author
Ingmar Ohlsson, Swedish ambassador, former Under-Secretary of State and the right-hand man of then Prime Minister Göran Persson (fictitious name)
Anders Pihlblad, well-known political reporter and commentator, TV4
Tiina Rosenberg, well-known Gender Studies professor and feminist, former non-professional politician (Feminist Initiative)
Gudrun Schyman, top politician and party leader (Feminist Initiative, former chair of the Left Party)
Cecilia Stegö Chilò, professional board member, former journalist, and former minister in the Swedish government (the Moderate Party)

Ireen von Wachenfeldt, former chair of ROKS (National Organisation for Women's Shelters and Young Women's Shelters in Sweden)

Partners listed in alphabetical order:

Floorball Dad's wife
Kennet von Wachenfeldt, vicar, husband of Ireen von Wachenfeldt

The journalists who have been interviewed may also be regarded as elite individuals in a Swedish context. The selection of these interviewees was based on three criteria:

1 In spite of their limited number, these people together represent a broad spectrum of Swedish opinion-building news media, such as broadsheet newspapers, tabloids, and public-service media (radio and TV).
2 During their long professional careers, they have had extensive experience of covering media scandals.
3 They are all well known, influential, and politically orientated.

Journalists listed in alphabetical order:

Heidi Avellan, political editor-in-chief, *Sydsvenska Dagbladet*, the largest broadsheet in Southern Sweden (independent Liberal)
Anette Holmqvist, political reporter, *Aftonbladet*, one of Sweden's most influential and oldest evening tabloids (independent Social Democratic)
Mats Knutson, political reporter and commentator on *Rapport*, one of the two largest news programmes on Sveriges Television, public-service television
Pontus Mattsson, political reporter and commentator, Sveriges Radio's news desk *Ekot*, public-service radio
Margit Silberstein, political reporter and commentator, *Aktuellt*, the largest news programme on Sveriges Television, public-service television
Niklas Svensson, political reporter and commentator, *Expressen*, the other of Sweden's two oldest and most influential tabloids (independent Liberal)

A source-critical, detailed survey of both the material and the method is provided in the Appendix.

1
In the middle of the media storm

This part of the book presents fundamental themes in the interviews with the central figures of the scandals and their partners. I initially focus on the changes in everyday life that each scandal involved for those affected by it and the emotions it engendered. Initially, the emphasis is on the experience of actually being at the centre of a scandal and on the feelings of loneliness, guilt, shame, grief, and anger that came to dominate the lives of several of those affected. I will use everyday life as a starting-point, where a sweeping renegotiation of previously self-evident routines and patterns occurred in the wake of the scandal, and I also examine how things changed.

The food-and-sleep clock

To set the stage, you as a reader are invited to the home of Håkan Juholt who was at the time, in October 2011, the very hard-pressed party leader of the Social Democrats. Here incidents took place which, viewed in hindsight, come across as tragicomic. One such incident occurred when Juholt, completely unprepared and dressed in a T-shirt, was photographed at close range through the kitchen window of his ground-floor flat in a rental block in Västertorp, outside Stockholm. During my interview with him, Juholt illustrated his surprise at the time by opening his eyes wide and his mouth as well. He grinned with amusement when describing the incident, which was not at all funny when it happened but whose preposterousness made us both smile when it was retold. The picture taken by the photographer was not published; but it made Juholt and his partner Åsa Lindgren realise that very little in their lives from then on could be interpreted as 'normal' or 'the way things usually are'. Among other things, they crawled back and forth on the floor in and out of the kitchen to make coffee so that they would not be spotted by the photographers who stood in the street outside, their telephoto lenses at the ready. Opaque curtains were eventually put up, but of course the journalists remained there anyway, around the clock, physically just a few metres from the windows. This becomes even more problematic when considering how long their home was under surveillance.

> INTERVIEWER (I): How often were there people in the street?
> HÅKAN JUHOLT (HJ): It was constantly for a while, it came and went for a while. But I never noticed that they disappeared completely, so from October to January there was always someone there.
> I: That's quite a few months.
> HJ: Yes, there was always someone. Sometimes there were many, sometimes only a few photographers.
> I: From October to January?
> HJ: Yes, there was always someone in the stairwell, always someone outside.
> I: In the stairwell?
> HJ: In the stairwell. In the beginning they rang the doorbell pretty regularly, but I think it was SÄPO [the Swedish Security Service] that told them they weren't allowed to do that, so they stopped doing it. They took photographs into the building, into the flat. (M27102)

The pressure of the media is, as we already know, very great indeed in the initial phase of a media scandal. All the affected people and their partners told me in great detail about how bad they felt during the initial hunt, which is generally a downright physical experience. Among other things, these people supplied accounts about worry, anxiety, fear, sleep problems, and loss of appetite, as well as about physical sensations such as migraines, muscle pains, tremors, sweating, heart arrhythmia, skin rashes, stomach pains, nausea, vomiting, and, over a longer period of time, weight loss. Anders Pihlblad appears to have been especially badly affected when it comes to weight loss of an unhealthy nature. After the scandal erupted he lost his appetite. At first he quickly lost a number of kilos, and he then continued to lose weight at a slower rate. After a year, he had lost 18 kilos. Anders Pihlblad is a man of medium height, and at this time he weighed a mere 56 kilos. At his place of work, rumours began circulating that he had cancer. In order to tackle these problems he visited a doctor and a psychologist, as did many of the other informants. The treatment for most of them was therapy, sleeping pills, anxiolytic medication, or antidepressants.

Yet another example of how things may develop can be found in Peter Karlsson's story. He described how the initial hunt gave him severe nausea, quite physically, which led to his lying beside the toilet in his flat vomiting while the telephones kept ringing. An excerpt from the interview with him illustrates his circumstances:

PETER KARLSSON (PK): But the thing is that then I broke down, because that's when you get the physical shock. That's when you lie by the toilet vomiting. You're completely out of it. You're a physical wreck. You can't stand up ... .
I: So when the journalists come looking for you, then you're not at all in a fit state to answer any questions whatsoever?
PK: No. Today I understand that it's physically impossible to do that, because you end up in a situation like if there's a war going on. Doctors will tell you that all your defence mechanisms are switched on, like a hunted animal. So it's completely impossible to go out anywhere, you can't even go out to buy milk, because there's someone after you. You're so paranoid, completely nuts, it's impossible.[1]

Peter Karlsson was taken aback by the powerful reaction that literally floored him. He is not alone in having had this experience. Ulrica Schenström, former Under-Secretary of State for the Moderate Party and the right-hand woman of then-Prime Minister Fredrik Reinfeldt, describes a similar reaction in Anders Pihlblad's journalistic book, *Drevet går: Om mediernas hetsjakt* ('The hunt is on: On being hounded by the media') (Pihlblad 2010:8). In his work as a politician, Peter Karlsson had previously met others who had been affected by media scandals and thought, 'Get a grip, we'll deal with this!' without understanding the torment the person in question was going through.

One theme that emerges from the stories of the central figures is how their previously unreflective everyday activities regarding both minor and major matters came to a halt. The brakes were slammed on. They could not continue moving forward, as though the path in front of their feet had suddenly vanished. Not even the most elementary activity could be carried out with ease. Suddenly a visit to the supermarket, cooking dinner, and nightly recuperation in the form of sleep became projects that they had to goad themselves into doing. Peter Karlsson said that in connection with the development of the scandal, he invented a food-and-sleep clock so that he

---

1 There is no reference here, as it was not permitted to archive this material.

would not forget to eat and go to bed.[2] The clock consequently beeped several times a day with exact information about which meal it was time to eat and when he was allowed to rest – a kind of materialisation of everyday activities that normally belong on a routine, unreflective level.

> PK: I had the telephone. Then it rang at eight o'clock in the morning: 'Now it's time for breakfast!', Ten o'clock: A snack. Twelve o'clock noon: Lunch. Seven p.m.: Dinner.
> I: You had programmed that into the telephone?
> PK: Yeah, do you see? It's completely insane.
> I: A food-and-sleep clock.
> PK: Because then my wife got up and went to work, and you can so easily just stay in bed, and then you get completely depressed, you see.

When it became clear that his wife had broken down as well and lay sleepless at night, a couple of colleagues started up an emergency schedule which meant that every morning someone made sure there was breakfast and lunch in the fridge and every evening someone came home to the couple and cooked them dinner. 'I think they kept doing that for a month', he said. I myself have only heard of similar social support in connection with deaths and the subsequent period of grief, and perhaps the difference is not as great as it first appears.

Several interviewees testified to similar experiences, how their previously 'given' existence was transformed into an unknown and terrifying chaos where nothing was the same. Alfred Schutz uses the expression 'distance from the everyday' (Schutz 1989: 125) in order to describe this type of experience. In a crisis, he writes, the individual does not turn his or her back on everyday life; but because this person has for once been able to look at everyday existence and its components, his or her awareness of the possibility of doing just that is awakened, and this creates distance. Schutz continues: 'if his life (or what he considers to be the meaning of his life) seems threatened, he must then ask himself whether what just seemed so urgent and important is still so urgent and important' (Schutz 1989:128).

---

2 A figure in the Swedish children's cartoon *Bamse*, about a kind and strong (thanks to the ingestion of 'thunder honey') bear and his friends, has a food-and-sleep clock which governs the course of his day, whatever emergencies arise. This is sometimes inconvenient, as he is a preternaturally clever inventor whose aid is frequently needed.

What Schutz describes are the times in life when we are forced to pause, when we become visible to ourselves and other people in a particular way, where our previously so important tasks and our schedules containing plans for every hour of the day are transformed into a liquid state characterised by disorder and disorientation. Crises lead to a more theoretical attitude to what is our otherwise familiar, natural, everyday existence (Schutz 1989129f). The purpose of life is no longer obvious. We ask ourselves what we are doing here, who we are. It is as a rule unpleasant to be there, at a certain distance from oneself and other people. One theme that recurs in the informants' stories is precisely the distance that gradually arose in relation to other people. Loneliness is one of the most apparent and powerful feelings that found expression in their stories. Ulrica Schenström puts this experience into words in Anders Pihlblad's journalistic book, *Drevet går* (2010):

> People do not primarily suffer because there's no way they can defend themselves. Nor are they ashamed simply because they're being declared idiots in full-page spreads before the whole of the Swedish people. No. That's not what pierces you to the marrow. It's the silence. The silence from people around you. (Schenström, in Pihlblad 2010:9)

The paradox of visibility and loneliness

Each and every one of the affected people and their partners testified individually to tangible feelings of unreality and loneliness in the wake of the media scandal, a loneliness that was both voluntarily chosen and forced on them. Metaphors such as disappearing into a chrysalis, being shut into a bubble, being in a vacuum, or being the main actor in a surreal play were used. Kennet von Wachenfeldt, husband of Ireen, said that it caused him suffering to witness how his wife was made an outsider in their home town, something that was manifested in verbal attacks and averted, alternatively staring, eyes. It is a solitary and odd experience to be in a media scandal, even after the worst of the storm has abated. Loneliness expresses itself as separateness, which leads to a new form of visibility. Suddenly it becomes difficult to merge into the crowd. The interviewees had to either get used to being stared at in public places or remain indoors, within the confines of the home. Peter Karlsson expressed this experience in the following way:

> It's terrible going into a restaurant when everybody just stares at you. It takes years to get over people staring at you. It's completely insane. It's uncomfortable, and as you know people in this country

are not completely normal, you know when they see someone they sit like this [opens his mouth and stares with wide-open eyes]. And so you sit there with your spaghetti carbonara and then you just can't eat it because someone sits and stares at you and you get food on your face. It's completely insane, it's downright rude.

All the affected people testified to not being able to merge into the background any longer, and that was often described as a kind of torment. Tiina Rosenberg compared this experience to the protective function of anonymity in the following way: 'I find all these contexts when people ask me, "What's your name?" totally wonderful. "Hi, my name is Tiina Rosenberg".' This comment is reminiscent of the persecuted main character, Josef K., in Franz Kafka's *The Trial*, when in a famous scene he encounters the prison priest in the cathedral, a person he has not met before:

> 'You are Josef K.,' said the priest, raising one hand from the pulpit in a vague gesture. 'Yes,' said K., thinking how freely he used to say his name in the past. For some time now it had become a burden to him, and now people he had not met before knew his name; how good it was to introduce oneself first and only then be known. (Kafka 2009:151)

Several of the informants had previously enjoyed a large degree of anonymity in public life, but now they ended up at the centre of attention for everybody, and, in addition to this, in a compromising context where they were presented as mendacious, cunning, unreliable, crazy, or negligent. This eventually led to a new form of self-awareness. Being looked at from the outside caused the affected person to regard him- or herself critically, which could lead to the main figure in question developing self-centred traits. In the words of Anders Pihlblad,

> [y]ou become very narcissistic when hounded by the media. ... You sort of think the whole world revolves around you. You feel it as soon as you get on the underground train, and so on. Everybody looks at you all the time. And people did that anyway, maybe, but not more than usual, because I am after all a person who's been on TV and all that, but it became so much more obvious, maybe because you look for it too. You only think about yourself.

Many of the affected persons dwelt on the experience of being stared at. Some people with a superficial or non-existent relationship to the protagonist of the drama seemed to respond to the scandal by staring intently at the scandalised person from a distance. Others demonstratively averted their eyes. During the initial, chaotic period of the scandals this was not something the informants thought much about because it was as much as they could manage to get through the day; but in the narratives it is obvious that this was not a transitory phenomenon. They continued being recognised and people kept staring, long after the reporting had died down.

As time went by, it became clear that the people around them had begun to avoid them. Some friends refrained from calling them, invitations no longer arrived, acquaintances crossed to the other side of the street, colleagues turned their heads away and stopped saying hello, and it became manifestly difficult to find someone to have lunch with. Several of the interviewees described how people they expected to be supportive were nothing of the sort, which was experienced as shocking and painful. Because these so-called friends neglected to show compassion during the crisis itself, moreover, there was no way back later.

'Asocial responselessness' is a concept used by the greatly esteemed Swedish social psychologist Johan Asplund to describe situations where expected, everyday communication changes character, where a practised response fails to materialise and is replaced by uncertainty. In a face-to-face meeting, this often leads to a feeling of being put to shame in the person who is exposed to the responselessness. You do not know what to do next. Suppose that a person you normally say hello to every morning suddenly ignores your greeting. What do you do then? Repeat the phrase? Leave? Become upset? You probably feel dumb which, etymologically speaking, should not be understood in the sense of unintelligent but rather mute (Asplund 1987:13). When a fellow human being – Asplund uses the attractive phrase 'travelling companion' – does not answer your question or react to your greeting, he or she strikes you dumb, making you speechless. Although it was the other person who first demonstrated the dumbness, the responselessness is transferred to you, who also become dumb – an infernal exercise of micro-power, according to the author, who argues that the most basic form of power is exercised by individual actors in interpersonal meetings. Exercises in asocial responselessness can be extremely painful experiences, in particular when it is a person's travelling companion who forces him or her into this involuntary dance by violating prevalent codes of behaviour. Asplund goes so far as to call it a naked form of power that enforces pure submission (Asplund 1987:25). However, asocial responselessness always affects two people: the one who performs the non-action in question, and the person who is exposed to it. It is the reciprocality in the situations of social life that we should pay attention to. If we do, it becomes clear that the persons who previously used to greet me but now avert their eyes not only reject me but also their own selves, because I am not given an opportunity to recognise and acknowledge them either (Asplund 1987:17, see also Goffman 2008 [1972]:47–97). Existence cannot be confirmed unilaterally. For me to be able to confirm your existence, you also have to confirm mine. In the words of sociologist Erving Goffman:

> [A]n act that is subject to a rule of conduct is, then, a communication, for it represents a way in which selves are confirmed – both the self for which the rule is an obligation and the self for which it is an expectation. An act that is subject to rules of conduct but does not conform to them is also a communication – often even more so – for infractions make news and often in such a way as to disconfirm the selves of the participants. (Goffman 2008 [1972]:51)

The lifeworld is fundamentally shared. It is neither my private world nor your private world, nor yours and mine together. Rather, it is a world of common experience, that is to say reciprocal in its foundations (Schutz 1973:68). Against this, the interrupted communication and the experience of the protracted state of alone-ness in which a person affected by a scandal finds him- or herself seems a painful break in everyday existence against which it is hard to defend oneself. It just happens, in accordance with its own innate logic. A natural existence, where a person skilfully and routinely handles a flow of events and meetings with people, is replaced by anxiety. Nothing seems normal or simple any more, especially not spontaneous meetings with fellow individuals. The we-relation, where intersubjectivity within the lifeworld continually develops and is confirmed through planned and unplanned meetings with other people, is shaken to its very foundations. This leads, among other things, to my no longer being able to mirror myself in you, in the natural way that I otherwise do, or which we otherwise do with each other, because mirroring happens according to a dualist principle. Schutz puts it beautifully: 'The mirroring of self in the experience of the stranger (more exactly, in my grasp of the Other's experience of me) is a constitutive element of the we-relation' (Schutz 1973:66ff). Håkan Juholt described how, long after the scandal reporting about him had died down, he continued to avoid people's eyes and thus voluntarily refrained from the mutual mirroring:

HJ: Before, one looked at people when one walked down the street. Now, I almost always just look down, I never try to catch someone's eye or make eye contact. I don't want to see them looking at me, I don't want to ... so I look down.

I: Do you think that they're looking at you, that you are made visible?

HJ: Yes, I don't want that eye contact any longer, I don't want to see it.

I: Isn't that difficult?

HJ: Of course, it's really difficult, but that is the most obvious change. ...

I: Do you sometimes feel that other people are looking at you?

HJ: Yes, everybody does. It's OK, but I don't seek ... I opt out of it.

I: There must be a certain effort involved.

HJ: I've switched it off completely. (M27102)

Looking at oneself through the eyes of the Other is a deeply and universally human thing. In fact, it is innate in the knowledgeable human being, where knowledge refers to knowledge about oneself, that is to say an awareness of existing – an insight that has been developed in a plethora of philosophical works. It leads to the paradoxical circumstance that my foundation, my self, does not exclusively exist in me, but also outside me. A part of self-awareness thus has to do with seeing what the Other sees when he or she looks at me (Schutz 1973:66ff; see also Asplund 1987:17). This usually unconscious mirroring effect is, as Schutz writes, a decisive component of the we-relation which is now exchanged for an uncomfortable feeling of separateness, but also of visibility. The eyes that are averted or that silently stare at me single me out, making mirroring impossible, and therefore leave me to myself. The expression 'to stare someone out' says something about the inherent power of this weapon.

In this context, it may be worth reminding oneself of the meaning of late Latin *excommunicare* or *excommunicate* in English, which may even today be used in the sense of banning someone from the fellowship of a collective. A related phenomenon is *ostracism*, a psychological concept that can be used to explain the situation in which the people affected by a scandal found themselves, where asocial responselessness can be seen as an expression or a sign of ostracism. The word originated in ancient Greece, where a leading figure could be excluded from the community through a collectively agreed-upon form of exile or excommunication. The procedure was conducted by means of a vote, where each of the congregated citizens wrote down the name of the unwanted person on a shard of pottery, a so-called *ostracon* (*OED online*, s.n. 'ostracon'). This behaviour, that is to say the cultural tendency to exclude an individual who is felt to be deviant from or threatening to the social collective – because the person in question constitutes a danger to that particular collective – may be considered universal. It can take on a number of robust forms and variations, according to social psychologist Kipling D. Williams, who has written a book on this phenomenon with the telling title *Ostracism: The Power of Silence* (2001). The author describes the special mechanisms of ostracism as a display of aversive behaviour in social interaction among people:

> Unlike other forms of aversive interpersonal behaviors, however, for instance, verbal or physical abuse, ostracism can be characterized as a nonbehavior. Because of this, its occurrence is enveloped in several layers of ambiguity. For instance, targets may notice that they are being ignored and think to themselves, 'Is it actually happening or is it my imagination?' (Williams 2001:11)

The words used by those affected by a scandal to describe their situations are similar to the expressions that the informants in Williams's research used – as an experienced form of exile, exclusion, expulsion, or branding, communicated not least through the silence of and repudiation by the people around them, which means that ostracism as a phenomenon is simultaneously powerful, tangible, and shapeless. It can be unequivocal in its character – that is to say, a person who is exposed to this treatment clearly notices what is going on – but even so it can be extremely difficult to address, because the 'travelling companion' who performs the non-act can claim to be blameless if called to account. The so-called non-behaviour can, because of its inherent ambivalence, be denied, and thus does not have to be either explained or excused.

The branding and the escape

Several of the interviewees compared themselves metaphorically to vulnerable or persecuted groups in society in order to describe their experiences of exposure and loneliness. Ireen von Wachenfeldt felt that she became a victim of rape, where 'the media became like a perpetrator against me'. Ingmar Ohlsson, for his part, felt that he was presented as 'one of those who eat little children for breakfast'. Maja Lundgren said that she was portrayed as a lunatic, a hysterical woman, and was transformed into a scapegoat, while Tiina Rosenberg argued that she, like Frankenstein's monster, became evil personified. Another affected individual claimed that the scandal left a mark on the entire family, comparing the experience to the persecution of Jews and Roma. Variations on the words *sickness* and *death* recurred in the interviews, for instance in connection with interviewees describing their own degree of well-being or the reactions of the people around them. Several pointed out that they felt besmirched, dirty, contagious, and that 'they were bringers of death'. As we have seen, some people around them developed a talent in the difficult art of avoidance. That phenomenon calls for a deeper analysis, in which we will focus more on the role assigned to the central figure in this drama.

A person who has so-called 'blemishes' on her or his personal character, stains that are the result of, for instance, a lack of honesty or amoral behaviour, can become stigmatised in society, writes Erving Goffman (1990a [1963]:14). On the basis of the knowledge that we 'normal' people have, or believe we have, about a stigmatised person, we take discriminatory actions of different kinds, by which we effectively, if unintentionally, reduce life opportunities for the person in question. Here a kind of branding enters the picture. We believe by definition that a person to whom there is a stigma attached is not completely human (Goffman 1990a [1963]:15). This is particularly interesting considering that several of the people affected by scandals felt that as a consequence of the media reporting they became just that – dehumanised. That feeling is implicit in some of the comments reproduced above. Ingmar Ohlsson describes this experience as follows, in explicit terms: 'It becomes a kind of dehumanisation. You're not a person, you are a phenomenon, a figure.' Hanne Kjöller also used the word 'dehumanisation' repeatedly during our conversation, whereupon I asked what that actually meant. She answered:

HANNE KJÖLLER (HK): It means that I'm not a person.
I: And instead you become what?
HK: Perhaps an animal. A victim. That is, I become someone to bring down. There is no compassion for me, there is no empathy. There's nothing. It becomes a hunt. Like a computer game. I am nobody. I'm not a sister, a brother, or a colleague.
I: What do people want to do to you, then? You say 'bring down'? What does that mean?
HK: Well, I think I am supposed to break down.
I: Is that what is …?
HK: … Yes, in a way. You know, the power that the media have, it's so great. If thirty journalists decide to report a truth that isn't true, then it doesn't matter. You'll never be able to defend yourself. I'll never be able to escape the image that some people have created of me, no matter how wrong it is.

In connection with this discussion, Hanne Kjöller mentioned suicide as the ultimate reaction to a media scandal. She emphasised that she was never close to having such thoughts herself; but the experience of the scandal involving herself and those involving other people, whom she as a journalist has followed at close range, led to a realisation that it is plausible, even likely, that a major media scandal in Sweden could lead to a person's death. Among other cases, she referred to a well-known Norwegian case known as 'Tønne-saken' ('the Tønne affair'), which involved Tore Tønne, at that time Norwegian Minister of Health, who, after accusations of economic irregularities and a wide-spread media scandal, took his own life in 2002. This tragic event caused an extensive debate on press ethics in Norway (see Brurås 2003). What Kjöller also describes in the above quotation is a process of demonisation that is typical of media scandals (Allern & Pollack 2012a:187f). Maja Lundgren spontaneously used the word 'stigmatisation' in order to describe this experience, in the following way:

> MAJA LUNDGREN (ML): I felt as if that was the purpose of the hounding, to banish me in order to maintain order and defend honour, the honour of certain men. And I actually planned to move abroad. But I don't really want to move, I want to live in Sweden.
> I: And in this process you say that you felt that you were alone in a way that you haven't been before. Or?[3]
> ML: Yes. I have been alone before, but [now I was] alone in a different way, like, stigmatised perhaps you can say. Really.
> I: Stigmatised? How do you mean?
> ML: Well, kind of branded. Like some kind of witch. (M27093)

The feeling that the media reporting resulted in a kind of branding, banishment, and expulsion is something Maja Lundgren shares with the other informants. She felt prompted to leave the country, which brings up another recurring theme in the stories of the interviewees, namely escape. Several of them felt impelled to escape quite physically from the scandal reporting and all the attention. They went into hiding in their holiday homes or with relatives, or they went abroad. Phones were unplugged, doors locked, blinds drawn. Peter Karlsson, who has worked in politics,

---

3 Because the follow-up question is a leading question, it should be pointed out that Maja Lundgren, like the other informants, previously in the interview described a feeling of loneliness as one of the most prominent of her emotions.

has seen this happen many times, and he has also helped other people escape:

> I can say that today I'm a pro when it comes to taking care of people who have to get away from the media – a pro! It's almost like one of those secret-agent exercises, you know. It's not just a matter of disguising people, since you can't have the same car, for instance, because then the media will check the number plates. So you have to have other cars. Then they have to be driven around the country, because you have to move them from various holiday homes. I've done a lot of that [*laughter*].

An interesting emotional state came over us during the interview when Peter Karlsson told me about these scenarios of being hunted and escaping: we both found it hard not to laugh. He spoke about serious matters – the people who felt forced to escape were of course badly shaken – but there was a kind of irony and black humour in all this that made us both begin to laugh. Besides, the people he helped escape had disguised themselves, as had Peter Karlsson himself, which reinforced the element of absurdity. These were successful people he was talking about, men and women with status and power, who suddenly began to behave more or less irrationally. A more lengthy excerpt clarifies the mood:

> I: [*laughter*] Yes, well, it's exciting this thing where you disguise yourself and leave, more or less.
> PK: Mmm, but everybody does.
> I: Everybody does?
> PK: Yeah, yeah. Everybody I know has disguised themselves [*laughter*]. I myself was chased around Djurgården [the Royal Game Park] by *Expressen* and their photographers. ... And then suddenly a reporter jumps out of the bushes, and I'm out walking with my friend Klas. And I just go, 'AAAARGH!' and start running across Gärdet and he [Klas] yells, 'YOU ARSEHOLES!!' [*laughter*]. In hindsight, I don't know if I was the one they were after. They could have been after the royal family.

When Sven Otto Littorin told me about his experiences of escape, the mood in the room was characterised by seriousness. Grimly, he described in detail how reporters from *Aftonbladet* pursued the getaway car that he and his then partner were travelling in. The first two weeks were pure escape, he said. They switched cars at night, dumped telephones in litter bins, and sought temporary refuge in the forest in a holiday home belonging to a friend's in-laws. He described it as 'entering a second childhood' during such extreme circumstances. The reptilian brain is at work. He claimed that he would literally have crawled under a table from pure fright if the journalists had stepped into the house where he was hiding.

> SVEN OTTO LITTORIN (SOL): [We were at the electronics store] Expert in Årjäng. We were there to buy two of those burner phones, because our relatives had to be able to reach us. Evin, who was my partner at the time, walks into Expert and comes face to face with a wall of TV sets with my picture on them. And there I sit in the car with my jacket collar turned up, a cap, and sunglasses. It was like in the movies. It was disgusting. During this time the publishing continued, every bloody person in Sweden wanted a piece of me and I wasn't in a fit state for anything. It was … interesting.
> I: You were not in a position to answer questions at that time?
> SOL: Hell, no! I couldn't sleep, eat, drink … I was a total wreck. Via an acquaintance I managed to find a district medical officer in Årjäng who prescribed tranks. It was horrible, awful.
> I: Did you suffer any lasting physical or psychological damage?
> SOL: Oh, definitely. People say, 'what doesn't kill you makes you stronger', but I don't believe that at all. I will always have a pretty large scab, which I often pick at. That's how it is. I notice now that I'm becoming a bit …
> I: This is affecting you.
> SOL: Yes, absolutely. (M27095)

It is obvious that it is not just during the most acute course of events that the main figures of the drama experience fear and a need to hide. Peter Karlsson described how he, when the reporting had in principle come to an end, reluctantly went to visit friends in Copenhagen dressed in a scarf pulled up to the tip of his nose, sunglasses, and a cap pulled down far over his forehead. The trip had been preceded by his friends' assurances that it really was not dangerous to go out and have a beer in a neighbouring country several months after the reporting had died down. It is appropriate here to quote yet another interview section:

> I: What are you hiding from, then?
> PK: It's incomprehensible.
> I: You don't really know it yourself?
> PK: I said it the other day to a colleague, 'I saw this person walk around in strange sunglasses and everything. I've done it, too.' Like, it's so damn nuts. I don't know what I was hiding from. But hiding I was.

This behaviour can be linked to both the concept of ostracism and to Goffman's theory of stigma, since there are a number of ways for people affected by a scandal to respond to the unfavourable special treatment they receive. For instance, we saw how Håkan Juholt voluntarily refrained from making eye contact with people who stared at him when he was out in public. Another concrete response is to try to escape the situation. A third one is covering, that is to say, a desire on the part of the stigmatised person to conceal his or her stigma. In the case of an individual affected by a scandal this becomes equivalent to concealing, or hiding, oneself. It is obvious that people with visual impairments are not the only ones who use sunglasses in an attempt to protect themselves from the general values associated with the stigma in question (Goffman 1990a [1963]:125–8). According to Goffman, through these actions a discredited person accepts his or her stigmas as well as assuming responsibility for them. The purpose, he claims, is to reduce tension and make it easier for oneself and for other people to divert attention from the stains in question, so that one can devote oneself to what social intercourse should really be about. This process also includes interpreting the glances of other people, reading things into their eyes that may not actually be there, a feeling that 'they know', which leads to a form of self-stigmatisation. Thus the attempts of the person affected by a scandal to conceal him- or herself – through drawn Venetian blinds, eyes firmly on the ground, voluntary escape, isolation, and disguise – could be seen as a form of acknowledgement and accepting responsibility, a response to collective expectations. But this behaviour is likely to have an even deeper significance. On the basis of the ideas in Sartre's little book *Esquisse d'une théorie des émotions*, both covering and escape can be seen as illuminating examples of magical behaviour, an expression that allows us to understand the existential dimensions of fear. In a passage that deals expressly with escape as an answer to fear, Sartre writes:

> Ainsi le véritable sens de la peur nous apparaît: c'est une conscience qui vise à nier, à travers une conduite magique, un objet du monde extérieur et qui ira jusqu'à s'anéantir, pour anéantir l'objet avec elle. (Sartre 2002:43)[4]

A frightened person would thus be prepared to obliterate her- or himself in order to obliterate a threat to her or his existence. For

---

4 'The real meaning of fear is now becoming apparent to us. It is a consciousness whose aim is to negate something in the external world by means of magical behaviour, and will go so far as to annihilate itself in order to annihilate the object also'; Jean-Paul Sartre, *Sketch for a Theory of the Emotions*, trans. Philip Mairet (London: Routledge), 2002:43.

instance, fainting when facing a monster is an example of what Sartre calls magical behaviour. It is worth bearing in mind that there are cases where the protagonist committed suicide as a direct consequence of a media scandal (Bjerke 2012:165–81, is Brurås, Hjeltnes, & Syse 2003, Pihlblad 2010:145–63). We remember Hanne Kjöller's words from before. Johan Asplund would interpret this as a potential avoidance of self-obliteration (Asplund 1987:17). By engaging in magical behaviour and escape from the Other's exercise of power, I reduce his or her opportunities to take away my right to exist. I thus escape purely for the sake of self-preservation, which gives rise to the question, Can suicide be committed in an attempt at self-preservation?

The exercise of power can also take on more explicit expressions of aversion and hatred. Ingmar Ohlsson:

INGMAR OHLSSON (IO): Well, that's what became so exhausting. Before this started I was essentially a person unknown to the public. Now I became known to everyone.
I: Everybody knows who you are?
IO: Everybody knows who I am. And that leads to my not going out. I can't go out shopping; it's impossible. For a period of time I had to have bodyguards, because I've been threatened and because I've been beaten up. But, but, but ...
I: You were actually beaten up?
IO: I was beaten on three different occasions.
I: On three different occasions?!
IO: Yes, once in an aeroplane.
I: By private individuals who had got worked up about the reporting?
IO: And then I get bodyguards, and have them for a while, but of course eventually I can't take the responsibility for tying up lots of public resources. So what do I do? I simply don't go out.

Ingmar Ohlsson described how, because of the threats, he was driven from door to door in a car provided by the government for a period that lasted just over six months. He was exposed to all sorts of threats, and during several periods he had to have bodyguards protecting him. People spat at him in the street, and his car was vandalised (Pihlblad 2010:311). Because the media scandal came and went over several years, the acute situation with isolation as a consequence was also repeated later.

Ohlsson shares the experience of having received death threats with some of the other informants. Tiina Rosenberg testified about receiving such threats and also about threatening situations in public places, which led to her avoiding going out in public. She, too, was chauffeured – by her partner – from door to door between her home and her workplace for nearly a year. At her place of work, guards were hired. Not just she herself but also colleagues and family doubted that she was safe. When the reporting was at its most intense, her partner slept with a baseball bat at the side of the bed. Maja Lundgren, for her part, did not have direct death threats levelled against her; but in the newspapers people speculated that she might be so mentally unstable that she could be considered a danger to her own life. She personally experienced the media scrutiny as threatening in itself.

> ML: It's a feeling that one is about to be killed, sort of.
> I: A feeling that one is about to be killed?
> ML: Yes, one grows sort of weak at the knees and such things. One becomes anxious and so on. (M27093)

Gudrun Schyman used similar words. Among other things, she said that it was like being threatened with violence from which one cannot protect oneself. There was a kind of ringing in her body, her muscles tensed up, and she thought, 'This is it!' Ireen von Wachenfeldt spoke of an occasion during the intense phase of the scandal when a man on the underground demonstratively stood in front of her and spat directly at her. There were threats against her life as well on repeated occasions, via the telephone, email, and letters. The threats led to an intense fear of there being snipers up on the roofs who had a free line of sight into the flat where she lived. Ireen von Wachenfeldt described how she took refuge in her home in spite of not feeling safe there. She believed she had nowhere else to go, which in time had serious consequences: she refused to go out at all.

> I: By that time you hadn't gone out for several weeks, then?
> IREEN VON WACHENFELDT (IW): No …
> I: You isolated yourself?
> IW: You bet. … You know, it was as if I was walking around and around, sort of.
> I: Where did you walk around?
> IW: We lived so that you could walk from the kitchen and through the hall and through the living room, like this. You could walk around in the flat [pause].
> I: So you walked, did you?
> IW: Right, there I walked. (M27094)

The prolonged isolation eventually led to social phobia; that is to say, Ireen von Wachenfeldt became one with her stigma. She was terrified in the flat – of the roofs, the windows, the newspaper, the radio, the television, and the letterbox, the exits to the home, as it were – and at the same time she was terrified of leaving it. With the support of her family and of doctors, she was slowly and gradually pushed outside. Peter Karlsson for his part told me how he shut the world out by drawing the curtains and consuming massive amounts of TV series in accordance with completely newly created everyday routines. There he would walk around, as a kind of sleepwalker between his sofa and the TV, wearing pyjamas for the greater part of the day, fully aware of the journalists and photographers who were waiting outside the front door a few floors down. With grim humour, his friends called his plight 'the pyjamas bubble', ringing now and then to check whether he was wearing his nightwear or not. Once a day he sneaked out through a back door, in disguise, to take a walk – the big event of the day.

Anders Pihlblad described how during the most intense phase, when journalists were waiting outside the front door to the building, he pulled down the Venetian blinds in the kitchen window, through which one could see straight into his flat. Then he left his home for a time. When he returned, the Venetian blinds stayed down for six months, long after the storm had died down. His romantic relationship of some years' standing came to an end as well. One of the consequences of a media scandal on the personal plane is precisely that the partners of the main figures sometimes do leave. The scandal does not discriminate between family life and working life. 'It's actually the case that my life is destroyed by this', said Ingmar Ohlsson and underlined that it had caused both his professional and his private life to break down. The scandal reporting breaks into a person's everyday life on all fronts and changes its structure, sometimes forever. In Peter Karlsson's words:

> [s]o you have to remember that many routines, patterns, one's family, the people you socialise with – all these things are disrupted. And when that happens I think people can go under. I'm sure one can become a drug addict. But I was lucky enough to have my food-and-sleep clock.

Shame, self-contempt, and laughter

After a time, certain of the informants were able to return to their duties at work. Others were not. Losing one's job is a not uncommon consequence of a media scandal. A few years after the events, Peter

Karlsson could still remember the exact date when everybody else went back to work after a Christmas break while he himself stayed at home. For his part, Anders Pihlblad was welcomed back to the TV newsroom where he was employed, receiving support from his boss and most of his colleagues. Nevertheless, he continued to feel terrible:

> It intensified during this time, this enormous sense of self-contempt. A strong feeling of dislike for myself. But I didn't blame any of the people who were down on me, only myself. It took a while before I realised that this was exactly what was going on. Someone told me, 'You're going around despising yourself. Think about that. Why do you do it?'

Not surprisingly, self-incrimination is common in the stories of the interviewees. In particular, these self-accusations manifested themselves in the form of guilt and shame, feelings that appear to be the individual, emotional response to the stigmatisation, the asocial responselessness, and the ostracism, at least in some cases. The experience of not being wanted hits back at a person's own self; guided by other people's glances, he or she begins to look at him- or herself with a critical eye. Williams again:

> Being cut off, cut loose, cut down, and cut dead is perhaps the worst thing that can happen to us. I argue that the simple act of being ignored simultaneously attacks four fundamental human needs. Our sense of connection and belonging is severed; the control we desire between our actions and outcomes is uncoupled; our self-esteem is shaken by feelings of shame, guilt, or inferiority; and we feel like a ghost, observing what life would be like if we did not exist. (Williams 2001:6)

Tiina Rosenberg described it as a shame that was foisted on her from the outside, something she was expected to feel and act on the basis of, but which she resisted. Maja Lundgren was on a similar track and described it as primitive scapegoat-thinking, where the unity of the group stands or falls with a single person's being made to take the blame for everything and eventually being banished from the community. Ireen von Wachenfeldt experienced this as an incessant inner harping: How could I! I've ruined everything! I'm a terrible person! Peter Karlsson described the inner gnawing in a similar way, 'I've done something awful, I probably ought to die', connecting this experience to the articles about him:

> This silence [that people stop saying hello and getting in touch], which may often be because of fear and not spite, is of course connected to the image you then read about. So it takes a little while to realise that you're not the absolute worst person in the world.

The last sentence was said in irony, an irony which, together with a crass, black humour, appears in several of the informants' stories. Looking back, Peter Karlsson especially had the ability to see himself as a comic figure who disguised himself, wore sunglasses in the middle of winter, and behaved oddly when among people, as we saw above. When I listen to the interview, I am struck by how much we both laughed, in spite of the seriousness; 'laughter that sticks in your throat' is an expression that captures the feeling (Jönsson & Nilsson 2014:7–19). Our mirth was probably provoked by the carnivalesque characteristics of the media scandal. One's existence is temporarily turned topsy-turvy; a degradation takes place in public, hierarchies are dissolved, power is challenged, and roles are re-evaluated. At the centre of the spectacle is a person who has been made the object of ridicule and whose status has been altered, temporarily or permanently. The sometimes grim laughter that comes from outside singles out and separates. It can be merciless and ultimately change one's view of who one is. In the words of Swedish ethnologist Jonas Engman:

> [T]he fear of being laughed at, publicly disgraced, and destroyed also entails seeing oneself as a caricature of oneself, or perhaps even as a hyperbole. If we are disgraced enough, we seem to behave as though we were grotesque and we regress, perhaps in tears and anger. Laughter threatens to turn us into creatures with no control over ourselves, as though we have lost our humanity. (Engman 2014:21)

Laughter, too, no matter how innocent it may seem, can thus contribute to the experience of becoming dehumanised. Peter Karlsson, like several of the other informants, felt that it takes years to get over a media scandal emotionally and put it behind oneself, if one ever does. The following pages investigate the feeling of shame in some detail, considering the gaze of the Other in this particular context: how the people affected felt laughed at, stared at, and singled out, or, alternatively, actively ignored.

The shame that the gaze of the Other can engender is a phenomenon discussed in Sartre's texts. In *Being and Nothingness* (Sartre 1956:282–326), an illustrative and often reproduced scene is described where a man stands bent over with his eye to a keyhole, watching something on the other side of a door. Completely absorbed by his actions, he is at that moment unaware of himself. But when steps approach from behind, the man realises that he is in somebody else's field of vision, at which point he becomes aware of himself and quickly stops looking through the keyhole. A paralysing shame ensues. According to Sartre, this feeling does not originate in a realisation that the person in question has acted wrongly, but emerges because at that moment the man can see himself from the outside, through the Other's gaze, and he is ashamed of what he sees – that is, he is ashamed of himself the way he appears to the Other. But this shame also implies a kind of admission: I admit that I am as the other person sees me.

At a deeper level, Sartre says that the anxiety or fear that I may feel before the Other's gaze has to do with the fact that this person has an ability to make me an object and thus fasten me down and affix my person to a few selected qualities that are made to represent all of me. Without knowing my reasons or my inner motives, the other person transforms me into someone who looks through keyholes. The Other's gaze becomes a yardstick that measures me, and the judgement that follows is impossible to appeal against, completely independently of whether the image corresponds to my self-image or not. In other words, what I am ashamed of is how I appear to the other person, in spite of my being aware that this person's idea of me may be unfair, erroneous, and simplified. Ireen von Wachenfeldt tellingly described how she protected herself from the glances of her fellow human beings because she was afraid of being judged, a feeling that can still affect her, many years after the event:

> It says more about my own fear, that they won't like me. 'Don't judge me because that isn't really me. I'm really a very nice person' [laughter]. 'Like me for who I am.' It's a fear I have that they will think that I'm this personality that I'm not, the one that TV has brought out, that the media always bring out with their blazing headlines. I'm really very kind and want everyone to be valued the same [laughter]. I who can barely kill a fly. Jesus Christ. (M27094)

Sartre derives yet another example of the connection between shame and the Other's gaze from the story of the Fall. What is described there is, in reality, a basic fear of being surprised in a state of nakedness: 'And the eyes of them both were opened, and they knew that they were naked' (Genesis 3:7). The nakedness symbolises our vulnerable position as objects before the gaze of the Other. The Fall, according to Sartre, means being exposed, becoming paralysed and then becoming painfully aware of the fact that one is no longer a subject but an object before the Other: 'Pure shame is not a feeling of being this or that guilty object but in general of being an object; that is, of recognizing myself in this degraded, fixed, and dependent being which I am for the Other' (Sartre 1956: 288).

Several media theoreticians, not least those from within feminism and gender studies, have used the concept of the *gaze* in order to understand this power process in relation to modern mass media, in particular photography and film, sometimes with inspiration taken from Sartre, but also from psychoanalyst Jacques Lacan, philosopher Michel Foucault, and literary scholar Roland Barthes (see Mulvey 1975, van Zoonen 1994, Kress & Leeuwen 1996, Hall 1997, Casetti 1998, Hirdman 2001). Again and again they describe the power that a spectator has over an object that he or she looks at. The person who looks can to a great extent determine the significance and meaning of that object, without having to negotiate with it.

Interestingly enough, Peter Karlsson described an awareness of himself as an object above – that is, he spoke of how the unfavourable representation of him in the media manifested itself and also of how it was perceived by other people, something that, according to him, had the logical consequence that people did not get in touch with him. He was thus not only looked at by other people, he also looked at himself, thereby inevitably becoming a part of the objectification process. A paradoxical situation arises where the informants are simultaneously subjects and objects, exemplified above by Peter Karlsson's experience of shame at how he was perceived in public life.

Conversely, Håkan Juholt said that he never felt any shame, because in his view he had tried to correct the mistakes that had been made and had always striven to act in an honest and honourable fashion throughout his long political career. Perhaps that was the reason why he managed to retain his human dignity, which he feels that he did, in spite of his claim that many people wanted to take just that away from him. At the same time, he described incidents where the loss of control was pervasive and where an intense experience of having been transformed from a subject into an object presented itself, incidents in the course of which the possibility of influencing his own situation and adjusting his image in the media was taken from him. One such instance happened in connection with a debate among party leaders at a time when the scandal had reached its peak. On his way into the Chamber of the Swedish Parliament, he had to make his way through a large and agitated media posse. Inside the Chamber, the press gallery was full. All the attention was directed at him, the man who would, the media had predicted a few days before, soon suffer a breakdown. Speculation about his cancelling the debate, and about who would replace him, had been rife. This is how he described his experience of that day in October 2011:

> I myself as Håkan wasn't there. ... This is the only time in my life that I've had this kind of experience, of looking at myself. I mean, it didn't last long at all, perhaps just a hundredth of a second or a second. But I remember when the Speaker said, 'Address by Håkan Juholt', and I can so clearly see myself walking there. It lasted for a second, but nobody can take the memory of looking at myself from me. ... That's the only time in my life that I'm looking at myself from the outside. Very strange experience. I've never believed or thought about things like that [laughter], but I was actually a spectator of my own life there.[5] (M27102)

Might the intense media scrutiny have been one of the reasons why he had the first and only extracorporeal experience of his life then and there? The question is worth asking. He says that he himself as Håkan was not present. So who was really there? His body reacted and walked up to the lectern when he heard his name, he explained. At the same time he could see himself from the outside, watching himself walk towards the lectern along with the rest of the audience. It is as if at that moment he captured the essence of the experience of having been transformed into a figure, an actor in a play; and for a brief moment he stepped out of that role and instead became a spectator watching 'Håkan Juholt' act. He became, as he himself says, a spectator of his own life.

It is time to return to the concepts of guilt and shame. You feel guilt about what you have done and shame for who you are, write researchers James Lull and Stephen Hinerman in an early study of media scandals (Lull & Hinerman 1997). They believe that shame is a socially and culturally constructed emotion to a higher degree than guilt: 'It has to do with how others view the self as a longterm project' (Lull & Hinerman 1997:26). It also involves, as we have seen, a moral dimension: when you are ashamed of yourself and feel shame burning in your body, you embody, and thus also make visible, moral understandings. One of the main points the authors make is that traditional distinctions between guilt and shame have been eliminated as a result of the thoroughgoing medialisation of society.[6]

---

5 Also described in Loberg (2012:207f).
6 However, I want to call for caution when it comes to concepts like *medialisation*. They may lead the reader into believing that other periods, before the post-industrial era, were not medialised, which is a misconception. There is more on this in Chapter 2.

The media make moral transgressions visible to a large, interpretative community, and thus foist shame on the perpetrator. The public blaming and public humiliation of a single individual are, according to Lull and Hinerman, the central components of the scandalisation process. What was previously said and done in a limited context is taken out of its original frame of reference and through reporting made available to an indefinite number of recipients, who are given the opportunity to examine the life and personality of the guilty party closely in consequence of the media's generous conveyance of compromising intimate details (Lull & Hinerman 1997:26).[7]

Let us pause for a moment at the ritual element of these occasions of public shame. In his book *Communication as Culture*, mentioned in the introduction and originally published in 1989, communication theoretician James Carey opposes the then prevailing and simplified view that the actual transmission of information from one party to another is the goal of communication. Instead, his book proposes a ritual view of media and communication which is based on cultural, interpersonal relationships, a view where participation, sharing, and mutual association emphasise the connections between the word *communication* and words such as *commonness*, *communion*, and *community* (Carey 1992:18).[8] The broad concepts of *community*, *meaning*, and *identity* are central to Carey's research; and he examines them in great detail by, among other things, drawing on theories

---

7 One researcher who has made an in-depth study of the experience of mediated humiliation is psychologist and communication researcher Barry Richards, who in an article entitled 'Explosive Humiliation and News Media' makes an interesting distinction between shame and humiliation. Like Lull and Hinerman, he believes that shame as a feeling always invokes a moral dimension, and that shame is connected to the experience of guilt. They cannot be separated, he claims. A humiliated person, for his or her part, may feel completely innocent and free of guilt. He clarifies: 'You can be ashamed in your relationship to yourself; you don't need an audience to feel shame. Humiliation, in contrast, requires you to imagine yourself in the minds of others; it is the experience of an intolerable lowering in the world of others' (Richards 2009:63). However, it appears as though these emotions more or less merged for my informants. They experienced both humiliation and shame by turns, and if they were not ashamed they were aware of some people wanting to make them feel shame. In addition, Richards describes how the experience of public humiliation can lead to a need for payback and for getting revenge.

8 All these words originate in Latin *communicare* and *communis*, of which the first in English has the meaning 'to share' and the other has the acquired meaning 'common', 'public', 'general'.

about ritual. Carey regards the fact that both the word *communication* and the word *ritual* have religious connotations as an advantage. In his view, that circumstance exhorts us to think about media and communication as arenas where shared values, ceremonies, norms, and moral negotiations take place. Nine years later, he wrote the following sentence in a chapter in the anthology *Media, Ritual and Identity*: 'Rituals of shame, degradation and excommunication are official and sanctioned ceremonies in all societies from the simple to [the] complex' (Carey 1998:42).

In this text, Carey brings out the feelings of shame that are engendered in people who end up at the centre of particular kinds of dramatic, mediated events where a single individual is named and shamed, publicly stripped naked, and deprived of honour and reputation. These occasions, which he calls rituals of shame and degradation, serve to mark the shift in status of individuals from a higher to a lower rank – from respected to despised, from appreciated to disdained, from exalted to profane, from normal to deviant (Carey 1998:42f). These rituals are often successful in their intent, but not always. However, this is the very point of them, argues Carey: they are meant to cause experiences of guilt and shame and a feeling in the affected individual of being deprived of dignity, in the full glare of publicity. According to him, these types of rituals are also symbolic occasions where people are exiled. It can be an internal exile in the form of an expected withdrawal and an existence made invisible; this frequently comes across as partly voluntary actions, as we could see in the testimonies of the interviewees discussed above. However, the consequences of being made invisible are that civic privileges that the affected person previously took for granted are taken from him or her through a gradual exclusion from the community. This process can also assume the form of an external exile, where the person in question is physically moved from the common to the private through a kind of banishment and is placed in quarantine. Carey emphasises the importance of paying attention to and trying to understand the meaning of this type of public degradation ceremony:

> These are dangerous moments, particularly in the life of democracies committed to the avoidance of cruelty, for they are episodes of high, systematic and sanctioned misanthropy when the power of the state, public opinion or both is inscribed on the body. In testimony to a still fertile historical metaphor, we often call the search for victims to collectively subject to these rituals a 'witch hunt'. (Carey 1998:42)

Carey maintains that dangerous, punitive witch hunts of this kind cannot be justified or defended through utilitarian aspects as easily as other rituals – that is to say, rituals felt to be culturally necessary in that they lead to social integration and unity on moral issues about right and wrong within, for instance, a nation. Instead he encourages us to keep a watchful and critical eye on this type of phenomenon, because it is apt to reveal a more uncivilised aspect of people and of the communities they form.

Carey then elegantly describes how the actual stage for this type of ritual has been moved and changed over time. In primitive societies, such rituals were enacted in the town-hall square, the marketplace, or on the church green, where people who had been found guilty of theft, prostitution, lying, or similar crimes could be publicly displayed; they formed unambiguous embodiments of social norms and agreements, the purpose of which was to create order in the impending chaos. Today, argues Carey, these rituals take place in the public domain through the media (Carey 1998:43). In an almost repetitive manner, they turn up as a kind of interruption in the media rhythms that lend a certain structure to people's everyday lives. During the previous two centuries, he writes, these rhythms have had an increasing effect on people's everyday lives alongside other rhythms, such as liturgical and calendrical ones. In addition, each medium offers its own distinct temporal order in relation to its audience, confirming the current reality through rhythmical, repetitive reporting – that is to say, upholding the existence of an external world which is at bottom shared and common, at least on a symbolic level.

Today, Carey argues, these rhythms can be local as well as national and global – technological achievements breaking the boundaries that were previously perceived as comparatively fixed, such as national boundaries – and offer people a particular organisation of time: of the year, the season, the month, the week, the day, the hour, the minute. Nations, for example, he writes, do not only exist in historical time or in the present time, but also in media time, a point also made by anthropologist Benedict Anderson (Carey 1998:44; see also Anderson 1991). The place that makes up the nation – the physical place, that is – actually exists as border markings, land, lakes, forests, and cities; but it is to a great extent given its symbolic value through its mediation, where it is associated with events such as international sporting events, political elections, festivals, wars, crises, and similar occurrences, which give rise to what Anderson has called 'the imaginary community of the nation'. Only against this background do so-called *media events* become understandable. They have the capacity to unite people who have never met in real life, face to face, but who nevertheless identify with one another and feel an affinity for each other – people whose lives move along in a kind of harmony and coordination where I assume that the everyday existence in which I live is similar to the everyday existence in which you live (Anderson 1991). Mediated events of the more dramatic kind represent a kind of heightening of both pitch and emotional state, forming occasions that at least partly diverge from the expected, natural, rhythmic everyday flow of events and from the routine, habitual manner in which most of us consume media. In doing so, these events may mark a reinforcement, change, displacement, or reinterpretation of what Anderson calls imagined or symbolic communities.

Carey criticises Daniel Dayan and Elihu Katz's (1992) early studies of this kind of mediated, collective rituals, arguing that these authors, surprisingly enough, have neglected the regularly recurring degradation rituals that take up space in the media. The nation as a symbolic place is under continual negotiation, says Carey, where interpretations, values, opinions, religious convictions, political ideologies, and different groupings take shape and struggle for space on editorial pages, in the flow of news, and in popular cultural offerings. And in the multiplicity of flows and events in the public sphere, more distinct ceremonies with a dark undertone occur now and then: 'a marked rite of explicit passage when bodies are stigmatized, reputations destroyed and citizens expelled into a guild of the guilty' (Carey 1998:45). Carey refers to these processes of anathema as exercises in social cruelty. However, I would like in my turn to direct some criticism against Carey's account of just such a case, the analysis of which makes up the main part of his article – an article which, albeit interesting in many ways, is also too dense and therefore arouses my suspicions. Were there really no counter-voices? I want to emphasise that the kinds of degradation rituals that take place in the media should not be regarded as fixed or homogeneous. There would seem to be evidence for their existence; but criticism can be levelled against certain studies of ritual owing to their reluctance to acknowledge the ambivalence that in fact characterises these events. According to my way of looking at it, they are to be regarded as a form of cultural space for negotiation with ritual overtones rather than as ceremonies with a thoroughly settled form.

Lies and damned lies

On the other side of shame and humiliation, there is a more active emotion: anger. Tiina Rosenberg expressed these feelings in a single breath: frustration and anger over the fact that a kind of collective, insistent expectation would force feelings of shame on her. Long sections in a few of the interviews look like lists of names of individuals that the affected person felt had acted deceitfully, unprofessionally, or dishonestly. The closer in time the scandal was to the interview, the more evident was this trait, which is composed of both bitterness and feelings of revenge and injured honour. To me, who on these occasions had done my homework but was nevertheless an outsider, it was sometimes difficult to follow the reasoning and orientate myself in complex turns revolving around who said and did what and when. These outpourings had to do with the reactions of colleagues, friends, and acquaintances, but of course also with the actions of journalists. Frustration was expressed at how rigid the journalistic stories were during the scandal reporting. The informants claimed that they were treated by the people around them and presented by the media as persons different from who they are, and that they had little or no possibility to modify or resist these erroneous descriptions. A sense of powerlessness emerged.

Several people felt that the right to reply – that is, the right to make corrections – was rendered impossible because of the following circumstances:

1 Because the scandal followed its own logic, where the dramaturgy of the story seemed predetermined, the statements of the affected people were adapted to fit the inherent media order. Alternative and nuanced explanatory models were not given any space.
2 This in its turn had the logical consequence that the main figures became disinclined to give further interviews (see Allern & Pollack 2012b:17–21, Bjerke 2012:165–81). One could say that it is little short of impossible for an accused and scandalised individual on whom suspicion is cast to have the last word against a newspaper. 'The more one writes in one's own defence, the more smudged one gets by printer's ink' (Guillou 2010:549).
3 Yet another reason was the incredible pressure. To receive, every day, hundreds of phone calls from journalists whose questions were experienced as inquisitorial eventually resulted in telephones and email programs being switched off as people completely refrained from making any statements. Under such circumstances it appeared almost ludicrous to write, 'the newspaper has attempted to contact NN to ask for a comment'. The well-known Swedish

journalist and internationally established author Jan Guillou, just quoted, narrowed down the problem:

> When the hounding begins, the rule becomes that you should not check a good story because then you risk its falling apart. And the quarry is so overburdened with accusations anyway that no disclaimer from that direction a few days later has any credibility. (Guillou 2010:539)

All in all, there was little possibility for a protagonist to influence the course of events once it had started rolling. Erving Goffman touches upon this matter by emphasising the downside of celebrity for people who are in the public spotlight, where a limited number of facts about an individual can be blown up to dramatic proportions by the news media and then be used as a complete picture of him or her. In addition, if this very limited selection of information is of an unfavourable character, it can have serious consequences. 'We tend to impute a wide range of imperfections on the basis of the original one', he writes (1990a [1963]:15–16). It was precisely this situation that my interviewees protested against: the injustice of an incomplete image being presented as if it were complete, a single act being blown up and made to characterise the individual as a whole. Or, to return to Williams: 'the control we desire between our actions and outcomes is uncoupled' (Williams 2001:6). A lack of control develops, not least regarding our actions and how these are perceived and interpreted by the people around us. After having made a mistake, one would perhaps like to make things right; but this turns out to be difficult. The stickiness of the scandal is difficult to get rid of. Peter Karlsson expressed critical ideas about this:

> It's not as if a person has shot someone, or killed other people by putting poison in a big water reservoir. We're talking about people who have said something inappropriate on TV, paid a babysitter under the table, had wine in a restaurant, or not paid their TV licence. These are human things that can't affect anyone else. So many people have a sense of having done something that is so incredibly awful that they're expected to go into some kind of social exile.

Again one can see how the experience of loneliness and shame arises in the gap between the individual, his or her travelling companions, and the reporting of the media. The individuals respond to a kind of implicit expectation and 'go into some kind of social exile'. Seen in the light of the technological advances and expanding media business of the previous two decades, it may be added that scandals are repeated more often, develop more quickly, and include more actors today as compared to earlier times. This rapidity could be regarded as the greatest opportunity of modern journalism, but also as a curse. The new conditions surrounding publication involve challenges for correct news coverage where this intensified tempo entails an indisputable risk of getting it wrong – maybe not completely wrong, but not completely right either (Allan 2006:23–6, Carlsson 2008:121–38, Hartley 2011:343–74). This is very true indeed of the phenomenon of the media scandal, whose particular dramaturgy often means that news about a scandal is published at a hectic tempo as a consequence of the stiff competition among news producers. Every now and then, the upshot is that a so-called leitmotif is created on the basis of centuries-old myths in order to streamline and simplify the story, where heroes and perpetrators, witches and victims play central roles (Bjerke 2012:169). The Internet also has an incalculable influence on the duration of scandals, partly through the rapid and massive dissemination of a story, partly through the preservation of talk about it.

Several of the informants testified to how difficult it was to relate the public image of themselves to their experience of their own selves and their own identities. In the interviews, they returned to the feeling of unreality. 'That's not me!' they repeated, both to themselves and to other people. Tiina Rosenberg described this in an interesting way:

> Such an enormous gap opens up between the person I am, who reads emails and gives lectures, who certainly has a large audience, but who writes and works and has a family, goes on holiday, goes to the gym and exercises, walks with my Nordic walking poles, and so on. I mean, I can't see that there is anything spectacular in this. Other than that I can talk and write. Plus that I'm a feminist and on the political left, which collides with the prevailing political values that we have right now. But then I'm described as though I'm dangerous! A bit like the classic witch. Not just someone who should be burned, but someone who can lead other people to their ruin.[9] (M27092)

---

[9] For readers who have doubts about Tiina Rosenberg's description of how she, as a non-professional politician, and the then newly formed party Feminist Initiative (Fi) were portrayed in the media, I can recommend the analysis of political scientists Maria Wendt and Maud Eduard in the article 'Fienden mitt ibland oss: Kön och nation i pressbevakningen av Feministiskt initiativ' ('The enemy in our midst: Gender and nation in the press coverage of Feminist Initiative') (Wendt & Eduards 2010).

Håkan Juholt devoted a lot of time to telling me about the experience of having been deprived of his honour. In spite of journalists turning his travel bills and representation receipts inside out in the wake of the rent-allowance scandal, they found, in principle, nothing. Nevertheless, some news media, with the tabloids (called 'evening papers' in Sweden) at the forefront, managed to portray him as a dishonest and untrustworthy figure.

> It was so totally unreal, it was so incredibly unreal that people could claim and say just about anything about me. ... I have always accounted for my receipts. And then they describe me as the complete opposite. Of course I carry that with me, to the end of my days. It hurt me, it wounded me very much. It wasn't a political scrutiny, it was a scrutiny of me as a person, that I was generally unreliable, dishonest, lying, and deceitful. Of course it hurt. (M27102)

Most respondents testified that it was sometimes difficult to hold on to one's self-image while being publicly pilloried as a liar, a lunatic, or a villain. Among others, Maja Lundgren put this feeling into words:

> It didn't happen terribly often, but I sometimes thought, 'What if they're right?' What if this image they paint of this person who is sometimes weak and fragile, sometimes spiteful and greedy, what if it's true? It reminds me of one of those drawings the Surrealists used to make, that's called an 'exquisite corpse', where one person paints the head and then you fold [the paper] and continue with the body and then the legs and so on. I turned into that kind of figure. A monster. And at the same time, when I think deeply about my intentions, I know they were wrong. (M27093)

And in the words of Anders Pihlblad:

> When you gain a bit of perspective it's almost as if you're looking at another person. That's how it is. Because life for me is divided into a before and after this affair, with this scandal. That's absolutely how it is.

It may be worth pointing out that politicians and other so-called elite individuals are not the only ones who have a persona to preserve in public life – we all do. We construct our selves, our identities, by acting on the stage offered by everyday life. By presenting ourselves in a particular way in front of other people, we try to control and govern the information we convey, the information that forms the basis of other people's impressions of us. Goffman argues that we should be aware that the impressions of reality which are conjured up during our appearances on this stage are brittle and fragile phenomena 'that can be shattered by very minor mishaps' (Goffman 1990b [1956]:63). The image of me may come to be coloured by the mistakes I make in social life. Through my travelling companions' ability to appraise and evaluate me, I may experience losing control over the person I believe I am and wish to communicate to other people. I may feel unjustly judged for my actions, which I myself perhaps regard as exceptions and atypical of my personality. This social, communicative process is reciprocal, however. In the same way, I have an ability to appraise and judge you on the basis of your mistakes, or for that matter refrain from doing so. In this way, power is evenly distributed.

On the basis of the informants' experiences of taking on the leading role in the drama of a scandal, one can draw the conclusion that power in this context is very unevenly distributed. Through the tools of language, a particular character is chiselled out which is very difficult to alter once it has taken shape. It seems as though a collective force takes over journalism in connection with a scandal, where even individual journalists who would usually have held back stop doing so. The threshold is gradually lowered, and it becomes permissible to say or write just about anything about the main protagonist (Bjerke 2012). In Jan Guillou's drastic way of putting it, 'regular source-critical rules are eliminated when the hounding begins, and basically anything becomes permitted, if only one can land another blood-splattering blow. To the cheers of the crowd' (Guillou 2010:537). At a certain stage, it no longer seems necessary to have any evidence for claiming that the main figure has a dubious character or that he or she is a threat to social stability and should resign – if there is a post from which to resign – especially not if one is an editorial writer or a columnist (Pollack 2009:99–120, Nord et al. 2012). A scandal whipped up by editorial writers and pundits will inevitably be both more brutal and harsher in its tone, writes Jan Guillou. In advocacy journalism, he argues, a brutalisation of news reporting occurs in the context of media houndings as the truth and relevance requirements are set aside (Guillou 2010:520–4). When mishaps, to use Goffman's term, are exposed in public life, analysed, emphasised, and confirmed on the media scene by a number of influential media actors – whose status is not least determined by their having the opportunity to act on this particular stage – a form of deadlock occurs. Hanne Kjöller expressed a certain dismay at how, in the context of scandals, influential journalists take the liberty of using their own media platforms in order to carry out personal vendettas, something she herself strictly refrains from doing. She saw it as impossible to use her own forum, the editorial page of *Dagens Nyheter*, in order to defend or explain herself. 'I can write letters to the editor, I can write debate articles in other newspapers', she maintained, this being an act of respect vis-à-vis the readers, who are interested in relevant and impartial reporting rather than mudslinging. This, however, was not at all what was offered to citizens when the reporting about herself unfolded in the media, she said:

> There's no room for professional reflection either. There's no room for reflecting about things such as, 'Is this relevant for our readers?', 'Is it true?' Everything must sort of [be published]. It's a snowball. People are completely caught up in the hunt, and that's the journalistic shipwreck.

One example of what Hanne Kjöller calls 'mass psychosis' was the day when the news got around that she had cancelled her day-long seminar during the big Göteborg Book Fair. In fact, the date of the seminar had been moved owing to a funeral, the date of which had been fixed before the media hounding started. The change of dates had thus occurred several weeks earlier. Nevertheless, the whole thing led to intense reporting in the news media with the recurring headline 'Kjöller ställer in' ('Kjöller cancels'), in spite of the publisher's investing a lot of time in explaining to journalists that this was not the case at all. Consequently, one may conclude that the news fitted well into the dramaturgy of the scandal reporting, and the fact that it was not true was overlooked by a large number of news producers.

However, there are studies indicating that journalism is not always quite as conformist as might be believed at first. The 'hounding' metaphor risks overstating the uniformity of the reporting (see Jenssen & Fladmoe 2012). Some little time into a media scandal, a comparatively polyphonic conversation among different actors takes shape – not least in the advocacy material, where opinions clash and apologias in defence of the affected person are also formulated. To an even greater degree, the media audiences' responses to a scandal are characterised by diversity (Wästerfors 2005). It is interesting to note that the main protagonists hardly notice this while it is going on – *all* voices, whatever their points of view, are components of the scandals at whose centres they find themselves.

Family, love, caring

As I have shown, several of the informants described profound changes to their social lives as a consequence of the reporting.

Seemingly stable relationships of many years' duration, both private and professional, came to an end. As we have seen, the interviewees expressed surprise at how quiet and lonely their lives became. But on the other side of the silence, the betrayals, the averted eyes, and the absent phrases of greeting, there were people who chose to step up. Håkan Juholt:

> *HJ*: But no, the telephone fell silent really fast. There were of course those who surprised me, both in the party and outside it, who I didn't think would get in touch. One's friends are always there, but those who are sort of in the circle beyond one's friends, they surprised me. The corner I thought would be full was empty, and the corner I thought would be empty was pretty full.
> *I*: A rearrangement of the furniture.
> *HJ*: Yes, totally. Completely. That's a perfectly correct description. (M27102)

Real friends showed they cared and could be trusted, at any rate for Juholt; but other than that social life was characterised by surprises. The circle outside family, friends, and acquaintances harboured surprises as well. Strangers in city streets walked up to the main figures of the scandals in order to express empathy and dismay at the reporting in the media. At times they initiated physical contact by hugging, touching the affected person's arm, or caressing their cheek, a behaviour which sometimes caused fear and sometimes joy. A sense of having one's integrity violated was mixed with an invigorating experience of acknowledgement. In any case, it became apparent that exposure in the media had transformed the persons concerned into public goods, into people about whom one could have any opinions one wanted and to whom one could do whatever one liked, the boundary between the private and the professional having dissolved.

The significance of these types of attempts at making contact is, according to Goffman, that they turn the individual concerned into a person to whom strangers, without any particular reflection, can take the liberty to speak 'providing only that they are sympathetic to the plight of persons of his kind' (Goffman 1990a [1963]:28). In these types of contacts, the person at the focus of the attention is apt to try to anticipate what is going to happen by assuming a crouching, defensive position or by avoiding public environments altogether. The discomfort of being exposed increases in connection with strangers suddenly feeling called upon to establish contact because they emphasise the peculiar nature of the situation with their caring and their comforting words. One thing is clear, though:

In the middle of the media storm

natural, spontaneous direct contact with other people has come to a complete stop (Goffman 1990a [1963]:25ff)

At this point, I would like to invoke a personal memory. A fair number of years ago, I was sitting at Arlanda airport in Stockholm waiting for a domestic flight heading south. The newspaper billboards that day were adorned with the face of Allan Larsson, former Minister for Finance in the Swedish government and at that time the chair of Sveriges Television ('Sweden's Television'), who had been caught up in a dispute with Maria Curman, the Managing Director of the same public-service television company. Their conflict had clearly taken the step from the backstage region to front of stage, and it had begun to assume the shape of a public scandal (Goffman 1990b [1956]). The waiting travellers helped themselves to free copies of newspapers, the crackling of thin paper and the vague scent of printer's ink framing the otherwise passive moment of waiting. Time dragged itself along, people glanced at their watches, their eyes now and then turning to the counter where they hoped a flight attendant would soon show up. But suddenly the indolent mood changed, not rapidly, but nevertheless palpably. It was something to do with the way the bodies moved, how the energy in them increased, how the murmur rose. I looked up and was surprised to see what several of my fellow passengers had already noted: right at the gate was none other than Allan Larsson, sitting down among the waiting travellers. Unlike many of us, he refrained from taking a newspaper from the newspaper stand. The change in atmosphere was almost physical. Our collective attention was now completely focused on Allan Larsson. Swedes are a discreet people, so most of us tried to hide our curiosity; but it proved to be almost impossible not to stare at him. I myself made certain efforts in that line, but it turned out to be very hard to concentrate on the newspapers in my lap. Instead, I repeatedly glanced furtively in his direction. I remember it as a titillating experience that he sat there very close to me while at the same time, a bit further away, I could see him depicted on the newspaper billboards with a grim look on his face. Somehow, it was fascinating that he managed to be both flesh and blood and billboard material in one and the same everyday moment. The thought crossed my mind that maybe I should speak to him. But what would I have said? Instead, I joined the other travellers in attempting the difficult art of paying no attention. How Larsson experienced the situation could not be read from his facial expression. In any case, the particular charge that arises in a room when all the attention is directed at a person who is written about in the papers was very clear, as if this person had ended up directly in the spotlight. The unreflecting, quiet spirit of community ceased to exist as 'we travellers' was replaced by 'we travellers *and* Allan Larsson'. The affective mood did *something* to us at that moment, to use the terms of geographer Ben Anderson (2009:78). Affective moods are indeterminately suspended between subject and object, 'impersonal in that they belong to collective situations and yet can be felt as intensely personal' (Anderson 2009:80). According to Anderson, 'atmospheres have ... a characteristic spatial form – diffusion within a sphere. ... we can say that atmospheres are generated by bodies – of multiple types – affecting one another as some form of "envelopment" is produced' (Anderson 2009:80).

Returning to the narratives of the people affected by scandals, it was not surprising that the support from their families was what bore them through the crises. When they held, family ties could even be strengthened as a consequence of the exposure. It was also when family came up during the interviews that the voices of some people broke with suppressed anger or grief. It appears that much can be borne in the form of violations of one's own integrity, but when one's children or aged parents get dragged into the game, that is the last straw. Håkan Juholt again:

> They didn't hesitate to go home to my 80-year-old mother and photograph her. They visited my children's schools to question my children. They stopped their teachers. If there is an open season there is an open season, then you can do whatever you want. (M27102)

Juholt was not alone in having these experiences. Several of the informants told similar stories about how journalists had called or gone to see ex-partners, former classmates, siblings, cousins, parents, and children. In some cases, children were addressed by reporters right beside the school playground, sometimes in order to prevail on them to comment on their mother's or father's behaviour or to get information about where the parent in question was. When I brought this up with Niklas Svensson, reporter at *Expressen*, he questioned the veracity of these stories. If such things occur they are accidents at work, he claimed. Reporters look for contact information on the Internet. It is not unusual for them to find several telephone numbers listed for the main protagonist, whereupon they call these numbers. In these cases, said Svensson, there is a risk that they end up speaking to a child, because the children's telephone numbers are listed under their parents' names. What contradicts this kind of explanation is that several of the children claimed, in front of their parents, that they were actually called on, spoken to, and/or questioned by journalists, in physical meetings. Whether or not this is true, children and other family members were dragged into the scandal in an emotional sense. Their fear and worries were doubtless the heaviest burdens for the informants to bear. Juholt recounted how his son's anxiety and care for his father both moved and tormented the elder Juholt:

> My youngest son was still living at home. He felt that I was being bullied. He felt bad, because he saw me as a victim of bullying. He said expressly that it was bullying, he used that word several times. He felt bad because nobody stood up for me. Why didn't anybody hit back? How do you feel, Dad? I could wake up in the morning and get up to work around six, and then find I had a text message that he'd sent around two at night. He wrote how much he thought about me and how much he loved me and things like that. So he took that responsibility. He took responsibility for his dad, that I should feel OK. (M27102)

Suddenly the roles were reversed. A teenager took care of his weary and stressed-out parent. The son represented parts of the functionality in everyday life that had been lost, and among other things made sure that his dad combed and put styling mousse in his hair in the mornings. The informants described scenes showing how children were pulled into the media scrutiny because it was taking place physically outside the home. Cecilia Stegö Chilò:

> When the news about the TV licence broke and I got the whole posse outside in the street, then it wasn't easy for the children. The eldest one dealt with it pretty well, but the youngest refused to go out. It's also a sensitivity thing for a mother when her children don't feel well. Who pays the price for this? You're supposed to be some kind of strong, female politician – tough, smart, focused, cool. And then your children are affected, and at once you're a tiny, helpless nobody.

Family ties also entail the latent presence of a kind of infection process; that is to say, the stigma in question can be transferred from the protagonist to the people who are in her or his closest circle, like rings on water. '[This is] a relationship that leads the wider society to treat [them all] in some respects as one', claims Goffman (1990a [1963]:43). It is their house too that is being watched, their telephones too that keep ringing. Goffman's book includes a moving letter sent to an advice column, published in 1961 in the *Berkeley Daily Gazette*, which portrays this infection in a telling manner. The letter puts its finger on how the mechanisms of avoidance risk affecting not just the scandalised person, but also his or her close relatives:

> Dear Ann Landers,
> I'm a girl 12 years old who is left out of all social activities because my father is an ex-convict. I try to be nice and friendly to everyone but it's no use. The girls at school have told me that their mothers don't want them to associate with me because it will be bad for their reputations. My father had some bad publicity in the papers and even though he has served his time nobody will forget it.
> Is there anything I can do? I am very lonesome because it's no fun to be alone all the time. My mother tries to take me places with her but I want to be with people my own age. Please give me some advice — An OUTCAST. (Goffman 1990a [1963]:43)

That family members were pulled into the process and were, so to speak, infected by it became clear in the interviews with the interviewees' partners. But can the stickiness of the scandal on a social level cling to children as well, as the letter quoted above testifies? It looks very much as if this is the case. Ireen von Wachenfeldt felt that her own nadir was reached in connection with her children and grandchildren being pulled into the media scandal, in the latter case through the playground taunts of their classmates, geographically far from the epicentre of events. Her husband, Kennet von Wachenfeldt, said:

> **KW:** But we probably took it hardest when our grandchildren were told things like, 'Right, you're the one whose grandma thinks men are animals', 'we sure know where your grandma lives'.
> **I:** Your grandchildren heard this from other children?
> **KW:** Yes.
> **I:** So spreading rumours goes all the way down to preschool?
> **KW:** That's pretty much it. The first three years of compulsory school at any rate. (M27103)

It was the spreading of rumours at school and the covert threats to her grandchildren that made Ireen decide to write a book about the events (Wachenfeldt 2007).

Fellowship-of-the-hounded letters

Loathing and exclusion, love and care. The one does not exclude the other; rather, these phenomena seem to happen in parallel in a complicated, emotional interaction among human beings. We saw how Peter Karlsson and his family were embraced by the persistent empathy of his colleagues, which manifested itself quite practically in the form of cooked food and comfort. He is not the only one who has experienced this. Sven Otto Littorin, who himself initiated this type of caring arrangements for people who found themselves under fire, felt that he would probably not have made it had it not been for the people who stood there, prepared to hold on to and hug him. In the midst of the critical stage he discovered that he actually had a good many friends, 'genuinely sweet' ones, as he put it. He also claimed that this had been a literal life-saver for him during what he calls a state of crisis. One of the people who were part of this friendly group had gone through similar experiences and encouraged Sven Otto Littorin to act in the same way toward the next person to be affected. Littorin bore this in mind, and in January 2012 he wrote a long personal letter to Håkan Juholt. Later Juholt answered the letter with the following lines: 'I also want to take the opportunity to express my great appreciation for the letter you sent me when I was falling apart. Your warm humanity gave me hope and strength. I am infinitely grateful for this.'

Littorin and Juholt are not the only people who have been involved in this type of caring processes across party lines. In the midst of the most intense phase of the scandal reporting about Ulrica Schenström, at that time Under-Secretary of State for the Moderate Party, Schenström had similar support from Ingmar Ohlsson, former Under-Secretary of State for the Social Democrats. In the preface to Anders Pihlblad's journalistic book *Drevet går* (roughly translated, 'Open Season'; 2007), Schenström speaks about the particular significance of Ohlsson's words when she was at her most wretched stage. In compassionate terms he wrote, among other things, about how few people there are who think about the person behind the public role when the media hounding starts (Schenström in Pihlblad 2010:7).

By analogy with the rising number of public scandals within the political sphere, one can thus note the existence of this type of informal acknowledgement among affected people across party lines, something that calls for reflection. These *fellowship-of-the-hounded letters*, how should they be interpreted? Among other things, they signal awareness among politicians at a collective level about the vulnerability that comes with their role in a society where journalism does not just inform people about politics but also interprets, filters, comments on, and directs it, expressing special interest in the doings of individual political actors. The letters also suggest that the experience of being at the centre of a media scandal is not unique. It is an experience shared by a number of women and men, both within and outside politics. The letters, one may assume, take part of the sting out of shame by emphasising the shared nature of the experience. In doing so, they make the loneliness less acute.

In addition, Erving Goffman provides many detailed examples of how a marked individual seeks or is offered contact with other people who share the experience of a particular form of misfortune. It seems as though ties can form in the wake of exclusion. These relationships that spring from similar experiences are associated with ambivalence because they underline the marginalisation itself by virtue of their very existence. The first group of favourably disposed people are of course those who share the stigma in question. From their own experience, they know what it is like; therefore, they are able to provide a certain amount of guidance to a person with regard to ways of coping with the stigma, and they can supply 'a circle of lament to which he can withdraw for moral support and for the comfort of feeling at home, at ease, accepted as a person who really is like any other normal person' (Goffman 1990a [1963]:32).

The empathic fellowship-of-the-hounded letters in combination with the kindness of strangers emphasise that a stigmatised person 'must everywhere face being received as someone who no longer is what he once was' Goffman 1990a [1963]:91). When the discrepancy between an apparent and an actual identity becomes obvious to the affected person, his or her social belonging is undermined, writes Goffman. This insight leads to the person being cut off both from society and from him- or herself, 'so that he stands a discredited person facing an unaccepting world' (Goffman 1990a [1963]:31). Together with people who share the misfortune in question, however, he can lick his wounds and tell the whole sad story about his fate (Goffman 1990a [1963]:32).

To return to the question of why the phenomenon of fellowship-of-the-hounded letters arises now, in the twenty-first century, the book *Media and Public Shaming* (Petley 2013) can offer some answers. In this volume, a number of researchers and journalists describe how the development of technology, competition in the media business, and increased visibility in public life have led to a significant increase of risk for anybody to experience being publicly derided and scandalised, not least through social media, which exist in a kind of symbiosis with traditional media (more about this in Chapter 3). Questionable publications in digital forums where private individuals are portrayed as lunatics, predators, or simply as disgusting creatures can, so to speak, seep into the coverage of traditional media and then be justified by means of so-called public interest, an expression that is given a multiplicity of meanings, sales figures not infrequently controlling the interpretation (Petley 2013). The 'naming and shaming' part of the whole thing – that is, actions that are felt to be morally provocative are exposed in public life and embodied via a single, named individual – is easily recognised from media-scandal contexts. The social consequences are also well known by this time. For instance, Jacob Rowbottom writes in the above-mentioned book that 'successful' naming-and-shaming processes can lead to feelings of shame, isolation, and exclusion for an affected individual, as well as to a real loss of status that may last for a long time (Rowbottom 2013:1).

This research in combination with other studies indicates, as was mentioned earlier, that scandals are rather frequent in today's Western society (Allern et al. 2012, Thompson 2008). Besides, this frequency has increased. Both the visibility and the loneliness, as well as the direct – sometimes offensive, sometimes loving – actions to which the informants were exposed, can be interpreted in the light of what John B. Thompson (2005) has described as a new form of visibility in our time. It includes us all, he emphasises; but in his account he concentrates on the visibility of today's politicians in public life via the media and in particular TV, which has, he claims, created a particular form of vulnerability. The media not only offer opportunities for exposure, where political leaders can be applauded and supported, but also a number of opportunities for attacks and condemnation. In the paradigm of the new visibility, missteps that previously remained hidden, or were judged to be insignificant, can have fateful consequences. This mass visibility is characteristic of our time, argues Thompson. Differing from the visibility of earlier historical periods, it has, as a consequence, contributed to a form of intimisation of our leaders; we can see their features, study their physical imperfections in close-ups, hear their laughter, and note the nuances of their facial expressions.

> Hence the visibility created by the media can become the source of a new and distinctive kind of fragility. However much political leaders may seek to manage their visibility, they cannot completely control it. Mediated visibility can slip out of their grasp and can, on occasion, work against them. (Thompson 2005:42)

Media and communication researcher John Corner (2000) emphasises these circumstances in a fine analysis of politicians' ways of acting in public life today. His description of how they manipulate their personas directs one's thoughts to a kind of martial-arts-influenced dance where they duck and step forward, attack and caress, in turns. In general, there is an awareness among politicians of the exposure gains that are to be had by a person who ventures to step out of the official, professional role and be personal, not to say private, in interviews; at the same time, they are fully aware of the risks that such behaviour involves, where scandals and the encapsulation effect that they entail loom just around the corner (Corner 2000, Corner & Pels 2003; see also Kroon Lundell 2010).

How things change

In the above sections, we have seen how the home is both a place where media scandals take shape in a direct physical sense and a refuge from these very scandals – two things that are difficult to reconcile. Anthropologists and ethnologists have written substantially about the importance of the home to human beings and their everyday existence. They have investigated how the security that is connected with a home is generated and how that distinguishes the home from places in general. This happens, among other ways, through the practice of a multitude of habits and routines that take place there, in coexistence between people and things (see Miller 2011a). The late modern idea that everything is in a flow of creation should be complemented by the insight that most things happen many times over, according to an all but rhythmical repetition (Schutz 1973:99–242). The continuity of repetition in everyday life creates a link between a then and a now, a link which also extends towards that which we know nothing about, namely the future, leading, on some level, to our already being there.

Becoming the subject of a media scandal means an abrupt end to habits and routines and hence also to the unreflecting security that is engendered through the thousands of repetitive, everyday activities through which we continually create and re-create our lives, not least in our homes. The informants testified to a state of emergency that lasted for a surprisingly long time, a state which was at first characterised by chaos and confusion but which eventually, for some, led to a form of passivity. The home then became a castle where one could hide and lick one's wounds; but it could also be transformed into a prison under constant surveillance, a place where one felt watched and insecure but which one still could not – or did not dare to – leave. A paradoxical situation arose where people took refuge in their homes while feeling exposed there, an experience that continued even after the cameras were extinguished.

The introduction of Martin Heidegger's concept of 'thrownness into the world' into this line of reasoning makes it possible to trace a transitioning from being able to behave as an acting subject, expressed in the present-participle form 'throwing', to a more reactive and passive state, the past-participle form 'thrown'. In the latter form, a person is thrown into the world through no fault of their own; she or he is an object. This has to do with so-called *limit-situations* occasioned by conflict, suffering, and guilt, 'life-defining moments' where people meet 'the unspeakable, the limits of our understanding. What lies in the shadows, beyond our immediate comprehension and control' (Lagerkvist 2017:102). At that moment, a person is thrown out of what Schutz calls 'the social, natural attitude' (Schutz 1973:59), i.e., ordinary behaviour in the everyday lifeworld. While in that lifeworld, we are continually directed towards the future, a directedness that rests on the idea of an 'and so on' and 'I can always do it again' (Schutz 1973:35, 55). Suddenly, it becomes very difficult to lead a life orientated towards the future; it is hard to live 'normally', to act as one used to act, to plan as one used to plan. In the words of programme presenter Anders Pihlblad: 'It's completely impossible to have a normal life. Nothing felt normal in any way.' Peter Karlsson expresses this in a similar manner: 'Nothing becomes normal after having experienced this, it just doesn't.'

In this situation, everyday things – such as the daily newspaper, the calendar, the computer, and the mobile phone – may acquire radically new meanings, and they are no longer there to be interacted with in the way they used to be. They are no longer *zuhanden*, to borrow yet another concept from Heidegger; that is, they are no longer a reachable or usable tool (see Frykman 2012:99–103, Frykman & Povrzanović Frykman 2016:20ff). A person who has a calendar easily fills it with events and even, one might say, with encounters. Many of the interviewees, most of them high achievers, were skilled at precisely this. But now the calendar became unusable, a dead thing, a reminder of the sudden inhibition of everyday life, just like the mobile phone – this invaluable technical device for people with many meetings booked into their calendars – whose incessant signals now produced stress, even terror, and which was therefore switched off, alternatively transformed into a food-and-sleep clock. After the acute phase, the phone once more became tangible, but now because of its silence. Alluding to anthropologist Daniel

Miller (2008), we might speak of 'the discomfort of things', referring to that re-charging of objects which transforms them from 'ready-to-hand' creators of security and meaning to things one would rather forget, hide, and avoid.[10] Sartre argues that during a state of emotional turbulence, highly valued things can lose their inherent meanings and their natural places in everyday life. From having been charged with meaning, they become emotionally reset to zero (Sartre 2002:86f). Their owner's relationship to them seems to die in some way, or rather, in this particular case, to become charged with new meanings (Heidegger 1974:115).

Håkan Juholt described this re-charging in relation to the mobile phone in a thought-provoking manner. During his short and turbulent time as party leader for the Social Democrats, the phone became 'like a machine for solving very difficult tasks' which was busy round the clock. When the negative media scrutiny started around his person after a few months as party chair, things became, if possible, even worse. The tempo increased, and he was expected to answer new questions every minute, day and night. As soon as he hung up, the phone rang again. One section from the interview may be quoted by way of illustration:

I: It almost sounds as though technology kidnapped you for a while there?
HJ: Yes, completely, totally, raped me. It was brutal ... .
I: There were also expectations ... you couldn't switch off the telephone?
HJ: No. It was around the clock. All the time, round the clock. And the telephone very rarely meant something positive for me, very rarely.
I: So it was charged with ...
HJ: The phone was charged with negative energy. Out of a hundred activities, ninety-nine were problems or misery. It was very, very rare for me to use the telephone for something that was fun or enjoyable.
I: But you can do it now?
HJ: Absolutely, so now I'm in the process of forgiving the telephone and taking it back. But I only talk on the phone once a week at most. (M27102)

From having been speaking on the phone more or less constantly, Juholt today uses the phone at most once a week, usually not even that. 'I don't answer and I don't call anyone', he asserted. He does

---

10 The title of Miller's book is in fact *The Comfort of Things* (2008).

not even answer when family members call, but sends them a text message instead – a way of regaining control of technology. He described this as being a matter of preferring to see the people who are important to him, rather than talk to them through a device. A strong aversion to the mobile phone, which was previously allowed to take up so much of his time, became apparent in our conversation. Ingmar Ohlsson on his part recalled the new, unfamiliar fear of the daily newspaper that faithfully landed on his hall mat every morning:

> You try to shut yourself away from the world, but it goes so far that you don't even want go and get the morning newspapers inside the door in the morning because you know – what are they writing about you this time? It's such an incredible violation. It's damaging to one's self-esteem in general to be demonised in this way.

Other people drew up strategies so that they did not have to acquaint themselves with the things that were written about them, which may be hard enough when so many daily activities are tied to presence on the Internet. It takes a great measure of self-discipline not to click onwards, or in the words of Anders Pihlblad: 'One has to get away, one has to stop Googling one's name all the time.' Those who still had their partners during the scandal often had their help with the refraining and sifting procedures – not looking, not reading – a circumstance that indicates the loneliness which others had to endure.

Concluding comment

On the basis of the analysis of the emotions of people affected by scandals – the way they are expressed in the interviews – it is possible to establish that media scandals are by no means things that happen in the media only, an intra-journalistic phenomenon, but that they to a very great extent include interpersonal communication. The interviews do not only afford access to the inner, experienced dimension of the scandal; we also catch sight of the reactions of the audience – as experienced by the main figure – and how these interact with one another. People who read or hear about the scandal act in the social space on the basis of their impressions of the reporting. This may have to do with anything from raising their eyebrows, or talking about the event at home, to ignoring, staring at, or trying to make contact with the person who is being written about. In exceptional cases, there may be more aggressive, physical expressions, in the form of violence and threatening letters. The person who is at the centre of the scandal is, in his or her turn, compelled to respond to these implicit and explicit actions, as several examples have demonstrated.

The analysis shows how visibility and vulnerability through mass communication interact with the kind of communication that takes place in physical meetings among people. These communication paths do not exist independently of one another; rather, they are messily intertwined. Both people in the immediate vicinity of the informants and persons at a greater distance from them reacted and acted on the basis of the mediated image. In this way, visibility became a factor whose presence was felt in everyday life. This both obvious and exciting interaction among different forms of communication is of little interest to John B. Thompson, who, in accordance with sociological tradition, is content to use a macro analysis from a distance, where the people around whom everything revolves are relegated to the wings. My critique of his and other researchers' way of seeing the public scandal as a media phenomenon that takes place on its own, through traditional and digital mass media, is explained in greater detail in the ensuing chapters, among other things through a historical example.

2
Gossip, rumour, and scandals

In this part of the book, the analysis of the relationship between the interpersonal and the mediated dimension of the public scandal is deepened.[1] The preceding chapter made it clear that these dimensions are more or less interwoven, a circumstance to which media researchers have not paid a great deal of attention because they have, as a rule, chosen to focus on the media themselves, employing a narrow definition of the 'media' concept. In order to acquire an idea of the inherent mechanisms of the scandal phenomenon, the focus in this chapter is on how interpersonal communication influences and interacts with mediated communication. The overall question is: How is a media scandal possible? Through which media is it created? The text is divided into two parts: a detailed historical analysis and an analysis of a contemporary case. The point of departure is located in historical material, consisting of secondary sources in the form of literature, together with primary sources in the form of interview material and present-day media sources.

Mediated orality

The seminal work on the topic of media scandals is British sociologist John B. Thompson's *Political Scandal: Power and Visibility in the Media Age* (2008), which was mentioned in both favourable and critical terms in the preceding chapter. It is in many ways an insightful analysis of the history and particular characteristics of mediated scandals, but there are also some things missing. For instance, the author initially devotes some space to establishing the difference between the concepts of gossip, rumour, and scandal, in spite of just having confirmed the kinship among these words

---

[1] This chapter is a revision and further development of an article published in the cultural historical periodical *RIG* (Hammarlin 2013a).

(Thompson 2008:25–8).² A matrix that is presented early on in the book cannot be misunderstood: Thompson really does mean that a phenomenon that he calls 'local scandal' is distinctly different from a mediated scandal (Thompson 2008:61). In the former category, both the revelation and the disapproval are created through oral communication face to face, while in the latter category this happens through mediated communication. To my mind it is doubtful whether distinguishing among closely related words and phenomena in the way Thompson does enriches the analysis. In fact, I believe it becomes limiting. I would venture to claim that it is a mistake to see the processes of media scandals as separate from the everyday talk that is produced in face-to-face meetings, an idea that Lars Nord, a Swedish professor of political communication who has studied Swedish political scandals, seems to take as his point of departure: 'What differentiates the modern political scandal from the classic one is that the scandal no longer derives its nourishment from discussions and conversations among people, but is mainly conducted in the media' (Nord 2001:20).

There are several problems with this statement. First of all, it is unclear what Nord means by the 'classic' scandal, which he contrasts to the 'modern' scandal. The lack of clarifying examples and a historical anchoring leaves his claim unsupported. Secondly, there is an overemphasis here on a kind of distinction between media and people. Everyday talk – or, for that matter, gossip – among people is interwoven with mediated scandals and supplies them with nourishment, not least because people who work with media live and operate within a cultural context, just like everybody else. These people are, in their turn, in constant mediated as well as direct contact with ordinary citizens for tips and ideas about possible follow-ups and further investigation of the scandal. In addition, in everyday life in twenty-first-century Western culture, it has become increasingly difficult to draw clear dividing lines between, for instance, conversations via social media and 'conversations among people'. The following quotation from anthropologist Elizabeth Bird, who has studied modern mediated scandals, brings out the essence of the problem and forms a suitable point of departure for the continuation of the present discussion:

> Indeed, in many ways, the notion of 'scandal' is more firmly embedded in the oral, interpersonal dimension of our lives, rather than the

---

2 See the Introduction to this book.

media dimension (although these are closely intertwined). The media play the role of the storyteller or town crier, but the scandal gains its momentum from the audiences. (Bird 2003:31)

Consequently, it is everyday talk among people and its relationship to scandals that I try to foreground here, 'the chitchat that keeps social life lubricated', as sociologist Herbert J. Gans calls it. In this continually ongoing small talk, news about scandals may serve as raw material; but gossip and the spreading of rumours can also stimulate professional news distribution, something that Gans would describe as a commonly occurring meeting between everyday news and professional news (Gans 2007:162).[3]

By way of introduction, the word 'gossip' is in need of elaboration. Here I support anthropologist Max Gluckman's interpretation, in which he sees this type of moralising orality as an integral part of culture. He emphasises, among other things, the unifying function of gossip, insofar as people are brought together in discussions raised by the moral issues contained in gossip, even if views on what is right and wrong may differ. 'Gossip does not have isolated roles in community life, but is part of the very blood and tissue of that life', he writes (Gluckman 1963:308). The author uses gossip and scandal as a conceptual pair, 'gossiping and scandalizing', and continues: 'their importance is indicated by the fact that every single day, and for a large part of each day, most of us are engaged in gossiping' (Gluckman 1963:308).

This engrossing activity, which many of us neither acknowledge nor register because of its both embarrassing and everyday character, is a culturally determined process with particular, if unspoken, rules. For instance, it is, at least in Sweden, felt to be normal behaviour to lower one's voice or close one's door when discussing something compromising about a person who is not present. Gossiping is occasionally concluded with the exhortation 'Don't tell anyone!' – a kind of adjuration that confirms rather than hinders the ability of the spoken word to travel quickly and freely. An appeal such as 'Tell only a few people about this!' would have been more apt. The word *slander* is multifaceted. It is etymologically connected to the word *scandal*, as was mentioned in the introduction to this book,

---

[3] The news genre is complex and makes up its own field of research, and I will therefore not delve into this matter in greater detail. It is the scandal (which can indeed be considered a kind of news in itself) as a phenomenon that is at the centre of this book.

and covers expressions such as *bullshit, tittle-tattle, defamation, the spreading of rumours, gossip,* and *innocent small talk.* The word *gossip* has existed since the sixteenth century as a word denoting a person, usually a woman, 'of light and trifling character ... who delights in idle talk, a newsmonger, a tattler' (*OED Online*, s.n. 'gossip'). Since the nineteenth century, the word has also come to mean the act of gossiping itself. According to *The Swedish Academy Dictionary* (*SAOB*), the Swedish equivalent of the *OED*, the first evidence for the Swedish word *skvaller* (gossip) – which can be said to include both the concepts of *gossip* and *slander* – can be found in a version of the New Testament in Swedish from 1526, *Thet Nyia Testamentit på Swensko* ('The New Testament in Swedish'), also called 'the Vasa Bible'. Here *skvaller* seems to mean *fåfängligt tal* ('vain speech') (*SAOB*, s.n. *skvaller sbst*^{3}). The *SAOB* also points to the mobility of the word; one idiom is *löpa med skvaller* ('go around gossiping'). This idea can also be found in English, where Washington Irving's character Ichabod Crane owes his popularity to his being '[a] kind of travelling gazette, carrying the whole budget of local gossip from house to house' (*OED Online*, s.n. 'gossip'; the quotation is from Irving's 'The Legend of Sleepy Hollow', 1820). Gossip can be about the relationships of other people, and can be irrelevant but also disparaging. It can be equated with prattle and loose talk, but also with rumour and defamation. Gossip can be harmless, but also malicious. The *SAOB*, for instance, describes gossip as something disloyal and unsporting. One does not gossip about one's friends; that is, gossip would in this sense border on a kind of treason. However, anthropologist Max Gluckman, like many of his anthropologist colleagues, argues that gossip is socially valuable – indeed even necessary, because of the moral questions which it tends to encompass. When he himself gossips about friends and enemies, he is therefore aware of performing a kind of social duty, he writes, ironically continuing: 'but ... when I hear they gossip viciously about me, I am rightfully filled with righteous indignation' (Gluckman 1963:315).

The relationship of gossip to truth is complex. We can gossip without telling falsehoods or lying; the talk can just as well be about things of which we are convinced, but it can also, as has previously been pointed out, have to do with half-truths, fabrications, and malicious lies. Perhaps it is precisely this possibility and ambivalence that make people both spread and listen to gossip. For what if things were this way? Can it be possible? The old saw 'no smoke without fire' points to the driving force behind at least a certain type of gossip.

It never occurs to Gluckman to endeavour to differentiate between gossip and scandal. On the contrary, he writes about them as though they were deeply interconnected phenomena. To draw dividing lines between rumour, gossip, and scandal, as Thompson does, is perhaps necessary in order to delimit a research area; but between the spoken and the mediated, between everyday talk and public conversation, between the newsroom, the living room, and the street, if you will, there are quite a few new things to be learnt about this phenomenon. For this reason, I will pursue my inquiry in that direction.

Chronique scandaleuse

When examining the matter more closely, it becomes clear that scandals have been mediated for centuries, and that general person-to-person conversations about them have played a notable part in that process. In a historical perspective, the oral distribution of news should in point of fact be considered a form of mediation. By looking at mid-eighteenth-century France and England, I hope to be able to clarify certain similarities and connections between so-called modern and classic scandals (to refer to Nord's expression), in particular with regard to the oral dimension of this phenomenon.

Book historian Robert Darnton has investigated the history of scandals in great detail. He takes his readers on a journey to a smelly, noisy, and tumultuous, but at the same time organised, France during the Enlightenment, when news was conveyed through a complex media system. The assertion that we have recently entered the information age is the most misleading of all platitudes now in circulation, he observes (Darnton 2004). Paris at this time was abuzz with sound, life, talk, and a continually ongoing exchange of information. Songs were sung and poems recited, gossip passed from one person to another, rumours were spread, and the few newspapers in existence were read aloud (Darnton 1997, 2000, 2005, 2010). News distribution was a natural part of the many occupations of everyday life.[4] In order to find out what was happening, people would go to so-called *nouvellistes de bouche*, whose task it was to spread oral news. Darnton translates this French expression into *gossipmongers*. The word exists in several variants,

---

4 At least for privileged citizens of the male sex.

which he uses as synonyms in his presentation, such as *scandal-*, *rumour-*, and *newsmongers*. This is interesting in the present context and additionally underlines the kinship among these phenomena. These professional telltales could be found both indoors and outdoors, and they attracted large numbers of people who wanted to hear the latest about the latest. In the heart of Paris there was, for example, a large and splendid chestnut tree under which people gathered to partake of the news that was delivered; or people would congregate in one of the hundreds of salons and coffee-houses that existed at that time, where special areas were provided for rumours, gossip, and confirmed information.[5] People circulated within these areas, discussing what they had heard or read, thereby creating a kind of early newsroom (Darnton 2005:33, see also Holmberg et al. 1983:13).

Early journalism differed in a number of ways from today's manner of reporting events, not least because of technological developments and the professionalisation of journalism during the nineteenth and twentieth centuries; but certain things seem to have remained intact, such as a fascination with the sensational, scandalous, and personal. The contents of many of the pamphlets, ballads, and news books that were printed almost three centuries ago with the aim of spreading news were taken from the talk in the coffee-houses and dealt with unexpected, surprising, and shocking events, often involving people with high positions and prestige. They can be summarised as cautionary tales criticising those in power and constituting a form of popular entertainment. Anthropologists Elizabeth Bird and Jesús Martín-Barbero use the concept of melodrama to describe this genre which, they argue, brought in 'the "I can't believe it" dimension of life' (Bird 1997:115, Martín-Barbero 1993:112–20; see also Stephens 2007:90–115).

In particular, people in Paris were treated to gossip about Louis XV and his entourage. That might appear to be an innocent pastime, but in fact it was the direct opposite. Whereas press historian Mitchell Stephens (2007:94ff) depicts mediated gossip as a harmless *fait-divers* phenomenon, Robert Darnton argues that it has to do with popularly anchored means of communication which have at least to some extent been used in order to question the prevailing social order. This *bruit public* ('public rumour' according to Darnton)

---

5 This well-known chestnut tree was known as the Kraków tree, probably because of the heated discussions that took place beneath its branches during the War of the Polish Succession.

was closely connected with the formation of *l'esprit public* (public opinion), something the regime was aware of and feared (Darnton 1997:14–17).[6] Consequently, the French police were given the task of preventing the dissemination of rumours because it was understood that dangerous talk could escalate into scandals, which constituted a threat against those in power in the country at a time characterised by political change. Even if the King's sovereignty was total, public opinion – that is, the people – had a fair amount of influence over which ministers had to leave their positions and which could remain in their posts (Darnton 2004:110–19). In addition to regularly seizing blasphemous writings and meting out severe punishments for printers and publishers, the police also tried to suppress oral news distribution, another word for which would be gossip. The records of the Bastille which have been preserved for posterity speak about the arrests of individuals, quite a few of whom had some form of elevated social status, on the grounds of a type of crime called *mauvais propos* or *mauvais discours* (roughly, 'bad speech'). These entries could take the following forms:

16 April: the chevalier de Bellerives, former captain of dragoons, for discours against the king, Mme de Pompadour, and the ministers.
9 May: The sieur Le Clerc for mauvais propos against the government and the ministers.
10 May: François-Philippe Michel Saint Hilaire for mauvais propos against the government and ministers. (Darnton 2005:34; see also Darnton 2010:50–1)

It was arduous work to identify who had said what about whom, and many innocent people fell victim to the operations of the police. This did not prevent the number of arrests for bad speech from quickly increasing in number in the 1740s and thereafter. By means of a dense network of detectives with their ears pricked, the police collected information on what people were talking about in the salons, parks, and marketplaces, which resulted in long, detailed reports that formed the basis for the arrests.

Accounts of news distribution, public scandals, and politics in England at this time also suggest that gossip, rumour, and scandals were closely connected phenomena. Oral information about the excesses of the libertines – which to a considerable extent took place in special clubs designed for luxury living, erotic adventures,

---

6 The words *opinion* (public opinion) and *publicitet* (publicity) were also introduced into the Swedish language at this time (Holmberg et al. 1983:13).

miscellaneous unchristian entertainment, and the circulation of radical manuscripts – spread throughout the kingdom and also assumed written form in a literary genre that had been inspired by French scandal journalism. The collective name of this type of writing was the *chronique scandaleuse* – a broad genre within printed news distribution via so-called *nouvellistes à la main*. Darnton describes it in the following way: 'A muckraking and mudslinging journalism, which built up an account of contemporary history by tearing down the reputation of public figures, beginning with the king' (Darnton 2005:23). This was a journalism that makes the tabloid press of the 2010s appear tame in comparison, and as France moved towards the Revolution, the tone became even more hostile (Darnton 1997:14–17). Moralising as well as entertaining songs, verses, drawings, leaflets, images, and pamphlets told compromising stories about the people closest to the king, usually ministers, noblemen, and society ladies with alleged or real connections to the libertines and their scabrous way of life, all intended to annoy and belittle the king, George III. Historian John Brewer follows the progress during the 1760s of publicist and libertine John Wilkes, who tenaciously spread a form of propaganda geared to exposing the lack of sexual morals at court and connecting it to political malfeasance. The purpose of this vigorous literary genre, argues Brewer, was to expose political intrigue – whether true or false – which had previously been hidden from the public, putting these revelations to use in attacking the personal moral standards of the country's leaders and, by extension, their power and influence (Brewer 2005).

In mid-eighteenth-century Sweden, there were similar periodicals which produced person-orientated sensational journalism, one of which bore the telling title *Stockholms Sqwallerbytta* ('The Stockholm tattler'). There were political pretexts for this type of printed gossip, but some scholars maintain that the purpose of these publications was mainly financial gain. Scandals sell, then as now (Holmberg et al. 1983:26). In particular, poetry was written and gossip was spread about people with power and influence. As is the case today, it was privileged people in society who had to put up with this type of less than flattering verbiage, a circumstance that underlines the inherent meaning of mediated gossip and its relationship to power, according to literary historian Blakey Vermeule: 'Gossip is always concerned with power. It follows in the track of the great and never clings for very long to the down and out. People gossip up' (Vermeule 2006:105).

Eighteenth-century media scandals thus did not only exist in order to amuse readers or make money from journalism. The libertines wanted to relativise the established norms of society and were aware that texts with an erotic content could be regarded as attempts to spread atheistic ideas and prohibited criticism of the king. Just like the French, the English were aware of the risks involved in spending time in coffee-houses and salons, picking up news. This early form of scandal journalism also existed in the Nordic countries, where periodicals, pamphlets, poems, cartoons, defamatory ballads, and satire were employed as means of taunting those in power. New ideas according to which the press was an institution for discussion and enlightenment with regard to social issues emanated from England and France. Among other things, people learned from the French and the English methods of spreading criticism of contemporary society in the guise of satire, allegory, or caricature, because censorship made direct comments on political issues impossible (see Holmberg et al. 1983:13–44, Åhlén et al. 1986, and Carlsson 1967).[7]

All in all, this indicates that the gossip and scandals of a political nature that were disseminated, regardless of which medium was employed for the purpose, cannot be reduced to innocent prattle. They were part of the criticism levelled at a country's regime, which is why energetic efforts were made to silence the flow of words which, in spite of the efforts of the police, seeped into both texts and institutions, for instance the royal courts. A person's good name could be ruined if gossip was transformed into printed text; but oral rumours also constituted material for power struggles at court, writes Darnton (2005:25).

Gossip and scandals in today's media system

At least four considerations become visible in this historical example:

1 For centuries, mediated scandals have been used as tools for questioning the prevailing power relationships in society, not infrequently using humour as a weapon.

---

7 Here, too, it was dangerous to express open criticism of the authorities through the varying forms of media. Proof of this can be found in historian Karl-Ivar Hildeman's analysis of libellous writings in the Nordic countries, where court records show that people who wrote and performed compromising lampoons and satirical ballads could be condemned to banishment, or even decapitation (Hildeman 1974). This type of folklore intended to taunt power became increasingly widespread and refined as people from a larger number of social strata learned to read and write, and it is – as is well known – still alive and well today (see Broberg et al. 1993).

2 As a consequence of this, gossip, the spreading of rumours, and scandals were regarded as threatening phenomena by the authorities, an anxiety that still survives in our time.
3 For a very long time, scandals have been mediated, often in the form of news. This mediation has occurred in an advanced interaction with the communication that arises on an interpersonal level face to face, a kind of communication which should be considered a form of mediation on the border between the folkloristic and the journalistic.
4 This, in turn, indicates that media systems are characterised by interaction and continuity among old and new media. Older media do not disappear just because new ones emerge. (Harvard and Lundell 2010:8)

The different paths that can be taken by a narrative about a scandal seem to presuppose rather than exclude one another. Can this said to be valid in our own time as well? A truthful answer will probably be 'both yes and no'. No, because technology has transformed the opportunities for communication in such a comprehensive manner that it is difficult to draw any parallels at all (temporal rapidity). Yes, because people are cultural creatures, regardless of whether they live in the 1750s or the 2010s, and as such they are the same in some respects (temporal resilience). For example, people's need to both convey news and inform themselves of what is going on appears to be comparatively constant over time, and so is the way in which that is done: through communicative exchange via the available means and channels (Stephens 2007:7–16). In addition, gossip and scandalous news appear to be persistent phenomena that have a particularly marked effect on the audience, regardless of whether this audience was alive during the Enlightenment or lives in the post-industrial era. So let us not drop the issue, but instead investigate how gossip, rumour, and scandals move within the media circuits of today.

In order to do this, I would like to examine the concept of the *media system* and consider the following claim: by looking at the oral dimension as a part of the media system, we can catch sight of some things that would otherwise have remained hidden. The moment that communication among people, face to face, is seen as a more or less integrated part of the communication that is happening via (other) media, a number of new questions and speculations arise. This point of departure opens up new possibilities. An example of research along such lines is the attempt made by media historians Jonas Harvard and Patrik Lundell to construct an extended historical view of media systems where intermediary connections are made visible, and where the system is seen to make up the sum of the reciprocal relationships of the different media at a given point in time. According to them, the metaphor of the system could be seen as a methodological tool and a reminder of the connections among phenomena that cannot always be seen on the surface (Harvard and Lundell 2010:15). Two possible themes in relation to analyses of media systems are foregrounded by these authors: the spatial dimension and the social dimension. The first-mentioned dimension encourages examinations of relationships between the physical locations where media are produced and consumed and the imaginary spaces that are represented and distributed through the media. The latter dimension sheds light on the tension among actors, both face to face and within large organisations and institutions. Interest is directed at how the media system is used by actors, and at the symbolic communities of shared interests and values of which these actors hence become co-creators (Harvard and Lundell 2010:16). In the ensuing pages, these ideas will be tested on the contemporary media system, first of all with regard to how gossip, rumour, scandals, and news distribution can take place, something that raises further questions. Through which media, in a broad sense, are scandals created, and how do these media interact?

Digital town squares

Press historian Mitchell Stephens argues that digital technology has entailed a kind of return to an older form of news distribution where anybody can contribute to the news flow, or, in Stephens's own words, 'the ability of individuals, lots of them, to be newstellers' (Stephens 2007:14). In this respect, social media appear as a paradise of everyday talk where infinite opportunities for quick exchanges of information are offered, which means that they cannot be dismissed as trivial. This flow of information is not particularly honourable; rather, it is the mere background babble of the people in digital form where neutral information, revolutionary statements, and pure nonsense are mixed – background babble that may nevertheless have a decisive impact in sensitive situations. Protected by anonymity, gossip and the spreading of rumours flourish on forums such as the global Twitter, Reddit, and 4chan, as well as on their national equivalents such as the very popular – in terms of the number of users – Swedish Flashback Forum (see the introduction to this book). The unsorted quantity of voices makes these digital town squares into perfect breeding-grounds for news where rumour and gossip can be published at a much earlier stage than in traditional newspapers, because digital town squares often lack an editor with responsibility for content and do not have to adapt what they publish to rules pertaining to press ethics. In newsrooms, no matter how self-assured they may appear to be, it has therefore become a matter of prestige to use social media as a research tool in daily journalistic work.

Social media also shine a light on the vagueness of the boundaries between oral tradition, written text, and mediated communication, for how should one regard the special language forms of the Internet, which some linguists have classified as hybrids of speech, conversation, and writing? What is, for instance, a chat conversation – spoken text or written speech (Dresner 2005, Baron 2010)? A few years ago, the periodical *language@internet* devoted a special edition to investigations of the numerous conversational and oral features in the type of communication encompassed by the designation CMC, *Computer Mediated Communication*, which is text-based (Herring 2011). Any attempt to construct a boundary where oral tradition ends and printed tradition begins – or where conversation face to face is seen as something completely different from conversation via computer programs – appears to be fruitless (see Stephens 2007:7–47). Oral and written forms of expression have existed in parallel – or, rather, been entangled – over the centuries, fertilising one another; and they continue to do so today. Philosopher Paul Ricoeur has, for instance, claimed that writing is an activity that runs parallel with speech, but occasionally writing takes the place of speech and appropriates it (Ricoeur 1988:35f).

The traditional daily newspaper, which has gone through a metamorphosis over the past few decades and is now much more than just text on paper, may serve as an example here. Transformed into a complex multimedial meeting place, where the Internet, television, radio, and telephone converge, it is a typical example of communicative development in our time, where writing, conversation, talk, images, and actors are mixed into an unorthodox melange. In addition, like the *nouvellistes de bouche* of yesteryear, today's journalists talk intensively during their working hours, both with one another and with other people. The hunt for news springs from a continuous flow of communication by way of face-to-face meetings, telephone calls, emails, text messages, chat messages, and tweets. There is quite a lot of prattle and gossip even in the most respectable editorial offices. That statement is not intended as a critique of journalism; the point is that the connection between everyday small talk, gossip, rumour, and news lives on, at least to a certain extent. For instance, an attentive local reporter knows that it is the proprietor of the local grocery shop one should call in order to find out if something interesting has happened. This person, if anyone, overhears what newsroom staff usually refer to as hot topics, that is to say, the things people are actually talking about.

On a fundamental level, the exchange of news today happens in the same way as it always has, namely through interpersonal communication. The technological advances do not seem to have brought about a cessation of everyday small talk and oral news distribution among people. If anything, some kinds of technology have gained ground precisely because of our pressing need to communicate with one another, by offering a greater number of accessible pathways for the flow of words. In the next few pages, I conduct an empirical examination of these conditions in a case where we follow the progress of a modern Swedish scandal, from gossip and rumours among ordinary people, journalists, and politicians on to the blogosphere and then out to the big newsrooms and, finally, into the everyday life of the affected individual. This takes us back to a dramatic twenty-four hours in contemporary history, which occasioned an unusually long-lasting and far-reaching media scandal in Sweden.

The rumour about Under-Secretary of State Ingmar Ohlsson

In connection with the earthquake in the Indian Ocean and the subsequent tsunami disaster on 26 December 2004, when around 250,000 people, including 543 Swedes, lost their lives, the work performed by the Swedish Prime Minister's Office was exposed to heavy criticism in the media. An opinion shared by many people was that the authorities had reacted too slowly and unprofessionally, and had lacked a sustainable disaster plan just when it was most needed. Comparisons were made to other countries, for instance Norway and Italy, which had been on site quickly in order to rescue people in distress and take care of the deceased. The Swedish government appeared sluggish, with a clear lack of direction and practical ability.

During this time Ingmar Ohlsson worked as an Under-Secretary of State, a highly placed civil servant, and as such he had an important role to play in the actions of the Prime Minister's Office. In his capacity of decision-maker on duty on the day in question, and as the right-hand man of the Prime Minister at the time, the Social

Democrat Göran Persson, Ohlsson became a central figure in the public debate. A summary of the media scandal surrounding Ingmar Ohlsson cannot be provided here, because it came and went with varying intensity over several years. For that reason, the ensuing pages focus on a minor part of it, the part that had to do with a rumour about a mistress.

After the catastrophe, media attention was directed at Ingmar Ohlsson's claim that he had visited the Government Offices, Rosenbad, during the actual day of the disaster. He also said that while he was there, he had used the telephone and the Internet to inform himself about the situation in Thailand, where thousands of Swedes found themselves in something that resembled a war zone. Among other things, he claimed that he had spoken on the phone to Under-Secretary of State for Foreign Affairs Hans Dahlgren, something that Dahlgren denied. Dahlgren's version was supported by telephone records, and during a hearing in the Standing Committee on the Constitution (KU) in 2006, two years after the tsunami disaster itself and in the midst of an ongoing election campaign, Ohlsson said that he was no longer sure of the information he had supplied previously (Government Committee Report 2005/06:KU8).[8]

The rhetoric from many actors was harsh and condemnatory, not least from the political opposition. Among other things, the conservative daily newspaper *Svenska Dagbladet* provided space on its opinion pages for opposition politician Carl Bildt (Moderate Party) – also known for his international missions as a peace negotiator and for his role as Swedish Foreign Minister (2006–2014) – where he claimed that it was beyond reasonable doubt that Ohlsson was lying during the high-profile hearings in the Standing Committee on the Constitution, and that Ohlsson had been telling lies all the time. The end of Bildt's text is dramatic: 'If we accept the lie today, we have sanctioned the lie tomorrow as well. Then we are looking at a systemic change into the realm of mendacity' (editorial on 21 June 2006). The hearings eventually came to an end, but some questions remained unanswered, according to many critics. Where had Ohlsson been on the day in question? Had he really visited the Government Offices? Was he trying to hide something?

---

8 A disaster commission later arrived at the conclusion that Ingmar Ohlsson had not been particularly focused on the tsunami during the initial period of slightly more than 24 hours following the disaster, and that his performance had been inadequate, something that deserved criticism (Ministry of Finance 2007:44).

As a consequence of the questions that had not been cleared up, a rumour began circulating in the newsrooms of the evening tabloids. Suddenly the Prime Minister's Office received a torrent of telephone calls from journalists, all of whom wanted comments concerning the oral information that Ohlsson had in fact been at the house of his colleague Jane Davidson (fictitious name) on the day of the disaster. As a result of vigorous denials, nothing was written about this matter at the time; the established media chose not to publish because the rumours remained unconfirmed. But the gossip and the spread of rumours did not stop. They lived on on the Internet, where some right-wing campaigners had decided to influence the election campaign by pushing the issue further. For example, in February 2006, a blog called *Right Online* published information that Ohlsson 'supposedly' spent Boxing Day 2004 with Deputy Director-General Jane Davidson instead of working.[9] The language is significant here. It invites the application of a method developed by ethnologist Lars-Eric Jönsson and myself, where we as researchers make an effort to listen to *talk-like text* (Hammarlin & Jönsson 2017:93–115). When it comes to digital texts of this kind, but also the texts of news media in the context of scandals, we argue that it is important to pay attention to evasiveness, that is to say information from anonymous sources, information that seems to come from no specific sources at all, and claims formulated in the passive voice ('it is said') or in other ways with an unclear agency ('it is claimed', 'is supposed to', 'probably has', 'is likely to have had'). Conflicting information, disclaimers, and disagreements are also significant text categories which should be examined, with special reference to signals about rumours and gossip and how these can be connected to journalistic reporting. With support from the work of Robert Darnton, we believe that it is possible to identify and investigate the spoken word's colonisation of, and relationship to, written text (Hammarlin & Jönsson 2017:93–115), a process that I will explain in greater detail below.

The blog hinted that Jane Davidson and Ingmar Ohlsson had a romantic relationship. Among other things, the blogger in question, liberal lobbyist Johan Ingerö, had been inspired by the harshly criticised but successful (in terms of the number of visitors) site Flashback, where a so-called thread had been started around the

---

9 Archived remnants of the blog can be found here: http://rightonline.blogspot.se/2006_05_01_archive.html (accessedd 7 March 2019).

same time by an anonymous writer. The thread began with the following post:

> It is rumoured in the corridors of the Ministry for Foreign Affairs that one of GP's [Göran Persson, Prime Minister at the time] Under-Secretaries of State, I***** O*******, was not at all at the Government Offices on Boxing Day after the tsunami, but at the house of his mistress, J*** D*******, Deputy Director-General at the Prime Minister's Office. In order to hide this, our good IO was pleased to lie about cycling down to the office and carrying out great deeds in order to save Swedes in distress. Against this background it is not difficult to understand that very few of his colleagues met him in the office.[10]

A rumour circulating in the corridors of the Ministry for Foreign Affairs will, through the murmur of an indefinable number of voices, find its way to the people. Alternatively, it is a popular rumour that finds its way upwards through the social hierarchies. It is probably a matter of circular movements. On Flashback, the rumour is made visible and in some way real through its continuously preserving, albeit variable and chatty, thread, where a kind of dark popular humour combined with an explicit mistrust of politicians takes shape. This kind of humour is typical of political satire and similar to the libellous writings against the authorities that Darnton and Brewer describe as accompanying political scandals 250 years ago, exemplified by the following quotation:

> Well, what do you know, she's quite handsome, isn't she ... Then I understand why the man with the 'non-existing chin and the shifty eyes' didn't prioritise the tsunami disaster. Surely it's more or less an established fact these days that he spent the night with the woman in question? Let's hope he's married and his wife doesn't know, otherwise the scandal factor will be considerably lower ...[11]

A certain amount of covetousness is expressed here. The writer is hoping that the whole matter is going to turn out to be thoroughly disreputable so that there is a 'proper' scandal, something that goes on for a long period of time and may serve as a source of amusement,

---

10 Thread: 'Skvaller om en viss statssekreterares närvaro på Regeringskansliet' ('Gossip about the presence of a certain Under-Secretary of State at the Government Offices'), Member: 'Monarkisten' ('The Monarchist'), 16 February 2006, #1.

11 Thread: 'Skvaller om en viss statssekreterares närvaro på Regeringskansliet' ('Gossip about the presence of a certain Under-Secretary of State at the Government Offices'), Member: 'Petter Utas', 16 February 2006, #14.

self-satisfied glee, and conversation. However, the whole post is likely to have been written ironically, as indicated by the use of an emoji. It is also worth noting that the gossip about Ohlsson's mistress has here been transformed into 'more or less ... established fact', but with the hesitant 'surely' inserted as a reservation and with a question-mark at the end. I interpret this not simply as a sign of gossip but as gossip *per se*, with patent elements of orality and conversation, where hesitation and possibility may be seen as the very engine of this kind of talk. The question 'Can this really be true?' is conveyed to the reader who is thus encouraged to pass it on, in order to gain clarity. However, truth is not as important as the talk about the event and the opportunities for moral reflection that it offers.

There are also posts that criticise the media, written by people who argue that the Flashback thread was in fact created by tabloid journalists in order to garner more information about the rumour – a dubious research method, according to members of the forum:

> Interesting that some person (a journalist at AB [*Aftonbladet*]?) first lets the 'bomb' go off at a 'more or less obscure site' (in the eyes of the authorities) such as [Flashback], in order to be able to take it to the general public later, through the newspaper.[12]

The blogger Johan Ingerö subsequently wrote several posts on the theme of 'Ingmar Ohlsson's mistress', and all at once the number of visitors to his blog multiplied. He said later in an interview that he was angry at the established media because they did not write about the rumour, although at least the tabloid people 'knew' how matters stood (Nilsson 2006). The gossip spread to some fifteen blogs, and it soon came to be a kind of truth that Ohlsson's difficulties in answering the question of where he was and what he was doing on Boxing Day were due to his having had an affair with Davidson. In connection with this, a tabloid-initiated hunt for Ohlsson began where nothing was said explicitly, but where receipts from his flights and restaurant visits together with Göran Persson and other government staff were scrutinised. The reporting was illustrated with pictures of Ohlsson and his colleague Davidson, side by side, and could take the following form: 'According to increasingly stubborn rumours, Ohlsson was not at all in his room at the Prime Minister's Office on this day, 26 December 2004. This information states that Ohlsson

---

12 Thread: 'Skvaller om en viss statssekreterares närvaro på Regeringskansliet' ('Gossip about the presence of a certain Under-Secretary of State at the Government Offices'), Member: 'ABZeta99', 16 February 2006, #23.

was at that time engaged in pursuits belonging to the personal sphere' (Hedlund and Svensson 2006a).

The similarity to the Flashback post above is striking. Even though the text merely, if insidiously, hints that Ohlsson was with his alleged mistress, it offers limited scope for doubt in combination with the publication of the pictures. It is interesting that *Expressen* explicitly describes its sources as rumours, and that it still chooses to publish them. It is also a diabolical touch that the rumours are referred to with the words 'this information states' in the next sentence, an expression that formalises them linguistically into a more established, neutral category of materials for journalists.

In fact, rumour as a genre – which is included within the broader category of gossip – should also be considered a form of news that does not inform so much as it orientates. People who partake in rumours are better able to find their way, and act, in the contexts in which they live and work. A discussion that is based on rumour is not so much about the event itself, true or false, as it is about what to think about the event. The rumour circulates because ignorance about the news could entail a form of danger, either physical or symbolic. One might say that the rumour acts as an alarm clock. People talk in order to know. In addition, a rumour is dependent on the media's attitude to it. Its duration and dissemination are determined by whether they choose to keep quiet about it or, conversely, allow it space in broadcasts and newspaper columns (Kapferer 1988:48–63).

Suddenly, the previous caution vanished and the evening tabloids, the morning newspapers, radio and TV programmes began to report the rumours about Ohlsson's alleged mistress. It was done in a complex manner, in the sense that it was the very dissemination of rumours and the ensuing denials that became the news in certain channels, exemplified by a news item from the Sveriges Radio (public service) news programme *Ekot*:

> Social Democratic party secretary Marita Ulvskog today accused the Liberals of having spread false rumours about Under-Secretary of State Ingmar Ohlsson supposedly having had a love affair with his closest colleague, Deputy Director-General Jane Davidson. According to the rumour, Ohlsson is supposed to have been with Davidson when the alarm about the tsunami disaster came on Boxing Day 2004.[13]

---

13 Sveriges Radio, *Dagens eko* ('The daily echo'), 18 May 2006, telegram.

The denial is full of conversational elements, such as 'supposedly having had a love affair', 'according to the rumour, Ohlsson is supposed to have been', and so on; their presence places the denial right in the middle of the flow of intense prattling that was going on about Under-Secretary of State Ohlsson at this time. The purpose of the denial may have been to limit the spread of rumours, but if anything it served to confirm and reinforce them, according to the motto 'everybody else talks about and reports this, and for that reason we neither can nor want to refrain from doing so ourselves'. The fact that one of Sweden's most reliable newsrooms chose to provide space for the rumour in their broadcasts can be seen as a kind of elevation of it, a confirmation of its significance which raised the rumour from the street to the serious newsroom.

The then editor-in-chief of the tabloid *Aftonbladet*, Anders Gerdin, claimed that the intense reporting in his newspaper had nothing to do with what was written on social media. In an interview at the time, he said that it was unacceptable that the Prime Minister's closest aide was unable to account for his activities on the day of the greatest catastrophe that had befallen Sweden since the loss of *MS Estonia* in the Baltic in 1994 (*Fokus*, 19 May 2006). *Aftonbladet* therefore chose to expose Ohlsson to particularly intensive scrutiny, although two years had passed since the tsunami disaster. Media analysts claim that this is the first case in Sweden where blogs affected media coverage during an election campaign. The united force of the bloggers compelled the established media to address the issue again (Nygren et al. 2005). But there was nothing new to tell, which is why the reporting came to revolve around rumours and gossip instead. And it was obvious that many more actors cultivated the rumour in addition to the bloggers. An intricate and agitated conversation went on among newspaper editorial offices, blogs, Flashback threads, and other social media.

To Jane Davidson and Ingmar Ohlsson, the reporting meant that they were forced into a protracted merry-go-round of denials. In an autobiographical book, Ohlsson writes that he felt disgust at having to call individual reporters at different newspapers in order to deny the rumours. He continues:

> The absurd and unpleasant thing about this affair is that the media immediately transfer the burden of proof to the victims, not to the people who are spreading the rumours. Having to devote time and

effort for a number of months to continually rejecting this modern variant of 'Have you stopped beating your wife?' is among the most repulsive things I have experienced.[14]

This part of the scandal, which he himself describes as its second phase – there is a third phase, too – came to an end with his asking for a time-out period from his position.

Hot topics

I met Ingmar Ohlsson for an interview in an anonymous-looking office at the Ministry for Foreign Affairs (UD) in Stockholm. The following pages focus on the spreading of rumours about him and Jane Davidson and on his recollection of those rumours as expressed during our meeting. Ohlsson describes the origin of the rumours as 'a hot topic', which in this case refers to loose small talk or gossip in the corridors that spread both in tabloid newsrooms and at UD:

> As far as I understood afterwards, this was what people were talking about. The first time I get to hear of it is from a cabinet minister, a Social Democratic cabinet minister who had met a former leading politician from the Moderate Party at the airport, and this politician had cheerfully told him about the rumour and that he had heard it from [a senior figure in his party]. 'And [this person] knows what's going on at UD', he says. That was the first time I heard it. So there was talk about it among what's known as the 'gossiping classes', that is to say, this coterie of leading politicians and journalists in Stockholm.

Ohlsson had previously said in public that the senior Moderate Party politician was behind the dissemination of the rumours, a claim for which he was attacked by some writers, among others Linda Skugge. A well-known writer at this time, Skugge did not pull her punches in her ironically formulated criticism which was published a year and a half after the hearing in the Standing Committee on

---

14 This is a translation of a passage from Ohlsson's book. Since 'Ingmar Ohlsson' is a fictitious name, it was not possible to use the person's real name in order to produce a reference here. The original Swedish version of this book used Ohlsson's real name – it would have been pointless to try to disguise it – but as the present publication is intended for an international audience and published Open Access as well as in print, anonymity for the protagonist was deemed to be preferable.

the Constitution, two years and nine months after the tsunami disaster:

> Poor, poor little [a diminutive of Ohlsson's real first name]. He claims that it was Big Bad [senior Moderate politician] who was behind the rumours about the Woman with whom [he] is said to have been canoodling instead of helping people in distress during the tsunami. But because 'both of them have denied' this claim, does that mean it's not true? Since when were a few denials enough for a claim to not be true? (Lagercrantz & Skugge 2007)

In fact, Skugge underlines the hopelessness of trying to check the spreading of rumours once it has started. If Ohlsson remembered things correctly, the rumour went through three links before it reached him, something that indicates a whispering game according to a traditional 'and then he said, and then I said' model. In addition, he indicated that gossip among journalists and politicians – 'the gossiping classes' – was not a coincidence, but a well-known, well-established phenomenon. Denials to the media led nowhere. The telephones kept ringing. 'That is ... a typical element of hounding logic,' writes Jan Guillou, 'that a lie can be repeated as many times as you want for as long as you want until it becomes the current truth' (Guillou 2010:546). Putting an end to the rumours required certain efforts on the interpersonal level. Ohlsson and Davidson eventually decided to conduct personal confrontations with the people whom they knew to have been active participants in the gossip:

> We were pretty quickly able to find out who talked most about this. So we looked up these people, one by one, and we talked to them and asked, 'Why are you saying this?' Very interesting experience. In total we talked to perhaps eleven, twelve people who we understood were instrumental in spreading the rumour. They may not have been the origin, because we don't know who started the rumour. But as I said earlier, they were instrumental in their manner of spreading it. It actually had a certain effect. And of course it was interesting to see who these ten, twelve people were. I can say that they were all men, and they were all older than I am.

Ohlsson felt that gossip and rumours of this kind often affect a woman more than a man. In an elitist, male-dominated world like the one at UD, it appeared to some men an impossibility that a young and, in addition, beautiful woman could have a meteoric career exclusively on the basis of her merits. There had to be another reason for the promotions, the speculation went. Apart from the fact that Ohlsson's antagonists wanted to render him harmless by sullying his reputation, suspicion was cast on Davidson because of her femininity, about which she could not really do anything, while at the same time her competence was questioned.[15] In our conversation we also touched on the stock phrase 'no smoke without fire', discussing the hopelessness of trying to prove one's innocence:

> I was often asked, 'Can you prove that you don't have a relationship?' That's a completely astonishing question if you think about it, and it all had to do with this 'no smoke without ...'. People saw us together all the time, and it's obvious that it can't just be a professional relationship, right, it has to be something else, sort of. ... We investigated the possibilities of bringing an action for defamation, because the damage requirement was clearly fulfilled. But then the lawyers say, 'You have to be able to prove it.' How the hell do you do that? You can't! There is no way. I mean, how you do it? How do you prove that?

Well, how would Ohlsson have been able to prove that he had not had a relationship with Davidson? By showing people text messages and emails that had never been written and never been sent? From a historical perspective, it is interesting that it was a rumour about a mistress that was put about in order to 'get at' Ohlsson. In eighteenth-century England and France, mistresses often featured in the spreading of rumours about the sexual activities of royalty and other people in power, with the aim of undermining their positions and amusing the listener. John Brewer (2005) provides several examples of this, as does Robert Darnton, who among other things follows the creation of the scandal book *Anecdotes sur Mm. la comtesse du Barry*, from oral gossip to hard covers. Darnton writes:

> [It] is really a scrapbook of these news items strung together along a narrative line, which takes the heroine from her obscure birth as the daughter of a cook and a wandering friar to a star role in a Parisian whorehouse and finally the royal bed. (Darnton 2000:9)[16]

---

15 These gendered processes within politics and other male-dominated environments have, coincidentally, been written about in an elegant fashion by political scientist Maud Eduards, in the book *Kroppspolitik: Om Moder Svea och andra kvinnor* ('The body politic: On Mother Sweden and other women') (2007).
16 There was a great interest in the promiscuous lives of kings, which were considered in relation to their political abilities. In a police report, written by a so-called spy and framed as a dialogue, we can follow the talking as well as the listening at this time: 'At the Café de Foy someone said that the king had taken a mistress, that she was named Gontaut, and that she was

Gossip, rumour, and scandals 99

Clearly, then, this is a long-established tradition, at least from an international perspective. The United States is much to the fore in this context; the Bill Clinton/Monica Lewinsky scandal in 1998, Anthony Weiner's sex-chatting in 2011, and the accusations regarding Donald Trump's alleged sexual harassment of women in 2016 are examples of sex scandals that have had global dissemination. But this type of rumour about mistresses and politicians, or, as in this case, a civil servant, is not common either in Swedish politics or in Swedish political journalism, rather the opposite. This was probably why the reporting about Ohlsson and Davidson occasioned a certain amount of debate concerning press ethics. Niklas Svensson, a political journalist at *Expressen* who was one of the reporters that urged on the scrutiny of Ohlsson, underlines the special character of this case, but at the same time confirms that gossip and the oral spreading of rumours always gather momentum when a scandal gets under way. Both anonymous and named sources, from so-called ordinary readers to actors connected to the event, contact the newspaper with a large number of tips regarding the main protagonist. It then becomes the task of the editorial staff to sort out this flow of information.

In professional terms, the criticism of the deficient handling of the disaster and the subsequent scandals led to Ohlsson's being deprived of his duties at UD. According to his own version, he was put in quarantine, something he describes as the hardest punishment of all. It took several years before he was allowed to work with qualified tasks again.

There is thus quite a lot of talk about the melodramatic stories supplied to us by the media, then as now; people sigh, laugh, guess, and problematise in the course of everyday conversations. 'A scandal

---

a beautiful woman, the niece of the duc de Noailles and the comtesse de Toulouse. Others said, "If so, then there could be some big changes." And another replied, "True, a rumor is spreading, but I find it hard to believe, since the cardinal de Fleury is in charge. I don't think the king has any inclination in that direction, because he has always been kept away from women." "Nevertheless," someone else said, "it wouldn't be the greatest evil if he had a mistress." "Well, messieurs," another added, "it may not be a passing fancy, either, and a first love could raise some danger on the sexual side and could cause more harm than good. It would be far more desirable if he liked hunting better than that kind of thing"' (Darnton 2004:110–19; the exact page is unfortunately not clear in the version of the text to which I have access, made available through the database of Lund University Library).

that is relatively longlived must enter the public conversation', writes Elizabeth Bird (Bird 2003:38, see also Martín-Barbero 1993:104). Bird has attempted to show this by interviewing so-called ordinary people in order to define their attitudes to media scandals, an issue that leads us to the interesting question of why such scandals exist in the first place and what purpose they serve. Taking the statements made by Bird's informants as a point of departure, these scandals seem to possess a special ability to bring out people's attitudes to and experience of morals and norms through the values and boundaries expressed in them (Bird 2003:32). She writes: '[t]he very questioning and speculation invited by scandal may help people discuss and deal with issues of morality, law and order, and so on, in their daily lives' (Bird 2003:39). This conclusion, which is in line with Max Gluckman's interpretation, is hardly controversial. The media scandal could be seen as a kind of tool that is used in everyday contexts in order to discuss what may be considered acceptable moral behaviour in a certain cultural context and at a certain point in time. When people speculate about scandals they seem to look for answers in their own life experiences, and in general they are more interested in people who have some form of bearing on their own lives: How would I act if it happened to me? What would the people around me say? What can I do to avoid ending up in a similar situation? (Bird 2003:25–47).

Sociologist David Wästerfors is on a similar track in his research on corruption scandals. He writes that it is impossible to separate people's responses to scandals from scandals as phenomena, and vice versa. The response from the surrounding community is a direct prerequisite for the development and survival of scandals. 'When somebody calls out "scandal!", somebody else has to respond to this exclamation, otherwise there will be no scandal', he claims (Wästerfors 2008:63; Wästerfors 2005). Wästerfors likens this collective response to scandals to Victor Turner's description of a social drama, where the response represents its redressive or corrective phase. After the crisis that arises because of the alleged or real transgression of norms in the drama in question, a playful and active state of symbolic vagueness ensues. Order is restored and symbolism is gradually rectified, and this is done in a number of multifaceted and contradictory ways, not least through the forms of conversation and discussion where rumour, gossip, fact, opinion, speculation, condemnation, apologia, humour, sarcasm, irony, and satire find expression. The voices are characterised by polyphony rather than opinion (Wästerfors 2005:153).

The spatial and the social dimension

At the end of this chapter, I want to reconnect to the concept of the system and to those comprehensive themes that Jonas Harvard and Patrik Lundell (2010:7–25) recommend for inclusion in investigations of media systems: the spatial and the social dimension. Beginning with the first, the development of the Ingmar Ohlsson media scandal obviously encompasses a number of physical locations and spaces, such as the home, the living room, the lunch room, the physical town square, the digital town square, a large number of newsrooms, and the Ministry for Foreign Affairs as well as other official institutions. It is interesting to follow how gossip moves among different environments, from an undefined public space – sometimes called 'the street' – to digital forums, newspaper editorial offices, the government, and public authorities. One purpose behind the detailed description of the Ingmar Ohlsson case in this book is to demonstrate how this talk may be considered significant and influential depending on who is gossiping and who is listening, when it happens, and what the tittle-tattle is about.

But what is the point of regarding the communication and exchange of information that occurs in all these places and spaces as part of the spatial dimension of a media system? Why not draw the boundary at the media themselves, the editorial offices, and the digital town squares? It is, after all, media scandals that are being investigated here. The answer is that such restrictions would be unnecessarily limiting, blocking the broader view. In an attempt to widen the media concept and, for instance, as was done above, put the linguistic content of media texts in relation to the movements, actions, and statements of different actors, interwoven flows of words appear which move on different levels in different environments with a noteworthy synchronicity. Taken together, they make up intermedial connections: they reflect and affect one another; they shape and develop one another; and they collaborate and interact with one another (Harvard and Lundell 2010:7–25).

The analysis above is a case in point. On a concrete plane, it showed how talk, rumours, and gossip, both in actual corridors and in social, digital media – and including actors from outside the media business – can be colonised in the written journalistic text, and how this in turn can give rise to further oral conversations. At a first glance, these intersecting routes do not appear; but by means of the system concept, our thoughts can be liberated from conventional genre divisions where mediated communication is routinely distinguished from interpersonal communication. That leads us on to the next theme: the social dimension that is connected to the spatial one. What actors move in these spaces and in these locations? If we include the results of the analysis in Chapter 1 in the answer to this question, an extensive network of people appears: those who have no relationship to the scandal and its main figure other than as a media audience, and those who do have connections to the protagonist. This second group comprises family members, friends, acquaintances, and colleagues who are affected by and who themselves affect the development of the scandal. Or, as Wästerfors asserts: if nobody out there responds to the call of the scandal, it dies. Few people would doubt the truth of that. If the competing newspapers do not pick up the thread, if reactions from the audience fail to appear, and if the tip-off telephone falls silent, the story ceases to be relevant for journalists to report about (the tip-off telephone may be regarded as a tributary to a major river of gossip).

Because of its incorporated orality, the scandal, seen as a media phenomenon, appears to be something that cannot be reduced to unambiguous causal connections. Instead, the complexity and interplay of forces should be acknowledged and studied, media hierarchies that are usually taken for granted being regarded as relative (Lundell 2010:98). In addition to the classic media that everybody recognises, a number of varying media forms have played a role for the development of the scandal, or, rather, for its very existence. In order to answer the question posed at the beginning of this chapter – how is a media scandal possible? – many phenomena that are traditionally placed outside what is defined as media must be included in the analysis. For the answer is that a scandal becomes possible through all these varying and interwoven forms of communication, all these actors and texts, all these movements and flows, all these spaces and locations, at a certain point in time, in a certain cultural context. It therefore seems almost uncontroversial to regard the gossip and the spreading of rumours in the corridors of the Ministry for Foreign Affairs and in the tabloid editorial offices – and thus also the actors moving in these spaces – as media in a long chain which are seen, if one looks closely at them, to make up a single composite system.

Nevertheless, one question remains to be answered: What imaginary spaces were created and re-created through the reporting on Ingmar Ohlsson? This question includes the symbolic communities of interest and value of which the media system is a co-creator at a given point in time (Harvard and Lundell 2010:16). The imagined community represented by the nation, is the less than surprising answer. The scandal, or rather scandals, surrounding the Under-Secretary of State were occasioned by one of the worst disasters in modern times with respect to the number of Swedes killed and injured. Newspaper material from the time contains a multitude of data and analyses concerning the nation's lack of ability to protect its citizens in the event of a catastrophe occurring at a great geographical distance from Sweden. Repeated comparisons were made to other nations that were quickly on site in the affected area with evacuation aircraft, crisis teams, and trained medical personnel. Interviews with affected Swedes on the ground in Thailand, who expressed anger and bitterness at the authorities' inability to act, were standard features in Swedish media directly after the event. The contrasts were emphasised time and again: pictures of apparently incapable and paralysed politicians with stony faces going in and out of the Government Offices were published next to photos of desperate people searching for their injured or dead family members in overcrowded Khao Lak hospitals. The words Sweden, Swedes, and Swedish citizens appeared frequently in the texts.

In connection with the mistress rumour a few years later, it was yet again an ill-concealed contempt for politicians that was expressed in the media material. If one includes the 179-page-long Flashback thread entitled 'Skvaller om en viss statssekreterares närvaro på Regeringskansliet' ('Gossip about the presence of a certain Under-Secretary of State at the Government Offices') in this material, a thread containing over 2,000 posts, this contempt becomes even more apparent. In this thread scorn was manifested not only for politicians but also for the cowardice of traditional media, as exemplified by the following comment: 'a wonderful mess of government spokesmen who get ever more deeply entangled in lies and the abuse of power, but the media will probably lie down flat in response to pressures from above'.[17]

The reporting about Ohlsson must be seen in that context. In connection with the tsunami disaster, he became a symbol for the cracks in the edifice of the nation. This type of response to scandal, characterised by discontent and condemnation, produces a variant of an imagined community, namely cultural intimacy. With reference

---

17 Thread: 'Skvaller om en viss statssekreterares närvaro på Regeringskansliet' ('Gossip about the presence of a certain Under-Secretary of State at the Government Offices'), Member: 'jaha jovisst' ('OK fine'), 9 March 2006, #121.

to this concept, which originates with anthropologist Michael Herzfeld, David Wästerfors writes that such an imaginary community is not based on self-esteem and honour but, on the contrary, on shame (Wästerfors 2005:164). The cultural communities of nations depend on both collective self-criticism and collective pride. In Herzfeld's own words: 'National embarrassment can become the ironic basis of intimacy and affection, a fellowship of the flawed, within the private spaces of the national culture' (Herzfeld 2005:29).

The role as an *exemplum*

The Ohlsson story demonstrates the varying, not to say paradoxical, functions of the media scandal as well as its inherent complexity: for centuries, gossip, rumour, and scandals have been employed as revolutionary material in order to question the prevailing order; but they have also been used as tools geared to upholding this very order through a collective maintenance of social norms and boundaries of a basic, almost religious character, such as 'thou shalt not lie', 'thou shalt not steal', and 'thou shalt not commit adultery'. In this collective pursuit, the main figure of the scandal is given the role of an *exemplum*. This concept has its origins in the Middle Ages, where the *exemplum* constituted a popular literary genre of its own, in which the lives of famous people were used as examples of either good or bad acts in a kind of moral, cautionary story (see Scanlon 2007). Becoming the object of gossip is the same thing as being chosen for the *exemplum* role (Stephens 2007:94). Few things give the public such intense pleasure as first jointly celebrating collective heroes, putting them on pedestals, and then transforming them into scapegoats, seeing them plunge to the ground and be destroyed. 'To fall from grace' is an anthropological idiom that describes the process in a graphic fashion: 'Grace, like honor, is associated with power and with royalty ... To lose power is "to fall from grace", "to be put down", "to go out of favor", "to be disgraced"' (Pitt-Rivers 2011:445). The Germans speak of *Schadenfreude*, a word that by combining *Schaden* (harm) with *Freude* (joy) explains the self-satisfaction involved in hearing about or witnessing someone else's misfortune. Ostracism, which was discussed in the preceding chapter, and its limits are also relevant here. The person to whom the role of *exemplum* is assigned is *de facto* noticed and included in the community; he or she is a person one cares about, even if the consequences can be both stigmatisation and branding.

Concluding comment

In conclusion, I want to refer back to Lars Nord's statement that was quoted at the beginning of this chapter: what distinguishes the modern political scandal from the classic one is that the scandal no longer derives its chief nourishment from discussions and conversations among people, but is primarily conducted in the media (Nord 2001:20). On the basis of the preceding discussion, one could maintain that this statement is not borne out. Similarly, John B. Thompson's chronological calculations, where rumours and gossip are said to lead up to a scandal according to a model based on some form of three-stage rocket, seems too linear to fit our motley reality (Thompson 2008:25–8). What emerges instead is a media system that is both complex and circular (Bird 2003:32).

In this section of the book, I have attempted to illuminate the context from which the media scandal springs. I have focused on the relationships between the written and the spoken, between the oral tradition and narratives in the traditional media, using a specific historical example in order to enhance our understanding of the contemporary world. From time to time, there have been expressions of surprise that some scandals never really caught on, even when they were considered to be serious. They somehow petered out, for unclear reasons. The usual explanation is that the story in question was difficult for journalists to narrate. My analysis of how a scandal arises, through a media system with extensive offshoots and a multiplicity of forms of expression, takes the line of reasoning a step forward: if a story is difficult to narrate to the person who partakes of the news, there will be no scandal. If the moral of the drama is obscure, there is nothing to talk about. In other words, it is the oral narration *per se*, the story-telling that happens wherever there are people, that gives the mediated scandal wings and determines its duration and dissemination. 'What? Is this true?' we exclaim, and pass on the story.

So what kind of journalism has been examined in this chapter? Gossip journalism? Tabloid drivel? Perhaps; but it is also a matter of political journalism on the border of popular culture, a political journalism which moves within the historically persistent and lucrative domain of spectacle, scandals, and celebrities, according to media researcher John Hartley:

> An endless succession of scandals, from royal mistresses to Monica Lewinsky, continually remind us that sex remains one of the most potent elements of political journalism. The staples of popular culture

– scandal, celebrity, bedroom antics – are the very propellant of modern journalism and therefore modern ideas. (Hartley 2008:687)

Celebrities and scandals form a persistent part of news journalism, bordering on the informal character of the spoken word. There are no indications that these circumstances are changing; if anything, an ultimate fusion seems to be taking place between journalism and popular culture in the digital age, where journalism not only studies popular culture as an object but also forms part of it (Hartley 2008).

In the ensuing chapter, the complex relations among different forms of communication will once more be at the centre of the analysis, but this time with an anonymous private individual at the centre of events.

3
Floorball Dad

This chapter is different from the others. This is partly because the main figure in the case that is described in detail here is an anonymous private individual, partly because the story can be included in the concept of *public shaming*,¹ with some folkloristic elements, rather than in that of a media scandal, although the two are related. Even so, the material is suitable for illustrating enduring relations between the local and the mediated, between text and talk, and between journalism and gossip.

The phenomenon of public shaming is growing. As I wrote in Chapter 1, it may be described as a pronounced increase in the risk of anyone being publicly derided and scandalised – not least through social media, which live in a kind of symbiosis with the traditional ones. On digital forums ordinary people, who do not hold any notable positions of power in society, may be portrayed as idiots, criminals, or simply as disgusting persons. In the informative and entertaining journalistic book *So You've Been Publicly Shamed* (2015) by British author and journalist Jon Ronson the reader meets them, one by one – the scandalised, condemned, fallen figures. True, some of them have managed to get to their feet again; but others are still lying there, seemingly forever crushed. Ronson takes up internationally known cases, at least in the Anglo-Saxon part of the world. One of them is the best-selling American popular-science author Jonah Lehrer, who was caught out having fabricated facts in some of his books, whereupon two were recalled by his publisher, Houghton Mifflin Harcourt (Ronson 2015:12–23). In connection with these revelations, Lehrer was thoroughly dragged through the mud, not least on Twitter; and in Ronson's book he says that not

---

1 See Chapter 1 for an exposition of this concept.

only his career is over, but his whole life as well.[2] Another well-known case that Ronson analyses is that of Justine Sacco, the young South African woman who wrote the now infamous tweet, 'Going to Africa. Hope I don't get AIDS. Just kidding. I'm white!' (Ronson 2015:45–61). In the book, Sacco claims – and she has said the same thing in a number of interviews – that she wrote the ironic tweet in order to draw attention to and make fun of Americans' ignorance and racist ideas about South Africa. As she wrote her post, just before boarding a plane from New York to Cape Town, Sacco had 170 followers on Twitter. When she landed eleven hours later, she discovered to her vast surprise that she topped Twitter's lists of trending hashtags, that she was condemned by Twitter users and bloggers all over the world, and that she had been fired from her job. At the airport she was met by a Twitter user she did not know who snapped a picture of her using a mobile telephone, a picture which was immediately published under a hashtag that had rapidly become popular, #HasJustineLandedYet, with the following text: '@JustineSecco HAS in fact landed at Cape Town International. She's decided to wear sunnies as a disguise'. Later she found that her name had been Googled 1,220,000 times during a ten-day period. Before her startling tweet went viral, her name was Googled on average thirty times a month (Ronson 2015:45–61).

On the whole, nothing new under the sun; public shaming processes have existed for centuries. During the eighteenth century and through the first decades of the nineteenth, such processes were expressed through pillories, stones of shame tied to the feet, public tarring and feathering, and public whippings, to mention a few of many creative manifestations (Ziel 2005:499–522). Walking around with a placard around the neck or writing on the forehead, where

---

2 However, he seems to have recovered somewhat. In 2016 *A Book about Love* was published by a different publisher, although with devastating reviews as a consequence, among other places in *The New York Times*, where Jennifer Senior reviewed the scandalisation of Lehrer rather than the new book. She writes: 'In retrospect – and I am hardly the first person to point this out – the vote to excommunicate Mr. Lehrer was as much about the product he was peddling as the professional transgressions he was committing. It was a referendum on a certain genre of canned, cocktail-party social science, one that traffics in bespoke platitudes for the middlebrow and rehearses the same studies without saying something new. Apparently, he's learned nothing. This book is a series of duckpin arguments, just waiting to be knocked down' (Jennifer Senior, 'Review: Jonah Lehrer's "A Book about Love" Is Another Unoriginal Sin', *New York Times*, 6 July 2016).

the crime was publicly admitted, were milder versions. In Swedish agricultural society there was a variant intended for so-called whores, that is to say women who had given birth to children out of wedlock and who were for that reason forced to wear a *horklut* ('whore kerchief'), also called a *horluva* ('whore cap'), on their heads – to mark their crime and their low social position (Frykman 1977).

From the latter part of the nineteenth century up until today, public humiliation punishments of this kind have gradually been phased out; but they seem to have been revived in the digital era, where the reach and speed of technology have changed the rules of the game for public shaming in quite a radical manner. To return briefly to Ronson's above-mentioned case: Had Lehrer fabricated facts in a systematic and purposeful manner, or had he merely 'embellished' his texts by adding and subtracting a little in a popular-science book, and in that case, was that really so bad? In the words of *New York Times* journalist Jennifer Senior: 'Errors in even the finest works of nonfiction are ridiculously common.'[3] And writing a certainly idiotic but nevertheless ironic tweet, is that really enough for a person to be dragged through the mud, be taunted by the masses, and lose her job? There is no rhyme or reason in public punishments these days, Ronson concludes. In an interview in the podcast *On the Media*, he argues that the audience does not fully understand that an inflammatory public shaming campaign, which often has as its express purpose defending 'the underdog', can end in disaster, namely in a mob mentality that ultimately risks leading to ruined careers and lives for the people who are subjected to a collective administration of justice.[4]

The time has come for the readers of this book to familiarise themselves with a Swedish case of public shaming. This chapter places empiricism in the centre, allowing ethnography to flow while theory is put on hold. This is a tried and tested approach within anthropology. A large number of scholars could be named here, but I find the studies of Michael Jackson, Kathleen Stewart, and, within the media field, Daniel Miller particularly inspiring. I see this chapter as a kind of further development of Ronson's important book, which has no doubt increased general knowledge of the public-shaming phenomenon. Here, too, a case is investigated in

---

3 Jennifer Senior, 'Review: Jonah Lehrer's "A Book about Love" Is Another Unoriginal Sin', *New York Times*, 6 July 2016.
4 *On the Media*, 'Jon Ronson and Public Shaming', 24 July 2015.

great detail; but the interpretation and the understanding of it are deepened with the aid of scientific perspectives.

The choice of method and the decision to make room for a consideration of this particular case were also occasioned by ethical motives. 'Floorball Dad' became a public, if anonymous, figure in Sweden. Swedish media depicted him as an almost incomprehensibly vile person whom other people took the liberty to explain, portray, and condemn. In that way, this chapter might be seen as a description from within, a sort of counter story, which affords insights into events that have not been known to the public before. I was not personally present when, in an unusually cold winter month, the events took place that will now be reconstructed and described. Like most people, I first learned about them through the media. The ethnography on which this chapter is based is made up of telephone calls with key actors, extensive and wide-ranging media materials, material from the authorities, letter and email correspondence, telephone records, press releases, and two recorded in-depth interviews – one with 'Floorball Dad' and one with the less well known 'Floorball Mum'. In the account below they are called *the mum* and *the dad*. All private individuals and journalists in the following account have been made anonymous, as have the sports clubs and the towns in which the events took place. Of course it is possible to uncover the facts of the case – all you need to do is Google them – but the use of fictitious names is a tried and tested technique which researchers can use in order to emphasise the complexity of the context and the chain of events, rather than focusing on the actions of single individuals. As in other parts of this book, emotions lead the way into the analysis.

Confusion

Could the rumour that was now spreading like wildfire have anything to do with us? Could it be our son whom the coach had met? The family who lived in Ängsbacken (fictitious name) racked their brains during those January days. The son of the family, Martin, then eleven years old and equipped with both ball control and a winner mentality, had been deeply disappointed by the loss of a game during the major floorball tournament that had been played during the weekend in the city of Dala. He had run from the field in anger just before the final whistle. His dad, who was also one of the team leaders, and who had driven his son and a teammate to the tournament, walked around in the big arena after the game looking for the boy. It was not the first time Martin had displayed his athlete's temper, so his dad was not particularly worried. He will soon show up, he thought. But the minutes went by. The players began to be ready to go home. A certain concern began to make itself felt. One of the coaches of the team also participated in the search.

After a while the dad found Martin. He was sulking indoors on a window seat, in his match clothes. The dad gave him a change of clothes and said: 'It's time to go home now.' The boy persisted in his sulk, whereupon the dad added: 'There's no need to be angry with me, I haven't done anything. And you played a smashing game! But let's get the car and go home now. The others are waiting.' But Martin was still angry and disappointed, and threw his club demonstratively on the floor. The dad kept his patience and said: 'Take your stuff now. I'm going to the car now, at any rate!' A well-tested educational trick among parents. Instead of saying that you are leaving, you just do so, whereupon the child follows. Usually. But evidently Martin needed to cool off a bit more. The other player who was to be driven home to Ängsbacken stood by restlessly and waited, whereupon the dad decided to drive the car, which was parked at the back of the facility, around to the front of the building. Yet another reason for not waiting for Martin was that another teammate wanted his sports bag, which was in the boot of the car. While the contents of the car were being rearranged, the dad's telephone rang. One of the team leaders had, once again, found Martin. After a while he showed up with the boy, who got into the car. The drive home could begin. And that was that.

But this is where the story begins. The next day the phones began ringing in the house in Ängsbacken. According to a rumour that had begun to circulate, a boy from the club was supposed to have been left behind in the January cold outside the sports facility in Dala. 'Did you get everybody home with you?' asked the coach on the telephone. 'Certainly, I had my son and another boy in the car as planned', answered the dad and began to ransack his memory for any other boy who might have been left behind by mistake, unlikely as it seemed. A telephone chain was set up within the club. Leaders and parents called one another and checked that everybody had come home in good order after the tournament. Sure enough, no child was missing. But Anders, a coach from another team, claimed that a boy had been left behind alone outside the sports hall. He told a friend who had a blog about the event. The friend, in his turn, sat down in front of his keyboard and wrote that a boy from the Ängsbacken floorball club had been left behind by his dad. The tone was highly emotional:

> When I went home today my friend Anders called me and told me something that makes me feel doubtful about the human race. He met a boy who plays in the Ängsbacken team for boys who are eight to nine years old. The boy stood outside the sports hall in -6°C cold and waited; unfortunately the boy probably didn't know what he was waiting for …
> Anders told me that he saw that the boy was shivering with cold, and that wasn't so strange, because he was wet and stood there in his match clothes. When Anders took him into the arena the boy started crying, his dad had gone off and left him there in the parking lot – BECAUSE HE HAD PLAYED SO BADLY!!!
> Anders called the parent, who confirmed that the boy had to fend for himself and that he had left him behind because he had played 'such a bloody bad game'. Now Anders got hold of the parent of another player on the team, who returned to Dala to pick up the boy … but what happens when the boy gets home to his dad?
> I hope YOU are made to answer for this and that you are barred FOREVER from a floorball hall, I'm ashamed on your behalf, floorball dad. My heart bleeds when I hear this, what does one do?[5]

This blog post was mentioned in the web edition of the local newspaper which chose to follow up the story and do two interviews, one with the coach Anders and one with the tournament manager, who supported the coach's story. They both felt that what had happened was unforgivable. Things like this must not happen. You do not abandon your child in another town, having taken him to task and told him to find his way home in the winter cold wearing nothing but his match clothes. That is child abuse. 'I feel sorry for the kid who has to come home to that parent', said the tournament manager in the interview. At the end of the article, it is made clear that a private individual had reported the event to the police (Söderlund 2012).

Then things began to happen. The big national tabloid *Aftonbladet* wrote about what had occurred. The same people were interviewed, but now the tone of voice had become harsher. What had happened was 'deplorable', 'alarming', and 'cruel'. Anders explained that he had hardly been able to sleep because of his worry about the child, describing the incident as 'the worst thing he had ever experienced'

---

5 The site where this post was published has now been taken down.

(Jönsson 2012). A number of national news articles, news features, columns, and analyses about the case of 'Floorball Boy' or 'Floorball Dad', as it came to be called, were published during the subsequent two days in, among other places, the major daily newspapers *Dagens Nyheter* and *Svenska Dagbladet*, the tabloids *Expressen* and *Aftonbladet*, the free newspaper *Metro*, the local newspapers *Upsala Nya Tidning*, *Göteborgs-Posten*, *Hallandsposten*, *Nerikes Allehanda*, *Smålandsposten*, and *Arbetarbladet*, on the web TV channel *Nyheter 24*, by the venerable 'TT' news agency, and on the TV news programme *TV4-nyheterna*. The public-service newsrooms also joined in the reporting: Sveriges Radio *Ekot*, the local Sveriges Radio channels, and the Sveriges Television news programmes *ABC*, *Rapport*, and *Aktuellt*. Throughout the reporting, the coach Anders remained the only primary source.

Back home in Ängsbacken, there was a growing sense that something was seriously amiss. The parents realised that the commotion could have some form of connection to their son, who had talked for a while with a coach from another team during his voluntary absence in the sports arena. Could there have been some sort of misunderstanding? Could the coach be referring to Martin? But according to the reports, Anders was supposed to have borrowed the boy's mobile phone in order to call the boy's dad, and Martin had not had his phone with him in Dala. It had been lying at home. In addition, Martin was found indoors, not outdoors, as the coach had said. Representatives of the Ängsbacken floorball club contacted Anders on the phone in order to straighten things out. The dad also picked up his phone and called Anders. He introduced himself with his first and last name, the mobile number being visible on Anders's display. The dad began by thanking Anders for having taken care of Martin, if it was him Anders had met inside the arena during the search for the boy. He also clarified that they had not left him behind in the way that had been described in the news. In fact, Martin had not been abandoned at all. 'He went home in the car with me a little while later', explained the dad, and ended by saying that if Anders had any questions or thoughts he was welcome to contact him at any time; all he had to do was call. 'I mean, you have my number now.' But things did not calm down after this, rather the reverse. This is how the dad remembers it:

> The day after, something really strange happens, because then he [Anders] contacts the media and says that Floorball Dad has called

him from an ex-directory number.[6] It's the same Floorball Dad who told Anders a few days earlier that his son had played such a bloody bad game that he could walk home. ... Then it becomes incredibly unpleasant, because then the whole story turns, suddenly it begins to be aimed in a particular direction. I feel, hear, see, and read. He's directing it against me. Now it feels incredibly strange. ... Now he's got to mean me! I call him up again to find out what's going on. But I can't get through. It's completely impossible to reach him.

It was at that moment that Martin's dad became 'Floorball Dad', the point where the evil figure was given a body. The whole thing was based on a misunderstanding, that much was clear both to the family and the Ängsbacken floorball club; but the threads of the story were already beginning to be woven and made to form an intricate pattern, so exciting and poignant that many people neither wanted nor were able to refrain from following its development. Initially, the denials from the club led nowhere; social media went along with the reporting of the established news distributors. On Twitter speculation about the case was in full swing, and Flashback Forum was in a lynching mood.

> The old man should be bloody glad nothing happened to the boy ... And what the hell are you thinking when you leave a little ten-year-old alone in the first place ... The bloody idiot should lose his right to be a parent. Anybody know who he is?[7]

This is a classic Flashback move that recurs in many cases where a person, guilty or not, is singled out on the forum: Give us their name! Where does the idiot live?! Can someone publish the address?! We're going to beat the living daylights out of the SOB!! Come on, mates! This is freedom of expression for real! In one of the threads about Floorball Dad – there are three – match lists from the tournament with the first and last names of the boys were published at an early stage, in the hope of being able to make the correct team and name public and expose the dad and his home address to public view and scorn.[8] Journalists, too, were looking for information on

---

6 See *Aftonbladet*, 9 January 2012, 'Fallet innebandypojken granskas av åklagare' ('Case of floorball boy examined by public prosecutor'), news article, author: Lisa Röstlund.
7 Thread: '10-åring lämnades utomhus av pappan pga dålig sportsinsats' ('Ten-year-old left outside by dad because of bad sports performance'), Member: 'Xiztec', 7 January 2012, #3.
8 More information regarding Flashback is found in Chapter 2 of this book.

Flashback. Even the family that suddenly found itself at the centre of events turned to this site to find out what was actually being said about them. They should not have done that. The dad again:

> That was the stupidest thing I did, the stupidest thing our family did. We began reading things on Flashback Forum. It was no fun at all, that; it was brutal. The nasty threat was there, of course. They began writing unpleasant things about looking up who we were. And they were incredibly frustrated, because they usually manage to do this pretty quickly. But they couldn't find out. They threw things out wildly. It's like a competition for them, fun and exciting. I don't think they have any idea what they do to people when they act in this way.

Anxiety, fear, and community

The fear of their anonymity crumbling kept the mum and dad awake at night. The thought that was spinning around in their heads, keeping sleep away, was that their son would suddenly turn into the poor 'Floorball Boy', a child who had experienced something so humiliating and horrible, and that the dad would be transformed into the cruel 'Floorball Dad', an obviously sick individual who should be deprived of the custody of his children. Every morning the parents woke up in fear and thought: 'Now it's happened. Now the tabloid cars and broadcasting buses are outside the door.' They cautiously peered out into the street. It was deserted and quiet.

Even at an early stage of the scandal, the parents were aware that the protection of their identity was crucial for how things would develop. They realised that they could have put an end to the news reporting pretty quickly by going out and telling their story to the media, but that would have been a very risky thing to do. The mum and dad were convinced that certain people would choose not to believe them, regardless of how much time they spent protesting their innocence in public. Many people had already judged them, people who preferred the heart-wrenching story to the truth. The sense of shame that is foisted on a person from the outside, a feeling typical of public shaming, never materialised in their case – the dad was innocent – but what did appear was a fear of what would happen if their names were connected to these alleged events, no matter how spurious they were. The literature on the topic proves them right. The stickiness of naming-and-shaming stories cannot be removed at the drop of a hat. If the family had gone public with their identities, the loss of control over their reputation and status would have been a clear and present danger (Rowbottom 2013:1–18).

One detail that is particularly fascinating with regard to this story is how the sports association chose to support the affected family. Not everyone knew against whom the accusations were increasingly directed, but quite a few people suspected it; there were enough children, parents, leaders, and coaches for someone to have leaked the information to the journalists who besieged the town. That was how the club chairman, Måns, described the whole incident, as a siege. But there were several witnesses who supported the dad's version, people who had seen with their own eyes what had happened that day in the sports hall in Dala. To the club, it was therefore obvious that the dad was innocent. Because the club chose to protect the family in the steadfast way they did, the pressure on the sports association's representatives became difficult to handle. A great many news teams were parked outside the club premises. Måns's telephone rang incessantly for several days and nights. All the reporters who contacted him wanted the name of the dad. Some of them were particularly stubborn and aggressive, and the leaders of the sports association felt threatened and harassed, said Måns. In addition, representatives of the club were contacted by a leading member of the local government who wanted to meet them in order to be informed about the incident.

In mid-January 2012, in the media-critical public-service programme *Medierna* ('The media'), the First Channel on Sveriges Radio, broadcast interviews with those most closely affected, among others with the dad, even though his voice was disguised on the radio. Additional features about the case of Floorball Dad were broadcast a week later. After each broadcast the hunt was on again, according to Måns. In a document he wrote in connection with the events, he describes the reporters' research techniques in the following manner:

> Journalists call parents at home. Through our homepage they find their way to the individual homepages of our training groups. Then they look up the names and telephone numbers for homes and mobiles via [the websites] eniro.se/hitta.se. The journalists are desperately looking for the dad, and when somebody answers they ask, 'Are you the dad?' Even I as chairman am continually having to take calls from journalists who want to find 'the dad'.

The tabloids were especially insistent, claimed Måns. At first the reporters wanted to find the guilty party, but as time went by things turned around. Now it was no longer a matter of exposing someone, but of giving Floorball Dad the opportunity to tell his version of the story. Somehow, it was only he who could untangle the mess that the social media and news media had created together. In addition, it would be a scoop for the news company that managed to publish the dad's own story, but the newsrooms were not so forthcoming about that. *Aftonbladet*'s way of dealing with the issue will have to serve as an illustrative example. This is what a reporter wrote in an email to Måns:

> Hello!
> I have sought both of you in order to obtain help with getting in touch with the dad.
> I know you feel you have been burnt by *Aftonbladet*, but in the present circumstances I ask you to put that aside and instead provide contact information for the dad.
> The dad has to be allowed to give his version of the story.
> I have never been told 'no' by the dad except via various representatives. I don't feel good about that. We are willing to let him tell his story in any way he wants, either by talking anonymously to me or by writing a letter where he sets down what happened. The letter will in that case be published, completely unedited if that is what he wants.
> Many versions abound, and the only way to 'kill' this story is by letting the dad speak.
> He doesn't owe anybody an explanation, but by giving his version of the story he can make the other rumours go away. There is a lot of interest, one can't disregard that. We want to straighten it all out, but in order to do that we need the dad's own words. He has never commented on this (other than anonymously without a voice in a radio programme). I'd be grateful if you'd pass this on.
> Sincerely,
> Anna

The sentence 'there is a lot of interest, one can't disregard that' is the public-interest argument that is often used when publishing titillating, but by no means vital, news of this kind – in the present case, moreover, with dubious credibility in respect of the source (Petley 2013:19–43). This type of email seems to have increased the willingness of the club to protect the dad. Leaders, coaches, and chairman stubbornly refused to give out his name. They formed a human shield around the family. When the dad and the mum related how the sports association stood up for, believed in, protected, and supported them from first to last, they were both clearly moved. The mum:

> I also have to give a lot of praise. It's completely amazing how many people actually knew about this. The whole team, all the parents.

There were a whole lot of people who were in on it. And then all the people who weren't in on it and who found out about it. And nobody leaks to the media. Everybody chooses to support us. Nobody leaks my husband's name. Nobody did. Everybody just ... well, kept quiet and supported him. It was completely amazing. Lord, how many good people there are, that's what I feel. The goodness.

A child's sense of vulnerability

Relatives and family tried their best to protect Martin from the reporting in the media and from the continuously ongoing conversation about the boy who was left behind and speculations about what had gone wrong. This proved to be difficult. Every hour of every day was spent talking about what had happened, and a clever lad understands and draws his own conclusions. He was convinced it was all his fault, in spite of his parents' repeated attempts to persuade him that that was not the case. It had all been due to his terrible temper. If he had not become so angry and run off after the game, this whole incomprehensible and troublesome situation would never have arisen. That much Martin understood. He grew quieter and kept physically closer to his parents than usual. The dad again:

I: Can you see him reacting?
THE DAD (D): Yes, he starts being very much so that he likes to climb into my lap and wants to wrestle with me. He acts like a dog who is ashamed. He doesn't quite know how to behave. He's different from how he usually is. So he's absolutely affected by it. Both my wife and I feel that. It's no fun, it's difficult for him. And though we say it all the time, that this has nothing to do with him ... [pause]
I: But he knows that it's connected to ...
D: He knows the whole story, he knows everything. We talk about this around the clock, everybody's talking about this. It's all we ever talk about. Sitting there and explaining to all our relatives. ... No, it's incredibly exhausting, all of it. Then the next round begins, and the pressure gets to be so great that the police have to investigate this.

The police repeated their message in several news media: they would like to get in touch with the dad; they wanted to get to the bottom of the matter, which was now on the public prosecutor's desk – the classification of the alleged crime was 'abuse' – but so far they did not know who the dad was (Röstlund 2012). The police also mentioned the hundreds of telephone calls they had received from journalists, but also from so-called ordinary people. Rarely had a case been the cause of such great interest from the general public. The police in Dala:

> I can't remember any previous event when we've received that many calls, it's completely extraordinary. It's the behaviour that many people have reacted to. And if it happened the way it's said to have happened, then it is shocking. But we don't know that yet. [9]

Once again the family felt that they had a responsibility to try to sort out the questions that had come up, not least in order to support the club, which was going through a kind of crisis. For this reason, the mum took the initiative of writing an email, in consultation with the dad and in his name, to the police in Ängsbacken where they gave an account of the course of events in Dala, and in which they stated that their son might have been mixed up with another boy. Whatever the case, the stories – the mediated one and their own – differed so widely that the incident could not possibly have anything to do with their son. There were several eyewitnesses who confirmed their version, they emphasised for safety's sake, and they provided their contact information should the police want to know more. The tone in the email was obliging and matter-of-fact. Perhaps they would never have sent it if they had known beforehand what the consequences would be.

The police interrogations

Rumours had begun to circulate in the small town. Apparently people who were connected to the family were called in to the police for questioning, one after the other. Gradually the police came ever closer to the innermost circle of the family. Eventually Martin's mum and dad walked around waiting impatiently for their own telephones to ring. There was no longer any doubt that they were suspected of a crime, so they might as well get it over with. Waiting was, in any case, worse. When a police officer finally did call the dad, he felt a certain sense of relief, at any rate initially:

> Then suddenly a policeman calls me after all. 'Well, you know we have to investigate this. But I want you to know that we've had your son in for questioning for two hours now in the morning.' [Pause] 'What the hell are you saying??!!' That was upsetting, let me tell you. Incredibly upsetting. And then they told me how everything

---

[9] TT, 9 January 2012, 'Utredning om lämnad pojke' ('Investigation of boy left behind'), news article.

had been done, so I was rather quickly put at ease about that bit. They had to do it that way, and I understood that afterwards.

Martin had been escorted out through the back door of the school. It was done with all due circumspection. None of his friends in the fifth grade suspected anything. A teacher first accompanied him to a secluded room. There Martin was invited to shake hands with a man who introduced himself as his lawyer. The man gave him a business card, which he put in his pocket. Two more people were there. They introduced themselves as police officers, but they were in plain clothes. The three of them escorted the boy out to an unmarked police car. At police headquarters, a lengthy questioning of the boy followed. A child psychologist from the social authorities noted what Martin said and did during the questioning. Because the persons who were suspected of a crime were his parents, neither of them had been contacted. Nor, for that matter, had anyone else – family member, relative, or friend – been informed about the questioning of Martin. When the mum described how she herself was taken in for questioning, just after she had found out that her son had sat alone at police headquarters for two hours, she remembered physical sensations in particular: how her legs and hands shook and trembled, and how she had tunnel vision in the interrogation room. She was unable to focus properly on the questions. All the time her thoughts revolved around her son, whom she had still not been allowed to see.

Later, as required in accordance with official procedure, the family was also made the subject of an investigation by the social-welfare office in the town. The case was quickly dropped. When the parents summed up the course of events, they commended the actions of the authorities and the school. Staff and officials carried out the jobs they were employed to do with respect, discretion, and care. Martin himself was not particularly distressed by the police interrogation; on the whole, it had been rather exciting to be at police headquarters. Nor did the actions of the social authorities leave any marks. The other things – the totality of it, as it were – were worse. The boy was still convinced that he had done something unforgivable in Dala on that day in January, considering all the commotion that ensued. That conviction was hard to dislodge.

The pale cast of thought

In mid-January the public prosecutor closed down the preliminary investigation, and the police published a press release in which the decision was justified and the course of events was described.[10] The son had been sad when his dad did not meet him at the front of the sports arena where he was waiting. The coach Anders from Dala saw the weeping boy and tried to comfort him. The dad, on his part, sat in the car waiting for his son at the back of the arena, which is where one of the leaders of the club had promised to take him. The dad had never had any intention to leave his son behind in Dala. Whether or not the coach had spoken to the dad over the boy's telephone was not important, according to the police, because it was the dad's actions that formed the basis for the assessment of the case. There was no longer any suspicion that a crime had been committed.

Long before the legal decision was published, reality had caught up with the lie – or, more correctly, caught up with journalism. Less than twenty-four hours after the very first publication in the web edition of the local newspaper, a few source-critical posts showed up on Flashback. In that respect, the writers there were much quicker to reconsider compared to the traditional media on the Internet, as is exemplified by the following posts with their critique of journalism:

> I doubt the whole story. I think it's a bluff! This Anders character has faked things to get attention. In the Ängsbacken floorball club they don't have any information about any incident and nobody other than Anders has any info! Fake story![11]

> Have the media fallen for a bluff? Does the rapidity of the new flow of information make journalists sloppier about checking that the stories stand up before we publish?[12]

This is not the first time that members of the forum, or citizen journalists if you will, display a knack for source criticism.[13] By

---

10 Swedish Prosecution Authority, case no. AM-3575–12, 17 January 2012. 'Utredningen om den övergivna pojken läggs ned' ('Investigation about abandoned boy discontinued'), press release from the Swedish Police Authority, 18 January 2012.
11 Thread: '10-åring lämnades utomhus av pappan pga dålig sportinsats' ('Ten-year-old left outside by dad because of bad sports performance'), Member: 'chribsson2', 8 January 2012, #626.
12 Thread: 'Den övergivna innebandypojken från [Ängsbacken, fictitious name] – har media gått på en bluff?' ('The abandoned floorball boy from [Ängsbacken, fictitious name] – have the media fallen for a bluff?') Member: 'bkb1000', 9 January 2012, #1.
13 As an example, it may be mentioned that the Flashback investigators were given the Sveriges Radio award 'Årets medieorm' ('The annual media snake') in 2011 precisely for their source-critical ability and dedication to research, which had led to the revelation that Norwegian nature photographer Terje Hellesø had cheated when creating his internationally acclaimed photographs.

virtue of this powerful net-based crowd-sourcing, which is able to assemble hundreds or thousands of members in one individual thread, Flashback is very good at seeing through underhanded methods, among others those that can be found within established journalism whose shifts, exaggerations, and downright errors are regularly scrutinised. In this regard, one might say that today's journalism is faced with a choice: either it can be transparent and open to criticism from these quarters, and make that criticism visible in its own channels, or it can ignore the criticism by getting on its high horse and only using social media of this kind when such usage suits its own purposes (Noppari et al. 2014).

In a way, it was only to be expected that nuances would appear quickly on the forum, because what is published there is gossip engendered by a number of actors. It is a form of conversation of which one purpose, among others, is to jointly examine issues of this type – that is, matters with a moral resonance – where mulling over something in dialogue with other people is the actual point. Since the essential function of this chatty text form is to test arguments and points of view, preferably on the basis of an apparently real case, 'on-the-other-hand'-arguments are automatically given more space than in established journalism. The reporting of the traditional news media belongs to another genre which cannot be said to be characterised by openness and a testing approach. In spite of the transformation of journalism that was caused by digitalisation, the products of journalism in the form of features, articles, news items, columns, and analyses are still comparatively fixed in shape and rather monological.

In addition, journalism has a documented preference for 'good stories' like this one – that is, local, sensational, entertaining, and personified news with a negative slant which comprises a dimension of unpredictability. The news that works best is culturally familiar and contains elements that confirm our prejudices while offering something unexpected. In this case, the story of Floorball Dad fitted in with earlier debates in Swedish public life about so-called sports parents who urge on their children, putting them under pressure. At the same time, this dad surpassed most people's notions concerning the havoc that a sports parent can create.

In tandem with the prevailing anger against the cruel dad, the Flashback threads overflowed with empathy directed towards the boy. No child should have to endure such treatment! That was the essence of most of the posts. The writers stood up for his dignity and his rights, demanded action and punishment for the perpetrator, and brusquely rebuked all the 'net trolls' who commended the dad for his tough educational strategies. Taken altogether, this is tortuous reading matter. One could say that Flashback promoted the dissemination of the story; but the forum also contributed source-critical perspectives by questioning its credibility at an early stage. Even so, it was the blog of Anders's friend and Flashback that *Expressen* blamed when the story was about to fall apart. The newspaper excused itself by claiming that the blogger and the forum had pointed to the wrong club – a statement whose most notable characteristic is that it indicates where *Expressen*, and other media too, originally obtained their information (Josefsson 2012).

Many months later, some of the features in Sveriges Television news programmes *ABC*, *Aktuellt*, and *Rapport* were found by the Swedish Broadcasting Commission to have been in breach of the regulations concerning accuracy.[14] During the following spring, the floorball club contacted a psychologist from the Swedish Armed Forces who was an expert in crisis management. Under her guidance, the management, the leaders, and the dad met in order to jointly sum up the situation and process their feelings, reflections, and experiences. This provided a kind of closure. However, the mum still cannot let go of the story entirely. Although several years have passed since the dramatic days played out in the town I have called Ängsbacken, she still, with some regularity, occasionally finds herself looking for information about Floorball Dad on the Internet. She says she is looking for redress. For instance, she wishes that the general public would have been told that the alleged telephone conversation between her husband and the coach in Dala never took place. Martin's mobile phone had been at home during the entire tournament; consequently, Anders would not have been able to call the dad from the boy's telephone, which Anders claims to have done. Because this was never made public, the speculations could continue, the mum maintains.

News legends

How should we understand the story about Floorball Dad? What kind of narrative emerges in these flows of communication? The comparatively firm structure, dramaturgical simplicity, dramatic

---

14 The Swedish Broadcasting Commission, decision of 11 June 2012, reg. no. 12/00116.

content, and drastically presented main characters of the story link it to an older narrative tradition. Is it a modern fairy tale or a tall tale? There are features indicating a connection to both of these genres within folklore, but most of all the story gradually seems to have taken on the form of an urban legend. Unlike the fairy tale, this type of story takes place in a non-fictive world, in a reality we recognise as our own. In addition, it is narrated as though the events that take place are real; and it frequently involves something sensational or frightening which could happen to the readers themselves in their everyday lives (Dégh 2001). Also, both the dissemination and the number of storytellers are more comprehensive in comparison to the fairy tale as a genre, because anybody can pass on an urban legend – no particular rhetorical skill is required in order to relate it. A legend is characterised by its particular form where the world that is portrayed is apparently realistic, but closer examination shows it to be heavily stylised, simple, and pronouncedly visual. It sticks in your memory and is easy to pass on. It also seems as though the vitality of legends is not affected by time. Unlike orally narrated fairy tales, legends are told as much and as often today as in the agricultural society of the past; and then as now, they say something important about the things that move under the surface of the reality in which we live. The overall purpose of legends is to convey knowledge and confirm already established convictions, religious beliefs, and norms, but also to give nourishment to social relationships and conversations (Guerin & Miyazaki 2006).

Folklorist Bengt af Klintberg, the grand old man of Swedish research on contemporary folklore and modern urban legends, makes a very important point at an early stage in a book he co-authored with folklorist Ulf Palmenfelt, *Vår tids folkkultur* ('Folk culture of our time', 2008): 'One must realise', writes af Klintberg, 'that the recorded texts of legends are artefacts; in reality the legend exists as *a continuously changeable, oral communication between people* (af Klintberg & Palmenfelt 2008:17, emphasis added). I would like to underline the meaning of this quotation because I find it particularly significant: a written-down legend hence exists through and because of oral communication which takes place in physical meetings between people, face to face. That is where its actual origin lies, irrespective of the more fixed form it eventually assumes. In addition, af Klintberg emphasises the kinship between legends and rumours; their function is often similar, namely that of conveying knowledge in a situation where there is in fact no official information to rely on. He stresses the newslike and processual character of rumours and legends, i.e., how they are created through people's complex and interlinked communication flows (af Klintberg & Palmenfelt 2008:17).

The story of Floorball Dad illustrates this in a striking manner. As in the preceding chapter, we have been able to observe the actual circulation of communication. In this case, too, it becomes almost impossible – and to some extent irrelevant – to draw sharp dividing lines between different types of talk: that which is contained in rumours and gossip spread in the course of interpersonal meetings in the local community; that which is written in threads on Flashback; that which is written in newspapers; and that which is produced by radio and TV channels. Rather, what is fascinating in this context are the intermedial connections which testify to the intrinsic complexity of the media system, where so-called ordinary people exert a not insignificant influence on the duration and dissemination of a story.

However, there are also notable differences. 'Floorball Dad' is not a typical urban legend. For instance, the point of origin of a traditional legend is often hard, not to say impossible, to pin down. There is a form of inherent pointlessness to the question that continually attaches itself to the legend, says af Klintberg: 'Has this happened at some point in real life, and in that case when and where?' (af Klintberg & Palmenfelt 2008:17). This is not the case with the story that is discussed here. Among other things, the course of events can be dated and linked to a specific place, where real, named persons once found themselves. This type of legend hence contains more traces of truth than a traditional urban legend, which in this case made it appear credible. The Floorball Cup actually did take place during a specific January weekend, and the three main actors of the drama – Floorball Dad, his son, and the coach from Dala – really exist and were demonstrably there when the tournament took place. It is also evident that something happened at this point in time in this precise location, something that gave rise to the legend, even if the question of exactly what that was has remained unanswered. I therefore wish to propose the concept *news legend* as a term which helps to capture the essence of a story like this one. The word is connected to already established concepts, such as the English *newslore* and the related *nätlore* ('netlore') in Swedish (af Klintberg & Palmenfelt 2008 and Frank 2011); but *news legend* serves to say something more specific about the particular form of the urban legend and about its relationship to modern journalism, where communication via digital media seems to constitute a distinctive driving force. To a greater extent than a traditional urban legend, a news legend is a hybrid form between news as a genre and the legend as a genre.

To recapitulate briefly, here are some characteristic features of a news legend:

1. unlike most other urban legends, it is confusingly similar to a traditional news item and singles out existing individuals, sometimes also naming them;
2. in spite of its fictive character, it takes its point of departure in events that can be tied to particular times and places;
3. it is disseminated via talk that is transformed into talk–text hybrids, for instance through social media;
4. it is reproduced in social media and picked up by established media, which rely more on text than on talk as a source, irrespective of the nature of the text in other respects;
5. it fits into the news-evaluation practices and format of journalism by containing unexpected, dramatic, scandalous, shocking, and/ or amusing features;
6. it is reproduced within journalism itself through, among other things, the phenomenon of passing-down among journalists and other newsmakers.

Passing-down and narrative contagion

This last point calls for some further comment. There are several established source-critical tools that concern dependency – that is to say, how influences of different kinds change and form a person's depiction of a specific event that he or she has experienced in person – and that can be connected to the course of events surrounding the so-called Floorball Dad. One of the most common forms of dependency is referred to as *narrative contagion* by Swedish social scientists Mats Alvesson and Kaj Sköldberg. The expression concerns a form of social adaptation where an influence from other stories that an informant has heard may have affected both the structure and the content of a report made by that informant, a report which is then passed on with new meanings and undertones. The authors emphasise that the persons who have 'caught' narrative contagion are themselves usually unaware of the dependency in question. They have, so to speak, adjusted their stories to agree with one another, without knowing when and how this happened (Alvesson and Sköldberg 2008:226–37). Closely related to this is the spreading of rumours, called 'passing-down' (*tradera* in Swedish) in the context of source criticism – that is to say, a piece of information is passed on in several stages. Investigating these concepts, Swedish journalism researcher Torsten Thurén writes about urban legends in his classic book *Källkritik* ('Source criticism') (Thurén 2005:56ff). These closely related phenomena are thus interlinked, one after the other: dependency, narrative contagion, passing-down, the spreading of rumours, and urban legends.

The way I see it, a news legend may arise by way of, and because of, narrative contagion and passing-down among journalists and other news providers. The Floorball Dad story supplies a telling example of a pattern of dependency among different media, newsrooms, and journalists, where information about a case is not only shared and retold but also apparently deemed to be credible because some other newsroom or journalist has published it before – a phenomenon that is not strikingly uncommon. Since Sveriges Radio and Sveriges Television broadcast the news, a long line of news producers seem to think it has to be true before giving it space in their own newspapers or broadcasts. And so it continues, at a high pace. To put it in more drastic terms, one could say that journalism sometimes stops *using* source-critical tools and instead *materialises* them.

Joining in this advanced game of whispers as a journalist is associated with certain dangers, however, as should be apparent to everyone. Gossip jeopardises the credibility of individual journalists and newsrooms or, worse, the credibility of journalism *per se*. It can also expose innocent private individuals – who, according to the rules of media ethics, should have enjoyed the most powerful protection – to suffering the full measure of which is hard for an outsider to grasp.

So is the Floorball Dad case a one-off, forming a category of its own, or does the news legend represent an expanding genre where the Internet offers a fertile ground for growth? The book *Newslore* by communication researcher Russell Franks presents evidence suggesting that this hybrid is in the ascendant. Urban legends that find their way in among professional news are hardly a new phenomenon, but one that appears to have seen a certain increase in the digital age (Frank 2011:3–30). The faster legends are spread and circulated, for instance through social media such as Flashback, the greater the possibility that they will find their way into the domain of journalistic news, which then inevitably becomes a part of folklore (Brunvand 1981:153). When this occasionally happens, the status of oral stories is raised, from the rudimentary and popular to the authoritative and authentic (Dégh 1994).

For a journalist, it is perhaps of even greater importance than it used to be to be informed about this type of popular phenomena – that is, about the possibility that very good stories with moral overtones that are easy to retell and spread among many people may in fact be urban legends. It appears to be especially important because these stories actually look like news and imperceptibly slide between genres. In order to be believed, they move between the incredible, like fairy tales, and the credible, like news. 'ULs [urban legends] should mimic the details of news (*who*, *where*, *when*) to be credible, while being *emotional* and *readable* like a fairy tale to be catchy and memorable' (Guerini and Strapparava 2016:171; original emphasis).

Fake news as folklore

The 'news legend' concept also invites a critical scrutiny of popular expressions such as 'fake news'. Some fake news is actually folklore, as has been persuasively argued by Russell Frank:

> As digital folklore, fake news is a story generated in a non-professional social context that uses the style of news either to parody the style, satirize issues and personalities in the news, or perpetrate a hoax or prank. Not all fake news is folklore, and not all the fake news that is folklore is digital folklore. (Frank 2015:317)

However, the Floorball Dad story does not fit into the scheme described in the quotation from Frank, especially not with regard to the idea that fake news as folklore involves 'intentionally false reports' (Frank 2015:316). Rather, the event that this chapter examines in detail underscores the intrinsic interrelations between witness accounts (which could be produced by anybody with a computer; in this case it was a blog post), traditional news reporting, and audience reactions to the news reporting. By way of oral communication such as rumour-spreading and gossiping, this set of interrelations gradually transforms the relevant news item into the form of contemporary legend, or, as I prefer to call it, news legend. Fortunately, new research is emerging within this exciting field. For instance, in 2018 the *Journal of American Folklore* published a special issue which addresses the relationship between fake news and folklore. The 'fake news' concept itself calls for careful examination. It affords folklorists an opportunity to evolve in-depth knowledge of how semi-oral, often norm-creating, communication in social forums on the Internet affect societal institutions and civic engagement. In my view, researchers should be less preoccupied with narrow genre definitions and instead focus more on the cultural, societal, and political contexts in which these stories emerge. For instance, folklorist Andréa Kitta provides such a context-based approach in her highly relevant studies of the growing anti-vaccination movement, calling for greater appreciation within the public-health services of the insights that folklore as a discipline is able to supply (see e.g. Kitta and Goldberg 2017).

Concluding comment

It sometimes happens that the preference of journalism for good stories trumps impartial and true news reporting. On these occasions, journalism's residence within popular culture and the roles of journalists as storytellers are, so to speak, made visible. Yet again, we have seen how gossip that takes place face to face is interwoven with gossip in digital form, and how this text–talk hybrid occasionally not only seeps into journalism but also constitutes its main source. Similarly, one can see how the stories of journalism penetrate into people's everyday lives, giving rise to everyday conversations in the course of interpersonal meetings. If they are exciting or even scandalous, the stories are passed on with raised eyebrows and an amused or concerned, 'Did you hear what they said on the news?' People can then elaborate further on the basis of stories like the one about Floorball Dad. Together with friends and acquaintances, they can reflect on how they themselves and other people have acted as parents toward their children. They can test moral questions, try out their arguments, and finally decide where they themselves stand. In this way, scandals and gossip may be of cultural service. Indeed, the question is whether we could manage without them. But these processes also encompass a kind of exercise of power, and every person who contributes to the dissemination of gossip and rumour should be aware of that. 'The talk surrounding an issue, the media, everybody's voices, the social media. It's frightening how powerful that is', said the dad, and continued:

> Just this, that one should think about what one does to other people. And what one says about other people. Perhaps one shouldn't revel in their misery. Because it can hurt a family very much, much more than anyone can ever imagine. That's the only reason why I'm sitting here at all, talking to you, that I hope and believe that it will lead to something good.

The mum and dad described to me how people in their surroundings, unaware of the course of events, can still to this day refer to Floorball Dad as a horrible figure, and on the basis of his dubious actions discuss norms surrounding the education of children, helicopter parenting, discipline, parenthood, and so on. The retellers of this news legend have at least one thing in common: they are all convinced that the events in the story have taken place and that the story is true.

Even the mere concept 'Floorball Dad' evokes memories and feelings in people. News audiences may not recall the whole story; but many people retain a vague recollection of Floorball Dad as some kind of monstrous parent who did something unforgivable to his child – a memory which assumes the form of *postulated legend*, 'a reference that calls to mind a whole legend' (Dégh 2001:405), as time goes by.

In conclusion, I want to emphasise that this case also affords insights into the nature of human vulnerability in a mediated, digital world. The legend finds support in the digital archives and becomes real and eternal through them, which may explain why the mum continues to look for information about Floorball Dad on the Internet although some years have passed since the events took place. As was pointed out above, she says she is looking for redress; but instead she is reminded, again and again, of the fact that the story about her husband and son has apparently been given eternal life on the Internet. The case brings out the existential anxiety that is attached to digital life. Amanda Lagerkvist writes: '[h]eightened existential anxieties about the ominous forever of data have spurred urges among the networked generations to be selectively deleted, and recent debates about the "right to be forgotten" warrant our serious attention' (Lagerkvist 2017:105). 'The right to be forgotten' is contrasted with 'the ominous forever of data'. The mum was in this painful position when I met her. She realised that the story of Floorball Dad would live on in the awareness of her fellow human beings, supported by the endless information banks of the Internet.

4
The journalists and the rabbits

The moment a person assumes the role of a reporter or political commentator and views a scandal through their eyes, the character of the scandal phenomenon changes inexorably. To a greater extent than the preceding chapters, this one will deal with journalism and politics as arenas and examine how the two of them interact today. It is especially politicians who are at the centre of public scandals, and for this reason it is mainly political journalists who through their work trigger and follow the development of scandals at close range. If one wants to gain insight into how a scandal appears from the other side and is experienced by journalists, it thus makes sense to turn to this particular group of professionals.

Research about the interlinked, extensive areas that deal with the commercialisation of the media and the medialisation of politics, as well as their potential consequences for democracy, may be said to make up a vital artery of journalism scholarship and media and communication science today, and I will partially write myself into these areas. What I want to contribute is an individual perspective on the development that so many researchers have studied critically and in detail, and, on that basis, investigate how this development is experienced by practitioners.

Culture continues to be a key concept. In this chapter, journalistic culture will come in for special attention – that is to say, the normative cement that creates coherence and meaning in the everyday lives of journalists, where spoken or silent agreements, rules, and routines govern journalistic work and the production of news.

The events surrounding Håkan Juholt, former party chairman for the Social Democrats, formed a recurrent component in my conversations with journalists. These events had taken place around a year and a half prior to my interviews. It was seldom I who raised this particular topic. Instead, the reporters were encouraged to let their thoughts range freely around a variety of political scandals.

The answer to the question of why this story kept recurring probably has to do with its exceptional character. Never before has a Swedish party leader – and, in addition to that, the leader of such a large party as the Social Democrats, which governed Sweden for so long – had such a brief and scandal-dominated career. Besides, some of the journalists I met had studied Juholt closely, both during the time of the media scandal and afterwards.[1] In this chapter, as in the others, attention is also given to a number of Swedish journalists whom I have not interviewed, but who have discussed and problematised the media-scandal phenomenon in various contexts within the framework of public debate.

The objectivity talisman

Having worked as a journalist myself for many years, I regard the use of emotions as a point of departure when analysing the work of journalists as virtually impermissible. Even so, emotions in relation to journalists' objects of study are precisely what I wish to investigate in this chapter, starting out from a question formulated by researchers Barry Richards and Gavin Rees, who have investigated British journalistic culture: How do journalists relate to their own emotional lives in the exercise of their profession, and how do they deal with the emotions of the people they encounter while doing their work? (Richards and Rees 2011:853). These two authors write that journalism as a profession, being of an expressive and creative character, naturally attracts creative people. On the face of it, one might assume that this would promote an emotionally reflective culture within the profession; but for various reasons, developments have gone in the opposite direction. Richards and Rees:

> The 'free spirit' side of journalism cultures is balanced by the influence of a certain construction of 'objectivity', one that precludes excursions into the emotional. For this and other reasons, the picture of contemporary British journalism, as seen in impressionistic overview, is of a professional culture relatively unaffected by the turn to affect. (Richards and Rees 2011:854)

The authors argue that the so-called affective turn has reached neither British journalistic practice nor academic research on journalism.

---

1 For example, it may be mentioned that Margit Silberstein, together with political scientist Tommy Möller, has written a book about Juholt (Möller and Silberstein 2013). Anette Holmqvist of *Aftonbladet* scrutinised Juholt closely, too. It was she who uncovered (among other things) the so-called rent-allowance scandal – one of the reasons why I interviewed her in particular.

Similar circumstances can be said to apply in respect of Swedish journalism which has been inspired by Britain, not least within public service, where the BBC has been an explicit model. The development toward an idealisation of an objective and politically neutral journalism includes a number of nations and can be traced back in time for almost a hundred years. It began in the 1920s as a backlash against the propaganda spread by mass media during the First World War, and it also led to the concept of 'news' being redefined by professional organisations, such as the American news agency AP, the Associated Press. Gradually, in America as well as in Western Europe, both journalism and the news it produced came to adhere to guiding principles such as objectivity, impartiality, specialisation, source criticism, investigative methods, and autonomy.

Since then, the objectivity ideal has been problematised by both journalists and researchers. Nevertheless, it remains strong within the corps of journalists and has, to borrow an expression from Richards and Rees, a 'talismanic force within journalism practice' (Richards and Rees 2011:863). The opening words of the Swedish publicity regulations originate in this yardstick, with keywords such as relevance, independence, impartiality, objectivity, accuracy, factual accounting, and even-handedness – all necessary components of what one might term good journalism.

Yet another related concept has of late gained a firm hold in Swedish journalism and is used in order to safeguard its autonomy and impartiality: *consequence neutrality* or the *principle of consequence neutrality*. This means that a journalist should not consider the consequences of publishing a text, a photo, or a video or sound feature. She or he should not be influenced or hindered by the possible consequences that might follow from the publication of this item. Many newsrooms in twenty-first-century Sweden apply this principle, which is explicitly articulated in rules and regulations, here exemplified by a section from the policy of the Sveriges Radio news desk *Ekot*:

> Our basic rule is that news dissemination is consequence-neutral. That a party stands to gain or lose because of our publishing something is no reason for us to refrain from doing so. We broadcast what is important according to the requirements of relevance and objectivity. It is not the news broadcaster's task to consider who is favoured or disadvantaged by a certain news item.[2]

---

2 https://sverigesradio.se/sida/gruppsida.aspx?programid=3113&grupp=20752 &artikel=5789843 (accessed 7 March 2019).

When I interviewed Mats Knutson, political reporter at the Sveriges Television news programme *Rapport*, he asserted the importance of being consequence-neutral in his work. If an event is relevant one should report it, and if it is not one should leave it alone, was his unshakable basic rule. In either case, one ought not, as a journalist, to allow one's emotions to govern one's decision. That could, for instance, lead to special treatment being accorded to people in power towards whom the journalist as a private individual feels sympathy or antipathy, and that would be disastrous.

A circumstance that might be thought to militate against these creditable principles is that journalists are, in all essentials, feeling creatures, like the interviewees on whom they depend for the production of news. That is not something to which journalists readily admit, however; still less will they speak to other journalists about their experiences in the field and about emotions engendered by those experiences. It is a so-called non-topic, or, as one of Richards and Rees's informants put it:

> [Journalists] rarely talk about this, because people don't see it as a priority. And it runs contrary to your training as a journalist almost; because your training tells you you're not the story. ... You talk about events but not as they affect you. (Richards and Rees 2011:858)

According to the results in Richards and Rees's extensive interview study among journalists, it was not deemed proper to openly convey your emotions to your colleagues, not even following traumatic experiences at work. That was regarded as odd and undesirable behaviour which was opposed to the neutrality ideal and might, in the worst-case scenario, throw a spanner into the works of the story itself. In fact, many of the journalists attempted to evade the researchers' questions, which had to do with the emotional experiences of working as a reporter. A disinclination to speak about feelings became apparent.

To be thick-skinned as a journalist seems to be a lingering masculine ideal which is encumbered with a number of paradoxes: Good reporters should have the ability to empathise, but should not allow themselves to be too much affected by the people they meet. Reporters should be able to convey other people's emotions without feeling very much themselves. Journalists should use a creative, preferably emotional language in order to attract an audience, but they should not themselves be affected by it. They should act rationally and matter-of-factly and stay neutral and objective, but at the same time use their intuition in their journalistic work, where a so-called gut feeling should control the evaluation of news.[3]

Richards and Rees analyse these contradictions, arguing that one of the most important findings in their investigation has to do with the ambivalence that is prevalent within the professional corps concerning the concept of objectivity. In some contexts the concept implied political impartiality while suggesting an emotional distance in others. Sometimes these interpretations of the concept merged with one another. The authors argue that the distinction between expressing one's personal values in the reporting and showing empathy at work was lost, and that both of these were felt to contaminate the sought-after and exalted objectivity. It was not uncommon for journalists to argue, on the basis of both traditional and simplifying ideals, that feelings *always* jeopardised impartiality (Richards and Rees 2011:860).

If, as a journalist, I feel too much – that is, if I allow my feelings to provide me with information about the world around me and about how I myself and my fellow human beings relate to it and to one another – there is a risk that I will enter into compromises that diminish my impartiality and my duty to talk about reality such as it appears as neutrally as possible. For this reason, it is better to hold on to objectivity, no matter what that might mean. That is roughly how this opaque principle seems to be conceived. When I contacted well-known Swedish political journalists, I was of course well aware of this ideal, i.e., that good reporters should not be influenced by their emotions in relation to the subject or the person about whom they report, especially not journalists who cover politics. I was thus not overly clear about being interested in emotions in relation to my research area, but we did speak about

---

3 In spite of the female dominance in the profession in Sweden (Statistics Sweden (SCB) 2010), the idea of the solitary, emotionally unaffected, adventurous, and unassailable male reporter seems to live on – a kind of archetypal journalist who embarks on dangerous escapades, putting his life on the line in his search for the truth, and who drowns his sorrows, if any, in a few glasses of whisky instead of broadcasting his emotions and seeking comfort (see Jarlbrink 2006 for an analysis of the so-called heroic reporter). Cherished as well as caricatured, this ideal type seems to exert a stubborn influence, and many journalists still use it as a basis for their quest for a professional identity. The macho style of the hack reporter, the hatchet man, and the foreign correspondent serve as extreme examples of a culturally shaped agreement within the corps of journalists: we don't think too much about feelings in this business (see Melin-Higgins 2004).

emotions, as this chapter shows in a variety of ways. First, however, I will step on the brakes a bit and problematise the basic concept once more.

Scepticism – media scandals, do they exist?

In my meetings with the journalists, it became apparent that a few of them felt called into question by me as a researcher. Among other things, my introductory e-mails had aroused negative feelings in some of them. This was accompanied by a desire to explain themselves – alternatively defend themselves – when we met, which in its turn awakened a willingness in me to do likewise. On some occasions, for instance, I explicitly drew attention to my own background within the journalistic profession, as though to signal my prior understanding of the work involved. However, on the whole there was a good atmosphere during the interviews, which in several cases began with a critical discussion concerning the very concept 'media scandal' and a broad conversation about different *drev* (media houndings), which was the term favoured by the journalists themselves. The line of reasoning presented by political reporter Margit Silberstein of the Sveriges Television news programme *Aktuellt* may serve as an example:

> MARGIT SILBERSTEIN (MS): I think it so easy to use the word *drev* [media hounding]. Of course I realise that when everybody moves in the same direction, that's a hounding. ... But I also think that the people who feel exposed, that they very easily reach for that word. That it is a hounding and that it is the fault of the hounding, we get to hear that a lot, at least I as a journalist get to hear it. It's the fault of the hounding and it's the hounding that has led to a certain development that perhaps ended in, well, Juholt's having to resign. There are many Social Democrats who think that way, that it was the journalists' fault that Juholt had to go.
> I: And don't you agree with that, you who have studied ... [Juholt]?
> MS: I agree that he was very heavily scrutinised, absolutely. That is a truth. But I don't agree that it is the, whatever word one wants to use, fault of journalism. But it was journalism that brought out various things, so in that way of course we contributed. Do you see what I mean?
> I: Yes, I understand precisely what you mean. What you're describing is that the concept itself can also be used as a tool to strike back at the media?
> MS: Yes, absolutely. (M27097)

From the point of view of the journalists, the term *political scandal* is thus to be preferred to other designations because it puts an emphasis on politicians as actors, rather than on the media and on the journalists. On the other hand, Silberstein felt that there is indeed such a thing as media hounding. She herself used the concept repeatedly during the interview in order to characterise what she described above as the occasion when all journalists move in the same direction. In the line of reasoning of political editor-in-chief of the daily newspaper *Sydsvenska Dagbladet*, Heidi Avellan, an ambivalence also manifested itself in connection with the concept:

> But that it appears to be a hounding, everything appears to be a hounding today. It's no longer the case that there are *Rapport*, *Ekot*, and five daily newspapers to take into consideration. Now there is a myriad of different [actors] who ask questions and make claims. And this chatter, this punditry, is huge. Then you can call everything a hounding, merely as a description of the extent of the scrutiny. But obviously that doesn't make the scrutiny less relevant.[4] (M27099)

In our conversation, Avellan questioned the careless use of the 'hounding' concept, claiming, among other things, that in public debate it had come to be a term that could be stuck on to almost anything. The moment the ground starts to quake beneath the feet of a politician and the extent of media reporting increases, interested debaters immediately interpret the situation as a hounding, in posts that may be politically motivated. When, for instance, a Social Democratic politician ends up in the media searchlight, party sympathisers generally think that the media are going too far; but when the accused person comes from the opposing side, the scrutiny is perceived as being justified and vice versa. The main problem is, she argued, that the purpose of the discussions is to devalue the journalistic work effort, often for selfish reasons.

Hanne Kjöller, editorial writer at the big daily newspaper *Dagens Nyheter*, agreed with this and argued that the potential suffering of the main figure cannot be allowed to determine the extent of the reporting. How it feels to stand there in the glare of the spotlight should not be a measure of whether journalists have gone too far or not. The reporting can be relevant and adequate anyway. In his or her capacity as a politician or another figure of authority, a person has a duty to admit to what they have done and come forward, no matter how unpleasant this may be. It may be edifying

---

4 See Avellan's comment in *Sydsvenska Dagbladet* (Avellan 2013).

that people are shamed in public, both on a private and a social level, she argued.

According to the reporters, the increasing number of scandals is thus evidence that journalists are doing their job. It could be seen as proof that the talk about the open society is not simply rhetoric, but is actually put into practice. It is sometimes pointed out that media scandals are an unknown phenomenon in dictatorships.

Media scandals are undeniably complex phenomena. On the one hand, they can be seen as a valuable scrutiny of power from which we as citizens in a democratic society benefit in various ways, and on the other as sensationalism and character assassination of individual politicians which risk lowering public trust in both politics and journalism. Today, high-level politicians must expect to be heavily scrutinised, and most of them regard this as a natural consequence of their choice of profession. However, it is possible to imagine that the fact that political scandals have come to be an increasingly frequent phenomenon will deter competent people from going into politics in the first place, especially as some scandals involve matters that are not especially serious. Former Minister of Culture Cecilia Stegö Chilò (Moderate Party) touched on this in her resignation speech after revelations about her unpaid TV licences:

> I also want to direct a warm thank you to all those people who have in different ways supported me and my family during some stressful days. I have been the recipient of a lot of warmth, but I have also encountered great anxiety: What happens to our democracy if there is only room for flawless people in our politics? This is a big and difficult question which I cannot discuss here. But I hope that my experiences will not deter people like me: women, entrepreneurs, journalists, and independent public debaters from developing their ideas, following their convictions, and engaging in party-political work.[5]

In spite of this anxiety, Cecilia Stegö Chilò evinced an understanding of the work of the reporters, not least because she herself had worked professionally as a journalist for many years and had presented her own revelations about the abuse of power by politicians. Regarding the initial reporting about herself in 2006, she said:'[i]t was of course completely correct, they did nothing wrong from a publicistic point of view with respect to work on and publication of news. Of course it was above the fold!'[6] Stegö Chilò understands

---

5 Press release, Prime Minister's Office, 16 October 2006.
6 'Above the fold' is a journalistic expression and that refers to the top half of the first page of a newspaper – a place that has traditionally been reserved for the most important news of the day.

the logic of the news and respects the journalistic duty of scrutiny, but was still critical of what she calls a witch-hunt. She felt that the mudslinging and the demonisation that followed were shameful both for her and for the journalists involved, and researchers agree with her. Neither the publication of the news nor the criticism of the event in question is a problem in itself. The complications arise when the attention of the media turns into a collective hunt where both major and minor missteps lead to big headlines and the coverage grows to such proportions that it assumes the character of war reporting. This happens in parallel with shrinking perspectives and a one-sided use of sources, where the moral story eventually takes over completely and is presented as a simplified battle between good and evil, where the individual politician is depicted as representing the evil side (Allern and Pollack, 2012a:188). In a conversation with the current Press Ombudsman in Sweden, Ola Sigvardsson, he established the following points:

> If the issue is important and relevant to society, it is a good thing that many journalists and newsrooms move in the same direction, follow the course of events, and write about it. Then the hounding is desirable. The problem arises when the reporting becomes ever more attenuated and they still keep publishing as intensively. That's also when the affected person risks appearing as Beelzebub, that is, as a thoroughly evil person. (Telephone conversation, 19 September 2013)

Recurring in the interviews with the journalists was the assertion that neither the individual journalist nor the individual newsroom can control scandal reporting once it has gathered momentum. Perhaps the mechanisms of the hounding – which are, after all, acknowledged – are not good, but unfortunately the course of events cannot be halted. The process is beyond the control of individual actors. When I later listened to the interviews, the lines of argumentation made me think of the political term *TINA*, the acronym for the expression 'There Is No Alternative'. The following pages will investigate the significance of this fatalistic conviction in detail.

Undignified behaviour and a lack of independence

In all the interviews a good deal of time was devoted to talking about developments in the media market, in particular to what competition and digital development had meant for journalism. According to the reporters, that is where the answer lies to the question of why media scandals – a concept I nevertheless stick to – are becoming more numerous, and also why other kinds of political reporting have taken on some components from scandal reporting, such as personification, intimisation, and dramatisation.

Margit Silberstein of Sveriges Television initiated such a line of reasoning by establishing that over time it has become considerably more difficult to be a high-level politician, because the news is continuously being reported nowadays. All reporters write for the Internet; all newspapers produce web TV; and everything proceeds at a furious pace. 'It's an incredible tempo, so I definitely think it's more difficult. There is always some journalist showing up', she said. For the journalists, the growing competition and the intensified pace mean that it has become more difficult to carry out one's work in a satisfactory manner. More must be produced in a considerably shorter time and by ever fewer contributors. As a part of this, claimed Silberstein and several others along with her, it has become more difficult to refrain from reporting about certain events that receive a lot of attention in other media, not least in the context of scandals. This development within journalism will be discussed a little later, but let us first examine the journalists' experiences of the scandals.

Silberstein described detailed scenes where journalists crowded around a person who had ended up in hot water and looked as if they were suffering a great deal. When I asked a question about what emotions this experience in the profession awakened in her, she answered: 'I don't feel good about having that role. I really don't.' She continued:

> MS: There is something undignified in it, for the person who is exposed, but also for the journalist. You want to sit down like this and talk, but hunting someone ... it becomes so ... You stand there and wait outside the Chamber [of the Swedish Parliament] – Håkan Juholt had some party-leader debates that were incredibly hyped, then he comes out and we stand there with our lights, flashbulbs, and so on. It feels uncivilised, that's one way of putting it.
>
> I: What's the alternative, then?
>
> MS: No, if you want to be included, if you want to keep your job, you have to take part. So I don't know if there are any alternatives. Not that I can see. But you asked me to describe how I feel, and I don't like it. (M27097)

One does not refrain from participating in this type of reporting as an individual reporter, despite its being called both uncivilised and undignified. If one wants to keep one's job one has to take part, there are no alternatives, according to Silberstein. When I brought up the increasing number of mediated scandals in the Nordic countries and in the Western world, Pontus Mattsson, political reporter at the Sveriges Radio news desk *Ekot*, also emphasised the competition in the media market as an explanatory model: 'I believe the media competition has increased that [trend]. Information travels more rapidly and people are afraid of not keeping up, so one goes along instead of waiting to see what happens. The competitive element becomes clearer' (M27100). He then described – sometimes graphically, sometimes critically – what the coverage was like in January 2012 on the eve of Håkan Juholt's expected resignation, when journalists gathered in groups outside the Social Democratic party headquarters at Sveavägen 68 in central Stockholm. Mattsson was one of the reporters who stood there in the street, shivering in the winter cold, chasing news. After the fact he assumed a questioning attitude regarding the enormous resources that the media companies had spent in maintaining the surveillance outside the gate, a surveillance that went on for many days, round the clock, with little to show for it from a news perspective. He thought about what would have happened if the joint work effort had been invested in something else instead, such as more independent journalism.

> PONTUS MATTSSON (PM): Imagine the resources that were spent on people standing on Sveavägen hour after hour, day and night, waiting for a statement that never came, but, eventually, did come. Then I can feel that the proportions were distorted. I believe journalism in Sweden, the citizens, the newspaper readers, the radio listeners, would have got more out of all the overtime and salary resources if they'd instead been spent on journalists' trying to scrutinise the policies of the Social Democrats, for instance. Or the policies of some other party. But then there are a lot of things that make it impossible to resist. People want to know.
> I: What is it [they want to know]?
> PM: Well, the basic thing is that we want to know whether Håkan Juholt will stay on as party chair or not, it's a journalistic duty to inform people about this. (M27100)

Ekot is supposed to be a news leader. It is therefore impossible to refer to other sources at the symbolic moment when the party leader leaves his post. For this reason Pontus Mattsson, in spite of a certain amount of frustration, cannot leave Sveavägen and go back to his newsroom any more than the representatives of other media companies, who have an ambition to be news leaders as well, can do so. 'I'm supposed to stand there', he said emphatically. In principle, then, it was right for him to stay – even though he was, on a general level, critical of the massive coverage on the basis of what these resources, in the form of licence fees, time, and competence, could have been used for instead. On a more personal plane, between the lines Mattsson expressed a feeling that is perhaps surprising in the context, namely boredom. Apparently, it can be both tiresome and tedious to stand waiting for a statement that never comes. At any rate, it does not appear to be particularly exciting.

> PM: So when one of these stories has gone on for quite a while, then it just becomes sort of, at least I think so, a rel– [interrupts himself], then you want the whole thing to come to an end. I don't want to work with this issue any more.
> I: So what does the resignation mean to you as a journalist?
> PM: It means you can go home, something like that. (M27100)

There was no adrenalin kick during the drawn-out ups and downs surrounding Juholt for this experienced journalist, who rather seemed to view it as a necessary evil in his job to have to cover events of this kind together with thirty or forty colleagues. Instead he saw it as his duty to try to influence the situation by setting a good example and taking care not to contribute to the sometimes rancorous mood, neither in his actions on site nor in his reporting. However, the media themselves have no interest in putting a stop to this type of dramatised and scandal-orientated reporting, he maintained. On the contrary, many actors want to push the whole thing even harder, especially those media who have made dramatic revelations 'their thing'. Mattsson called this 'corporate branding'. 'Now there are new revelations!', 'We can do more!' Sveriges Televison political commentator Mats Knutson was on the same track. He too claimed that it has become more difficult for individual actors to refrain from participating in this type of journalism.

> I can say something about that, because my opinion when it comes to scandals and affairs is that we [the political reporters] who work with this are usually more restrained, even if we take the crap when we're criticised. Internally in the newsrooms, when we talk about what to do, we often argue against reporting about it, but the pressure becomes so great via other media that our editors and the people who sit there, internally in the newsroom, they feel that we are being left behind. Everybody else mentions it, and we don't. (M27096)

Anette Holmqvist of the tabloid *Aftonbladet* thought along similar lines, claiming that the change in the business is tangible. With her twenty-three years in the profession, she is able to put developments into perspective, and she argued that it is 'as different as chalk and cheese' with respect to the intensity of news dissemination, both at a general level and in the context of scandals. During the most recent decade, more and more newsrooms have emerged that consist of a growing number of sections, with one news team for each section. In spite of this, neither she herself nor her colleagues at her paper can refrain from reporting; the idea would be almost absurd. Not even TV4 reporter Anders Pihlblad, who has himself been the subject of a media scandal, sees any solution to the problem. An individual newsroom neither wants to nor can refrain from reporting on an event that everybody else reports on to a massive extent. That would mean renouncing their fundamental duties as news producers.

These experiences emphasise what we already knew, namely that the structures within journalism are generally superordinated to the individual's ability to influence journalistic production, where the collective awareness of the newsroom and the influence of the editor-in-chief and other managers have a dominant impact on the assessment and selection of news, at least in Sweden (Hultén, 1999:96; see Nygren 2008:48f, and Wiik & Andersson 2016:465–84). Mats Knutson, Margit Silberstein, Pontus Mattsson, Anette Holmqvist, and Anders Pihlblad testified that they – in spite of their undisputed standing as individual journalists – cannot refrain from reporting on matters that news editors, senior editors, and producers have deemed to be essential, even though they would sometimes like to. Specialist reporters usually have a high degree of autonomy in the exercise of their profession, which means that they themselves can control and influence what will end up as articles and features; but in spite of the special position of these informants, they seem to adapt to the logic of the newsroom when the chips are down. In fact, they not only expressed an understanding of and a loyalty to the prevailing order, they also defended it, doing what was expected of them at the end of the day. It is true that a form of resistance appears in the answers in the interviews, but this seems to be more rhetorical than practical.

The art of justifying one's actions

I didn't like it at all, but I had to do it. Most of all I wanted to leave, but I stayed anyway because it was expected of me. I actually said no, but somebody else decided I should do it anyway. It's in the nature of the job to act in this way. Everybody else does it. The profession requires of me that I act in this way, if I don't I will lose my job. I have a duty to draw attention to those matters that everybody else draws attention to. I only expose other people's errors. It's not really a media scandal because it is the politicians who have made a mess of things.

This is roughly how the reasoning of the journalists could be summarised. How are we to interpret these recurring interview answers? In the terminology of sociologists Marvin B. Scott and Stanford M. Lyman, they are examples of *accounts*, i.e., explanations that implicitly or explicitly excuse an act. In order to describe the functions of this linguistic phenomenon in everyday life, they themselves use language that is almost poetic:

> Our concern here is with one feature of talk: Its ability to shore up the timbers of fractured sociation, its ability to throw bridges between the promised and the performed, its ability to repair the broken and restore the estranged. This feature of talk involves the giving of what we shall call accounts. (Scott and Lyman 1968:46)

We are hence dealing with commonly occurring linguistic constructions which come into being in contexts where the actions of a person give rise to surprised or critical questions in other people, with the aim of preventing more questions and, by extension, conflicts. These constructions are especially apt to materialise in connection with modes of behaviour that the people surrounding an individual deem to be unfortunate, unnecessary, unsuitable, or inappropriate. Scott and Lyman argue that accounts serve as verbal links or bridges between people, links which we, usually without thinking about it, use in order to bridge the gap between our expected actions and our actual actions and make them comprehensible. Below, these linguistic models will be investigated more closely in relation to the journalists' statements.

Scott and Lyman initially divide accounts into two categories: excuses and justifications. The former is generally used in order to mitigate and alleviate the issue of responsibility in case someone's actions are called into question. A subcategory among the excuses, called *appeals to defeasibility*, corresponds to the journalists' answers to the interview questions in that the journalists often dwell on the impossibility of the situation, where they, despite their knowledge about and criticism of the mechanisms and consequences of media scandals, nevertheless acted the way they did – because their free will was limited. Such explanations are common in stories about coercion as well as about undue influence (Scott and Lyman 1968:47f): 'I had no choice but to do as I was told' is the essence of this position. In this and similar lines of reasoning one can discern an element of fatalism, which is expressed more clearly in the type of excuse that Scott and Lyman call *scapegoating*. They describe it as follows: 'Scapegoating is derived from another form of fatalistic reasoning. Using this form a person will allege that his questioned behavior is a response to the behavior or attitudes of another' (Scott and Lyman 1968:50).

It was linguist Kenneth Burke who coined the expressions *scapegoat mechanism* and *scapegoating* in order to describe the actual linguistic act where a party is exposed to undeservedly negative treatment by another party, with the intention of attaining some form of relief for the latter (Burke 1945:406ff). His interpreter René Girard (1986) refers in his texts to the transgressions of norms that may occasion scapegoating, transgressions consisting in actions carried out by an individual or group which in some way offend or violate the values, ideals, and existential principles of the majority. This usually has to do with a number of unspoken expectations or presumptions – which may be more explicitly expressed through norms and rules-of-the-game – concerning the kind of behaviour that is considered good or bad, right or wrong, permitted or forbidden, appropriate or inappropriate, and that is usually organised within the framework of a culture. Many examples of the relationship of media scandals to scapegoating mechanisms have been provided in previous chapters of this book. A scapegoat may be said to be on the opposite side of what people at a certain point in time within a culture identify as good behaviour. He or she has done something that violates the rules, or has certain character traits which are seen as transgressing some norm or norms, and should be punished for it. The person who administers the punishment is thus carrying out a sort of social duty and therefore escapes punishment her- or himself.

In other words, journalists are only acting at the behest of someone else. Pushed to their logical conclusions, long lines of argument presented by some of the interviewed journalists adhered to a pattern: first, it was questioned whether media scandals exist in the first place; then, in spite of everything, their existence was acknowledged; after that, criticism was levelled against the phenomenon; and, finally, it was claimed that those who end up in a scandal only have themselves to blame. According to a recurring line of reasoning, the transgressions of people in power are the causes of the scandals, and for that reason the resulting developments are their fault. What journalists do is expose mistakes already committed. They neither can nor should be held responsible for the consequences of that exposure. In addition, these consequences would not have had to be so serious if only politicians had learned to handle these types of events in a more reasonable manner. A lot of suffering for individuals who have ended up in hot water would have been preventable if people on the political side of things had acted rationally and professionally, and so on.

Not untrue, indeed; but the answers consistently lead away from the responsibilities of the journalists, and that, according to Scott and Lyman, is their very purpose. Scott and Lyman's 'justifications' are closely related to this attitude. 'To justify an act is to assert its positive value in the face of a claim to the contrary', they write (Scott and Lyman 1968:51). This category includes four subcategories that are particularly interesting in the present context and will be briefly explained below: *the denial of injury*, *the denial of the victim*, *the condemnation of the condemners*, and *the appeal to loyalties*. The first subcategory includes explanations which amount to arguing that the damage caused by (in this case) a journalist's actions was in fact if not richly deserved, then at least inevitable. In that respect, the actions may be considered permissible. By implication, this entails a rejection of the possibility that the person who was exposed to the actions might be a victim of them (*the denial of the victim*). Scott and Lyman mention individual politicians as examples of people who may be attacked with the justification that they deserve the attack, mainly because every politician represents politicians as a collective. Regarding the third subcategory, *condemnation of the condemners*, Scott and Lyman write: '[u]sing the device of condemnation of the condemners, the actor admits performing an untoward act but asserts its irrelevancy because others commit these and worse acts, and these others are either not caught, not condemned, unnoticed, or even praised' (Scott and Lyman 1968:51).

In the interviews with the journalists, there was a repeated explanation to the effect that other people were already committing these actions which, when taken together, create a media scandal; consequently, the journalists – implicitly – neither have to, want to, nor are able to refrain from acting in the same manner. In addition, and in line with Scott and Lyman's results, a defence of this type of action usually originates in the fact that in public life journalists are not only criticised, but also applauded and praised. A conspicuous Swedish example is the tabloid *Expressen*'s so-called scoop from the autumn of 2009 concerning the previously mentioned Jan Guillou – an internationally established journalist and author – who was identified as a 'Soviet secret agent' on newspaper billboards and in headlines. The scandal writings, which in their entirety covered over fifty pages, were not only censured by the Press Ombudsman; they were also honoured with a Golden Spade award by the association Föreningen Grävande Journalister ('The association of "digging" [i.e., investigative] journalists'). The Golden Spade is a major journalistic award, and in this case the reason was stated as follows: 'For spectacular revelations that changed the writing of history about an icon within journalism and social debate.'[7] Since then, there has been complete silence about this ostensibly laudable change in the writing of history.

Since media scandals usually have a higher purpose and a kind of altruistic significance, namely that of 'exposing the people in power' and maintaining the morality of society (at least implicitly), transgressions on the part of journalists – as well as any personal injury caused by those transgressions – are justified. This type of reasoning is in its turn closely linked to the final linguistic neutralisation technique in Scott and Lyman's survey, the *appeal to loyalties*. 'Here the actor asserts his action was permissible or even right since it served the interests of another to whom he owes an unbreakable allegiance or affection' (Scott and Lyman 1968:51). Loyalty and firm ties grow strong among journalists, which is one of many expressions of the ideology that has been called the journalistic institution or journalistic field (see Bourdieu 2005, Petersson 1994, Ekecrantz 1996, and Broady 1988). The ideology of this institution comprises self-sacrificing ideals as well as elitist and populist components, where the ability of a journalist to expose and see through people in power is considered vital to democracy (Petersson 1994). According to this way of thinking, the public is distrusted and exalted at one and the same time. The public does not have the ability to find the necessary knowledge on its own and therefore needs the journalist, who holds 'the mandate of the public' to scrutinise those in power. The revelations published by the journalist form the crowning glory of this mission. But it is easy to forget that it is the journalist who decides which knowledge will reach the public, and also what conclusions should be drawn from the revelations.

---

7 The reporting was freed by the Swedish Press Council, PON, which felt that the headline '*Expressen* avslöjar: Jan Guillou hemlig Sovjetagent. Tog emot pengar av KGB' ('*Expressen* reveals: Jan Guillou Soviet secret agent. Received money from the KGB') had an unclear meaning. See Helin 2010, and Jan Guillou's book of memoirs (Guillou 2010:471–554).

Journalists have another strong tie of loyalty to their audience. Niklas Svensson, a political reporter at *Expressen*, was careful to point out that he and his colleagues at the newspaper ultimately had the mandate of their readers, which is a form of confidence that must be preserved and lived up to. If, for instance, the readers want to know what Under-Secretary of State Ingmar Ohlsson did on Boxing Day in 2004, well, then it is up to the newspaper to find out, even if the coverage means that Ohlsson will suffer personally. Loyalty to their readers justifies the tough scrutiny, including the publication of unconfirmed rumours, idle gossip, and newspaper billboards with the word 'LIAR' next to a picture of Ohlsson's face (see Chapter 2). As a rule, tabloid journalists are prepared to go very far in order to satisfy the wishes of their audience, Niklas Svensson asserted, and that seems to be true.

Mats Knutson testified to the existence of a degree of sensitivity to viewers' reactions to scandal reporting in the newsrooms at Sveriges Television. During the so-called *ministeraffären* ('the minister affair') in Sweden in 2006, when two newly appointed ministers were removed from office and several others were exposed to harsh criticism and were scrutinised in detail by the news media for months, the audience eventually had enough. Telephones in the newsrooms began to ring, and email inboxes filled up: 'Don't you have anything better to do?' was the indignant message according to Knutson, whereupon the extent of the reporting was reduced. Since then, the audience's influence over both reporting in general and scandal reporting in particular has only increased, especially because of the opportunities provided by digital technology for interaction and dialogue with the newsrooms.

In addition, the journalist tends to become the main figure of the scoop, where balanced information is pushed into the background in favour of the heroic deed. Håkan Juholt touched on this during our conversation. He repeatedly claimed that it is not the affected individual who is the main character in the ritualised drama that a media scandal constitutes. Another player has taken her or his place.

> HJ: The main character is the hunter, the quarry is secondary. I could have been any old animal. It's the hunter who is the main character, no doubt about it.
> I: It's the journalist?
> HJ: Yes, it's the person who lands the best-aimed shot, the one who hunts for long enough. They held no grudges against me, there were no journalists who had a personal aversion to me, absolutely

not. ... But it became a psychosis. ... And it was the hunter's own self-image [that mattered]. It was the columns of the political analysts, when they are allowed to stand and say that he'll be resigning tonight and then I didn't. How embarrassing that must have been for them. (M27102)

The concept of the ideology of journalism draws attention to the professional culture that is expressed through all the explicit or implicit norms, rules, codes, and agreements that regulate journalistic work. The following section examines these more closely, starting out from topical research on the development of the media business.

Honour, fame, and rabbits

It is well known that the most recent decades have brought unusual challenges for journalism, as the large traditional media houses with their flagship newspapers struggle to survive while journalism is increasingly devalued as a profession. The transfer from traditional, analogue news processing to 'the post-industrial organisation of newswork' (Deuze 2017:10f) is as tangible and challenging in Sweden and its neighbouring countries as it is in large parts of the rest of Europe and in the United States. At the centre of the theories on the post-industrial organisation of newswork are the particular challenges and opportunities which the digital era has brought to journalism on all fronts – technologically, economically, organisationally, ideologically, and culturally. Today, newswork takes up more and more space in formal or informal cooperation with the audience, who participate through 'a co-creative continuum ranging from sharing real-time information and providing eyewitness accounts, all the way to autonomously authoring news stories, shaping an emerging type of *networked* journalism' (Deuze 2016:11, original emphasis; see also Deuze 2005, and Beckett 2010). Within international media and communication studies, journalism research, and research on political communication, this development and the ideological influence of neoliberalism on the media – and, by extension, on journalism – have led to a plethora of concerned reports and scientific articles.

Studies show that commercial news criteria have been given increased space, even if the time-span involved is often a little too short to be fully convincing (Djerf-Pierre and Weibull 2008:195–214). When these 'changes' are discussed, researchers occasionally – implicitly or explicitly – proceed from an idealised notion of the 1960s. But it is neither new nor surprising that media scandals sell, and that journalism that sells is journalism that survives. Just as a reminder: the 2009 thesis of media historian Johan Jarlbrink, *Det våras för journalisten* ('Springtime for the journalist'), which describes the development of Swedish journalism from the 1870s to the 1930s, is filled with accusations against and ideas surrounding the unfavourable influence of commercial logic on so-called *smädesskrifvare* ('libellers') and *qvickhetsmakare* ('wit-mongers') and their best-selling scandal writings. Those two categories are contrasted to serious publicists who, on the basis of sound knowledge, educated and enlightened the public. In brief, journalism rests on commercial grounds (Jarlbrink 2009:55ff). In addition, it makes sense to regard the increase in scandal stories in relation to the larger number of actors in the market. The more people there are who are able to flush out these stories, write about them, and publish them, the more common they automatically become.[8]

Bearing these critical points in mind, it is still possible to make use of some of the figures and arguments that have been supplied by media researchers Sigurd Allern and Ester Pollack (Allern and Pollack 2009:193–206). They argue that scandal stories are considerably easier and cheaper to produce, and attract a larger audience, than investigative political reporting about complex circumstances; consequently, the number of such stories has grown. Or, in the words of journalist Mats Knutson, '[i]t's easier and more profitable to describe a scandal, which perhaps doesn't mean anything to society at large, than to give an account of a societal development that affects everyone' (M27096). In other words, scandals become a simple, effective, and cheap way of attracting the audience and competing for the limited space in the media market, where the characteristics of popular journalism are gradually being transferred to political journalism (Djerf-Pierre and Weibull 2011:294–310). The linguistic techniques that occur in scandal stories, where journalists endeavour to capture people's attention through high engagement value, an intensified narrative tempo, and a popularised and hostile conversational tone as politics becomes a more or less entertaining

---

[8] The testimonies of the journalists about increasing competition and a rising number of actors should also alleviate concerns, at least at some level, about the so-called crisis which journalism is said to be going through. Increasing numbers of journalists seem to work ever harder, if one is to believe the interviewees, but in a more widespread, varied, and indeterminate form than before.

spectacle, are useful in many contexts. Taken together, the increased scandal reporting could thus be seen as an example of an adaptation to a more crowd-pleasing political journalism that does not put too great a strain on the wallet while signalling that journalists devote themselves to newswork that scrutinises, exposes, and possesses relevance. By linking the adaptation to the market and the commercialisation of news to higher journalistic values, the scandal appears an almost ideal news product for media companies under pressure (Allern and Pollack 2012a:182).

The most important thing in journalistic competition, which has increased considerably during the two most recent decades according to both researchers and journalists, is and remains being first with the news. The competition and the contest among journalists and newsrooms are an established part of the professional culture and have been discussed in several studies (see Tunstall 1971 and Hartley 2011:98ff). Consequently, this is not a new phenomenon either; but it has become increasingly tangible, if one is to believe the interviewed journalists. A myriad of media actors, to borrow an expression from Heidi Avellan, are today fighting over space. The competition among these is not exclusively a matter of making money, but of acquiring a place in the sun, something that, of course, ultimately depends on economic circumstances. All media actors therefore have an interest in advertising themselves and their achievements in a way that, according to Pontus Mattson, has nowadays gone to extremes. As a part of this development, individual journalists have taken on roles as famous news anchors, experts, and social analysts. They have been turned into celebrities with shows, blogs, and image bylines that claim ever more space – a simple and cheap way in which to conduct journalism while marketing personal achievements.

The dream of many news producers is still to deliver news that everybody else quotes, sometimes called scoops, where, for instance, a revelation about the transgressions of a person in power at best fills newspaper pages for days on end, causes the public to come flocking, and impresses colleagues. When the revelation has been published, everybody tags along because nobody dares to sit on the sidelines – a powerful contributing factor to the reporting about a scandal very quickly becoming as massive as it is streamlined. I have already provided a number of examples of this process, but might mention my own research in this context; it shows how scandal stories adhere to a given dramaturgical pattern while being thin at a general level with regard to content, in the sense that the news keeps repeating itself.⁹

There is something ambivalent about news value being measured on the basis of whether other media actors give attention to a news item, while at the same time everyone wants to produce their own, unique news. The decisive factor for the importance of a news item within this competitive culture is exclusivity, which is – paradoxically enough – determined by whether or not competitors follow it up. On this basis, it is possible to conclude that a news item, no matter how important and unique, quickly loses its original value if it is not taken up by competitors (Hartley 2011:98ff). There is a field of tension between an ambition to be innovative and being obliged to write about the same things that everyone else is writing about.

An expression that has been used about journalism in order to describe the interdependence among media actors is that the field has come to be more and more *structurally biased*, competition for attention and funds determining what journalists report on and how it is done (Petersson et al. 2006:69–80). Structurally biased journalism

---

9 As previously mentioned, certain studies show that the conformity on the part of the scandals has been slightly exaggerated; there are counter-claims here at an early stage. This is an important observation. At the same time, the rewriting phenomenon shows up clearly when one analyses the scandals on the basis of form and content, i.e., how news items and articles grow legs and very quickly move from one newsroom to another while to a great extent retaining their original form during the move. Sometimes the effect is almost explosive, as when TV4 news anchor Anders Pihlblad in an interview on 30 October 2007 in the web edition of *Expressen* said the following about Under-Secretary of State Ulrika Schenström and her condition during the much-publicised evening at the restaurant, which led up to the scandal in question: 'She wasn't plastered, but she was damned merry.' This conspicuous quotation, which was picked up by TT, not unexpectedly became a favourite with editors and was published in almost every Swedish newspaper during the next few days, both in the TT format and in their own articles, analyses, and columns. It is true that there were variations in the material, not least regarding the extent of the coverage; but with respect to content, the reporting was extremely similar in the twenty-eight newspapers that reported the statement. Up until now I have studied five scandals closely on the basis of extensive media materials (see Appendix): the so-called Toblerone affair (Hammarlin and Jarlbro 2012, 2014), the 'Ingmar Ohlsson' affair (Hammarlin 2013a), the Pihlblad and Schenström scandal (Hammarlin 2013b), and the sex-related scandals surrounding both our present King Carl XVI Gustaf and King Gustaf V (Hammarlin and Jönsson 2017). I have of course also studied other scandals that are discussed in this book carefully, but have not analysed them systematically.

The journalists and the rabbits

turns inwards, reflecting itself in itself in an almost narcissistic manner, a point touched on by Pontus Mattsson. It is undeniably interesting that public-service media are also dragged on to this merry-go-round. Of course the Sveriges Radio news desk *Ekot* enjoys a greater degree of independence than the purely commercial news producers; but to forego the tempo, the very speed of the news flow, and, so to speak, to hop off while at full speed is fraught with danger. *Ekot* might suddenly appear fusty and outmoded, which would carry the risk of losing out with respect to status and confidence. Briefly put, one might say that only those who perish in the competition escape the rules of the game.

But does not the idea of the increasingly commercialised business of journalism risk obscuring the view? Journalist and author Göran Rosenberg (2000:39–47) does not hesitate when he writes that arguments of this kind embody a kind of evasiveness that is supported by a sometimes self-glorifying professional culture and should therefore be considered part of the accountability that was analysed above. It is simply not possible to see journalists as victims of circumstances when a media scandal occurs. They are not the rabbits, to use Rosenberg's vocabulary. They form part of the hunting team that hunts the rabbits. The first thing that happens during a hounding (a *drev* in Swedish; *drev* is the word Rosenberg uses) is that an intra-professional blindness to one's own defects arises as everybody moves in the same direction and therefore tends to look on what has happened in a similar way. This is partly because journalists use the already published news of their colleagues as source material. One observation thus gives birth to another observation which resembles the first observation, and so on. *Dagens Nyheter* editorial writer Hanne Kjöller calls this a stage of 'follow my leader' where journalists, apart from using reliable sources, have also begun to listen to and themselves disseminate gossip, rumours, and hearsay. Eventually, they cluster in a kind of excited mob where affiliation to the group stands and falls with supporting the 'right' opinion. She sums up: 'There is a critical boundary when the right opinion becomes disliking someone. ... It becomes like belonging to a football team, that is, whether or not one's going to belong to the winning team.' In addition, every participant in the hunt has a need to have his or her own particular contribution endorsed. 'Then', says Rosenberg, 'the risk is that the hounding becomes self-confirming, meaning that it hounds the wrong quarry in the wrong direction on the wrong premisses' (Rosenberg 2000:43). The hunt is difficult to call off, however. It arouses feelings of intoxication, excitement, and determination in many journalists: '[You] feel both the power of the pack and the intoxication of a burst of speed' (Rosenberg 2000:45). The energy of the hounding comes from a combination of different feelings and instincts that interact: the fear of missing a news item with significant prestige and attention value; the feeling of inclusion in a community where the values and ideals of one's own professional fraternity are promoted; and the competitive instinct that is at the very core of news culture, where the person who starts the hunt or gets to the trophy first at the end is awarded the Golden Spade. But over-eager participants in a hounding sooner or later mistake their own tracks for those of the quarry. That kind of hunt could end in a tragedy, writes Rosenberg (2000:43).

Feeling empathy

It is both interesting and problematic that individual responsibility seems to count for little with the interviewed journalists. They provide detailed descriptions of situations and circumstances that they, as individuals, are critical of and would prefer not to have to deal with; but at the same time they disclaim any responsibility by referring to a super-ordinated logic to which they have to adapt. This logic is embedded in language and can be made visible by means of Scott and Lyman's conceptual apparatus. 'The end justifies the means' is a recurring thought pattern. If the news is sufficiently important, and if a reporter wants to lead the news hunt as well as defend his or her place in the collective, that person will find acceptable reasons for stretching the limits of what would be considered dishonest during different circumstances. The 'end' is not always pretty. Swedish journalist Annika Ström Melin expresses this clearly and distinctly:

> Anyone who has worked inside the media factory knows that there are often less than noble motives behind various so-called exposures. Those who speak the loudest about the media's mandate of scrutiny and never hesitate to let other people be pilloried are sometimes those who themselves seem to have a need for justification or a position. A person who is looking for stardom or fighting to secure a permanent position knows that all newsroom managers love a really juicy scoop. In such a situation, all means may seem permissible. How should this partly inherent, destructive force be controlled? (Ström Melin 2006)

It is also obvious that Margit Silberstein was speaking as a private individual when I asked her about the actual experience of hunting an obviously hard-pressed individual and exposing that person to heavy scrutiny. When, in the above quotation, she said that she did not like it – that it felt undignified, indeed even uncivilised – she spoke as a fellow human being, not as a reporter. Word for word she said: 'I don't feel good about having that *role*' (emphasis added), which bespeaks a view of herself as from the outside. Most of all she wanted to be exempted from participating, she said. Then she seemed to re-enter the journalistic function; she donned a sort of psychological reporter's hat, declaring that she was forced to participate in this type of intense scrutiny if she wanted to keep her job. The rules of the game had to be followed. One could view this as her negotiating in real time with her individual responsibility, resolving to thrust such feelings as uneasiness, discomfort, and empathy to one side in order to be able to carry out her mission. In the nuanced little publication *Drabbad av journalistik* ('Affected by journalism'), Susanne Wigorts Yngvesson provides the following comment on this issue:

> Not all journalists strive to act in a morally defensible manner. They may think they have been given a mandate by their employers to do their best, which is often the same thing as being first with a piece of news. Other people can take the responsibility, i.e., the publisher. I do not believe in such a line of reasoning. Responsibility is basic for every single human being. Relinquishing moral responsibility amounts to making oneself less human. (Wigorts Yngvesson 2008:61)

In order to be able to assess where the boundaries for defensible behaviour are drawn, one will, apart from a professional framework, need self-knowledge, an ability to empathise, and the opportunity to judge the consequences of one's own actions, writes Wigorts Yngvesson (2008:59f). So instead of entering and exiting one's professional role, one should bring the moral values one has as a human being into the newsroom and allow one's private morality to harmonise with one's professional moral standards. If I myself can imagine acting in a certain way, it stands to reason that I should not judge somebody else for acting in that same way, argues the author, who investigated these issues in her doctoral dissertation through, among other things, a detailed study of the philosopher Emmanuel Levinas's ethical theory of responsibility.

Levinas describes the imperative nature of responsibility (Levinas 1985, 1989, 1998). It is impossible to step away from, he argues. This becomes especially interesting in the light of commonly occurring excuses and justifications, since these, according to Scott and Lyman, ultimately aim to *renegotiate* individual responsibility by mitigating and alleviating it (Scott and Lyman 1968:47). The point of departure in Levinas's philosophy, or view of life, is in the original ethical situation – that is, in the interaction between myself and others. According to Levinas, responsibility cannot be experienced – and therefore cannot be implemented – through collective agreements, because responsibility is personal. A striving for moral homogeneity, for example, by adhering to a mutually agreed-upon regulatory framework, limits the attention paid to the moral complexity of each unique situation and individual. Loss of uniqueness, claims Levinas, leads to a loss of responsibility itself. Instead of safeguarding what is unique, professional rules and an *esprit de corps* with elements of a self-celebratory culture risk turning us into role-players. So what would Levinas have said about Margit Silberstein's reasoning as described above? He could have emphasised that a person can never relinquish responsibility for the Other, i.e., a fellow human being. Every individual has a unique responsibility for the Other which is irreplaceable, a responsibility that, at bottom, makes me who I am. He writes:

> Responsibility is what is incumbent on me exclusively, and what, *humanly*, I cannot refuse. This charge is a supreme dignity of the unique. I am I in the sole measure that I am responsible, a non-interchangeable I. I can substitute myself for everyone, but no one can substitute himself for me. (Levinas 1985:101; see also Levinas 1989:83, 1998:149)

But what does a meeting with the Other look like? How does it come about? By way of the face, Levinas would have answered. I cannot meet the Other with dissimulation, he writes, only face to face. Levinas's preoccupation with the face as the very gateway to responsibility is fascinating. The skin on one's face is the most naked skin, the most exposed but also the most decent, he says (Levinas 1985:89f, Tangyin 2008). The face holds power and vulnerability at one and the same time; my power over the Other, but also the Other's power over me, my vulnerability when I meet the vulnerability of the Other. There is a state of dependence here: I need the Other. Without the Other I do not see the world, only myself. In other words, the Other has a particular power over me. But – and this is important – the meeting with the Other is not automatically symmetric or reciprocal. I cannot expect that the Other will also do for me what I do for the Other. In other words, the meeting challenges my selfishness and my will to dominate. For these reasons, the point of departure in Levinas's ethical theory of responsibility is that I always have a greater responsibility than everyone else in meetings with my fellow human beings (Wigorts Yngvesson 2006:242ff).

Göran Rosenberg regards the individual's independence of the group, and consequently individual responsibility, as a central part of journalism's original capital. In combination with a critical mindset, this is the *raison d'être* of journalism. He writes: '[t]he credibility of journalism is the credibility of its individual practitioners. Credibility is not created by intra-professional codes and rules. Least of all codes and rules that liberate the journalist from the responsibility to evaluate his or her own contribution' (Rosenberg 2000:46).

Niklas Svensson of the tabloid *Expressen* admitted that the coverage could go too far in scandal contexts and could be experienced as downright inhuman by the individual who is at the centre of the scandal. But that does not mean that it would be possible to stop trying to get in contact with this person around the clock, or to stop looking for her or him all over the country, in order to demand answers to a newspaper's questions. A lengthy section is quoted in order to illustrate how this reporter reasoned:

I: But can a person answer questions in that situation?
NIKLAS SVENSSON (NS): No, it isn't certain that you can ...
I: So one is really asking for the impossible?
NS: Yes, in certain situations I think that we in the media ask for the impossible from our politicians. In large-scale houndings or very extensive scandals, such as the Ingmar Ohlsson affair, where all the newsrooms are hunting in exactly the same direction. Of course it can lead to completely inhuman situations for the person we are all trying to reach. Obviously. I completely realise that, but at the same time I find it difficult to see how I as an individual reporter, or how *Expressen* as an individual media company, should let that keep us from trying to pose these questions ...
I: [*interrupts*] How does one solve this complex of problems then?
NS: It is a serious complex of problems, for an individual.
I: And partly also for the media companies, because you can't have the answers you want either.
NS: The alternative would then be to not ask any questions and not get any answers. Now we tried to ask the questions, but we didn't get any answers.
I: And then you do more right than wrong anyway, as journalists?
NS: Well, I'm not so sure about that. You have to look at it on a case-to-case basis. But in certain situations I think we should be self-critical and more cautious when everybody runs in the same direction. There is probably a good deal to be said for

trying to think about new paths for journalism in those situations. Of course when we have chased Ingmar Ohlsson for weeks with basically the same questions and we feel that we're not getting any answers to our questions, then maybe we should find another way to tackle the problem than just to continue chasing him.

I: That leads to a pretty insipid journalism, the way you describe it.

NS: Of course it does. ... It is an extremely empty journalism, absolutely. It certainly is. I think that all journalists have a lot to learn from earlier houndings and from earlier political scandals, and above all it is valuable to hear the politicians themselves relate after the fact how they experienced it. (M27101)

Several of the interviewed journalists expressed similar reflections. Anette Holmqvist at *Expressen*'s competitor *Aftonbladet* felt that the situation today for an individual politician can be horrible and once again used one of Håkan Juholt's well-covered press conferences as an example. She described how she herself felt panic at so many people being present in such a crowded space. People could hardly move in the room, which was packed to overflowing; the air was bad, and it was hard to breathe.

> Standing there in the posse, or whatever word we should choose. Being the target, even if people pose completely relevant questions. The simple fact that there are so many of us. It becomes intimidating. It can even become intimidating for oneself to stand there in the crowd and try to hold out one's tape recorder and shout out a question. Everybody's jostling and one can hardly get any air. That's how it is today. (M27098)

Margit Silberstein said that towards the end one could see that Håkan Juholt was suffering. His face showed that he was undergoing torment, which occasioned discussions in the *Aktuellt* newsroom as to whether they might take this into consideration in their coverage of him. 'But we didn't, and I don't think you should. It's sort of not our responsibility', she asserted.

Levinas's theory can hardly be given a more concrete framing. By averting one's eyes and thus abandoning the tormented face and looking instead to the self-affirming norms of the collective, individual responsibility can be negotiated away, without any further explanation. But of course it is not quite that simple. Silberstein did not relinquish responsibility, but shouldered it before the audience, the licence-paying TV viewers. She was also convinced that the reason why Håkan Juholt had ended up in a vulnerable position was his actions, which were not acceptable to his own party. There were a not insignificant number of mistakes that had put him in a precarious position. In other words, it was not a hounding created by the media against him. Their only task was to report about the mistakes. And Silberstein chose to do that, performing actions that she as an individual journalist could wholly stand up for on a moral level.

Reading my whole interview with Silberstein from start to finish at a later date, I feel that my representation of her statements sometimes seems unfair, or, in journalistic jargon, heavily biased. Throughout our meeting she was responsive, open, and humble, and she often expressed criticism of herself and the professional body to which she belongs. On a personal level, she felt for the politicians who had ended up in hot water. 'There is a kind of loneliness about these people as well, you can see how unprotected they are', she said. In such delicate situations she is cautious. She emphasised the importance of choosing one's words carefully and sticking to the facts, which is one way of expressing empathy. In other words, she took her humanity with her into her work. I broached the same issue with Mats Knutson:

I: You're not just a commentator, you're also out in the field. So you've met these people. Has that affected you at some point? Their expressions? I know, because I've interviewed them, that they feel really awful. Is that something you've reacted to on some occasions?

MATS KNUTSON (MK): Yes, sometimes. Of course one is sometimes struck by how haggard and vulnerable these people are in these situations.

I: What feelings does that arouse in you?

MK: Of course one reacts to it, obviously. But it isn't a matter of ... one mustn't let the reporting suffer. Because feelings are feelings. My comments on TV mustn't be affected if at some point I feel sorry for a person, or feel that that person looks like he or she hasn't slept during the last week. No, but on the contrary ... Perhaps it's a way of rationalising what one's doing. (M27096)

It seems as if my questions made Knutson hesitate a little. He went on to tell me that he has several times looked up politicians who have been affected by scandals and talked to them afterwards about their experiences, not in order to apologise but to try to understand the situation from their perspectives. At the same time, there is a degree of ambivalence in the above quotation, where the feelings that were in fact awakened were consciously ignored in favour of a so-called rational way of acting, which is consistent with the idea of neutral, objective news journalism. Journalism researchers Barry Richards and Gavin Rees sound a note of caution regarding this type of commonly occurring 'ready-made' line of reasoning among journalists. So what are the risks associated with such a way of thinking and acting, according to them? Within what philosophical tradition can this way of thinking be found? On the basis of their study, they draw the following conclusions:

> What we found ... is the particular danger that 'objectivity' as a lurking legacy of 19th-century positivism has for journalists in the emotional domain. Throughout our data there are repeated conflicts, ambivalences and confusions between empathy and sympathy, and detachment and dissociation. Underlying most of these is the belief, central to journalistic discourse about itself and largely uncritiqued, that emotion inevitably contaminates 'objectivity'. (Richards and Rees 2011:863)

In other words, the danger is that journalists take the positivistically influenced objectivity as a pretext for not exploring their own moral boundaries, because they feel that emotions can rub off on so-called consequence-neutral reporting. But one's feelings must be activated if one is to have some form of moral direction about how one should act. Both Richards and Rees's extensive interview study among journalists and my own limited one indicate similar results: journalists are not just unused to speaking, but also unwilling to speak, of feelings in relation to their own professional activities. They dismiss emotional expressions as something that should be kept in check and that must not rub off on 'neutral' and 'objective' reporting.

Of course, they share this niggardly attitude to emotions with many other professional groups; but there are circumstances that make this particularly troublesome when it comes to journalists. To a great extent, journalism works within an emotional domain in society and has a central role within what is usually called 'the emotional public sphere' (Richards 2012). It not only makes information available to a large audience but also filters it, shapes it, packages it, and gives in a particular slant, fairly often with the aim of arousing emotions, using language as a tool. For this reason, journalists need to reflect on their emotional skills and abilities, or what is usually called *emotional literacy* (Orbach 2001), to a greater extent than other professional groups. This is particularly important with respect to the journalism that is produced under today's arduous conditions where factors such as increased competition, insecure employment, news online, and round-the-clock coverage lead to a development towards a more intense tempo and a more brutal imagery, where the necessity for critical reflection about one's work becomes ever more apparent but is given less and less space (Richards and Rees 2011:864). 'The judgmental tone of voice is very harsh. It doesn't matter if it is in the entertainment pages or the sports pages or the current-affairs pages, it's very judgmental. It's harsh and judgmental.' That was how Håkan Juholt expressed the problem. In a cautious conclusion, Richards and Rees write as follows:

> While journalists cannot be held responsible for the feelings of the public, nor of those whom they have encountered when reporting, they could consider more how their own reports may influence those feelings, and whether different ways of framing reports may have different downstream effects. (Richards and Rees 2011:865)

Time and again the authors return to the myth of objectivity, in which rationality is a virtue, as an urgent problem within journalism because it misleads many within the profession into believing that there is only one way in which to report a story, *one* single truth. This intellectual construct partly liberates the individual journalist from assuming personal responsibility for his or her reporting. In fact there are a large number of angles to every story, an unlimited number of facts to compile, hundreds of adjectives, lots of images to choose from, and so on. An abundance of variety and an extensive freedom become apparent – a freedom that entails responsibility and, not least, encourages the individual to accept responsibility as a person. Media researcher Roger Silverstone is on this track in his research about media and morality. Every person has to be responsible for his or her own responsibility, because its character is binding. Each and every one who participates in journalism should therefore shoulder her or his own personal responsibility for the shaping of it, he writes: 'the proprietors, editors, producers, journalists of the world's media. They have to be responsible for their responsibility' (Silverstone 2007:134). In addition, a feeling such as empathy could – somewhat unexpectedly – lead to competitive advantages in journalistic work. In my conversation with Niklas Svensson of *Expressen*, a thought-provoking line of reasoning was outlined pertaining to the unexplored relationship between humaneness and news value. Another somewhat lengthy quotation is called for:

> NS: Our journalistic mission can be carried out even if we display a certain humanity, or at least think about how a person might feel. What can reasonably be demanded from this person in

        this situation? ... Are there any other angles? Is there another point of entry here? Another way of working?
I: If I interpret you correctly, compassion becomes a way out of the conformity?
NS: Yeah, something along those lines. I don't mean that we have to limit the extent of our publicity; we can maintain that. If there are still relevant questions to be posed, and it's a relevant scandal to report on, then the extent doesn't have to be reduced. But just as you say, away from conformity, we don't have to plough the exact same furrow as everybody else.
I: And then scandal reporting could actually become better?
NS: Yes, yes, yes. Absolutely. Definitely. If more newsrooms would dare to take the step out of that furrow where everybody else is standing, then the coverage will absolutely become better. I'm completely convinced of that. And then I also think that some people who are affected would afterwards feel that, 'Yeah, but *Expressen* asked these questions and I still got to say my piece there about this thing.' Those things that they afterwards feel they never got to say. That's what I'd like to get at. (M27101)

Compassion as a route away from conformity in the reporting – this thought turns some conventional ideas about news journalism upside down. And that is precisely what media researchers Charlie Beckett and Mark Deuze do in their thought-provoking, polemical piece 'On the Role of Emotion in the Future of Journalism' (2016:1–6). They claim that journalism, with the advent of digital technology and in an era characterised by networking and connectivity, has to confront the idea of objectivity and neutral reporting and consciously move towards a more emotional journalism. Why? Because objectivity is obsolete. Technology today means that news consumption to a great extent takes place on our mobile phones, where news is mixed in with a hodgepodge of other things: 'Today's news professionals have to work in this world where their craft is blended into people's digital mobile lives alongside kittens, shopping, sport, music, online dating and mating rituals, pornography, and games' (Beckett & Deuze 2016:2).

Journalism, these researchers argue, has to respond to the changes in news consumption in the digital era. It has no other choice than to adapt to 'this affective media ecosystem', where news is linked to emotions to an even greater extent than it used to be. Beckett and Deuze claim that we can already see examples of this shift and take the reporting about the situation concerning migration in Europe as an example, arguing that we are seeing 'the normalization of affect as a potent force for more effective journalism' (Beckett &

Deuze 2016:4). The credibility of journalism in 'the networked journalism age' is to an ever greater extent determined by its emotional authenticity, they say, as transparency and openness between news producers and news audiences appear increasingly essential. While they write in an exhortatory manner, they are clearly aware of the risks involved in an emotional journalism where sensationalism and transgressions risk diminishing reliability. 'The challenge for the networked journalist is clear', they write, 'how best to sustain the ethical, social, and economic value of journalism in this new emotionally networked environment' (Beckett & Deuze 2016:5).

Concluding comment

This chapter paints a complex picture of the relationships of journalists to the emotions that the exercise of their profession may evoke. On the one hand, emotions are something one should not concern oneself with, according to a mindset where traditional but nebulous ideals surrounding objectivity, impartiality, and neutrality form an explicit or implicit basis. If one actively explores one's feelings during meetings with – for instance – politicians, there is a risk that one might start to engage in positive or negative special treatment, which would be fatal for the reporting. On the other hand, very special feelings arise in connection with being on the scent of a scandal, and that obviously affects the actions of both newsrooms and individual journalists. Rationality as a virtue is swept away and replaced by a collective instinct for hunting and competition that is perhaps not experienced by all journalists – what Pontus Mattsson spoke about had more to do with boredom – but that becomes visible in the wake of a scandal in the form of an inquisitorial, one-sided, and repetitive journalism, manifested in heavily biased articles, a lack of nuance, the elimination of a right to reply, and a hunted protagonist who feels miserable for a long time.

It also seems as if unwillingness to allow the emotions that the profession engenders to show may lead to a disinclination to reflect morally on the scandal situation. The journalists whom I interviewed felt empathy with the affected person and sometimes also tried to express this by, for instance, showing more consideration than usual in their work. But actually leaving the hunted person alone – after relentlessly pursuing her or him for days or weeks on end, with ever more watered-down reporting as a consequence – does not seem to have been an option. Instead, a psychological reporter's hat was donned, like an item of protective clothing, against the emotional weaknesses of the unreliable private individual. Like Susanne Wigorts Yngvesson, I do not believe in such a division into private and professional roles. Moral responsibility is fundamental to each individual. Relinquishing this responsibility amounts to making oneself less human.

To some degree at least, journalists pawn their original capital during a media scandal, and most people realise that once the intoxication has abated. For this reason even successful hunts, where the quarry is brought down, usually occasion certain pangs of conscience among journalists when, under the auspices of Publicistklubben (the Swedish Publicists' Association), they afterwards debate the course of events in a self-critical frame of mind. That is when they call me and want me to speak about my research. Many journalists are thus aware of being caught up in behaviour based on group pressure and a common driving force, rather than on individual reflection and critical consideration, as is apparent not least from the analyses made by the journalists themselves that have been foregrounded in this chapter. A journalistic hounding is triggered when all the implicit and accepted coded signals of the news culture together signal a shift into hunting mode, when the equivalent of a rabbit is put in front of the equivalent of a pack of dogs, writes Göran Rosenberg (2000:46). Then it is difficult not to participate in the hunt, as it is sometimes difficult to justify the hunt afterwards. Clearly, though, individual journalists could profit from training their ability to recognise the rabbits and learn to resist the instinct to hunt them, not to mention what journalism as a whole would gain from such increased awareness. The last word goes to Mats Knutson of Sveriges Television: 'Even so, people think that we overdo it, that we are too harsh, that we push it too far. As a result, I believe it affects and diminishes [public] confidence in us when we go in for this type of reporting' (M27096).

Concluding words

In his famous meditation upon cities teeming with life, Italo Calvino wrote a couple of lines about the cultural recommendations and limits that are communicated to citizens in the signs that crowd together in street corners:

> Other signals warn of what is forbidden in a given place (to enter the alley with wagons, to urinate behind the kiosk, to fish with your pole from the bridge) and what is allowed (watering zebras, playing bowls, burning relatives' corpses). (Calvino 1997:11)

Only a tiny proportion of the cultural, regulatory system to which people must relate can be communicated through signs, whereas a considerably greater part of our understanding of the circumstances and restrictions of the community happens through informal talk, for instance in the form of gossip. The media scandal as a phenomenon is good at revealing these often unspoken and emotionally regulated cultural agreements. It makes the boundaries of cultural life visible, allowing us to examine those boundaries by talking about them and exploring them emotionally together. The precise location of the boundaries distinguishing the acceptable from the unacceptable, at a given point in time and in a certain context, is rarely crystal-clear from the start. If it had been, and the boundaries had been beyond dispute, there would have been very little need for degradation rituals in the form of mediated scandals and public shaming. The scandal serves as a point of support in everyday life, a foothold from which we can push off and look at vital questions together.

Emotions are both individual and shared, and they shape our understanding of ourselves and our travelling companions in the continuously ongoing social and natural flow of daily meetings between people and things. Emotions give us a collective direction, a joint cultural foundation on which to stand; they connect us to the surrounding world, situating us in the lifeworld. In this book, an empirical focus on what emotions *do* – both to people and to media, in a wide sense of the word – has contributed new insights into the media scandal as a phenomenon, but also into the media system, where a traditional interpretation of the 'media' concept appears so limited that it becomes downright misleading. The media system has also been studied empirically in this book; that is, it was not defined beforehand, but its nature was discovered as the research progressed.

This striving for openness and flexibility has to do with the conviction that a certain media fixation among some researchers is linked to a preoccupation with the present; but, as Robert Darnton writes: 'every age was an age of information, each in its own way' (Darnton 2004:119). The oral history of scandals has neither been replaced nor ceased to exist, but lives tangled up in the conversations online that interact with the movements in traditional mass media. Everything is then stored digitally and creates a form of vibration that can be heard into the future, a kind of variable *echo archives*. Today, everybody with an Internet connection can contribute to and influence the more fixed stories that are produced in the form of texts. I see gossip as a kind of democratic component in the media scandal which is not at all new and which in part challenges accepted ideas about the media system, where traditional mass media are customarily and through force of habit considered to possess the greatest power, a state of affairs that risks undercommunicating the power of audiences. If nobody responds to the call of 'Scandal!', there will be no scandal. Conversely, if viewers, listeners, and readers urge on the pace of the scandal, the intensity of the reporting increases. If they react to and act on the scandal in their everyday lives, it adds to the troubles of the person at the centre of it. If the audience grows weary of the scandal, the newsroom will adapt the reporting to suit this satiety. There is a degree of sensitivity here on the part of news producers, an ear to the street, if you will.

Science has, according to media researcher John Hartley, consciously or unconsciously adapted itself to the desire of journalism to come across as a serious activity, which has resulted in less attention being paid to some less than flattering journalism and ditto journalistic methods (Hartley 2008:689). I agree with him about this, as I do when he writes that large parts of journalism, including that produced by the news media, *is* popular culture (Hartley 2008:689). To view gossip, which takes place face to face, as an integral part of the spatial and social dimensions of the media

Concluding words

increases the understanding of the complexity and temporal resilience that characterise the phenomenon of media scandals. What I have wanted to bring out is the circular character of the food chain where gossip, journalism, the exercise of public authority, and political considerations form an intricate network, without clear hierarchies or directions for the flows of information. In this sense, gossip-influenced and gossip-dependent journalism is not by definition bad or inferior. Undoubtedly, more studies on news journalism need to be conducted with respect to its oral, informal methods – not least now, in the midst of the shift of journalism from industrial production to 'an emotionally charged networked environment' (Beckett & Deuze 2016 1). In earlier times, informal talk – gossip, among other things – was something that mainly took place through oral meetings face to face, whereas today informal talk is being transformed into a text–talk hybrid on the Internet, which, with its archiving functions, gives this hybrid a different weight. This is why we must all hone our source-critical tools – professional journalists, the audiences of journalism, and researchers into journalism alike.

The openness, availability, rapidity, and opportunities for preservation of the digital communication arenas have changed the position of scandals, gossip, and rumour within, as well as their influence on, the public conversation of citizens, with profound consequences both for individuals and for society. Dimensions such as dissemination, scope, and speed must be taken into consideration in order to understand this change, which has created greener pastures for fabricated news and conspiracy theories. There is doubtless a need for research geared to contributing to increased knowledge and awareness of the moral issues and problem complexes that follow in the wake of the transformed opportunities for gossip, the spreading of rumours, talk-in-text hybrids, and other types of orality in the digital media environment.

It should be added that scandal audiences have been given far too little attention so far. In order to understand mediated scandals in depth, we must achieve a better comprehension of how they are received and used by their audiences, as well as how they elicit the engagement of these audiences.

Today, the media scandal as a phenomenon is the subject of public debate as well as of scholarly analysis, as in this book. In addition, there are firms of consultants that offer their services to the main figures of scandals when the situation becomes acute. Possessing detailed knowledge about the particular dramaturgy of scandals, they are able to calculate beforehand what will happen and what protection the affected individuals will need. And now, within this emerging field, we also have the people whom Erving Goffman, with characteristic cynicism, calls 'a circle of lament' (Goffman 1990a [1963]:32), consisting of people who share precisely this type of bitter experience and write what I have called fellowship-of-the-hounded letters to one another. On this basis, one could draw a cautious conclusion that media scandals in future will see a reduction of their strength. Through public scrutiny and a loss of uniqueness, we might anticipate a devaluation of the scandal's effects in the form of exclusion and public shaming. When an unusual experience such as this one becomes more common, it will probably also become less threatening. At the same time, the functions for preservation on the global Internet mean that it becomes increasingly difficult for scandalised people to begin anew, to be given a second chance. In the digital era scandals are stickier than ever, being virtually impossible to wash off.

In addition, it is possible to discern a certain satiety in the Swedish audiences, at least when it comes to political scandals. It appears to have become more difficult for the media to whip up the public mood with a tepid revelation about a newly appointed minister. Perhaps this is due to the rigorous background checks that are routinely made within the parties before each new ministerial appointment, where skeletons in cupboards are revealed beforehand; alternatively, it may have to do with the audiences having grown tired of stories that no longer titillate or surprise. 'There are institutionalised ways and mechanisms for preserving an optimal degree of novelty, i.e., there are existing cultural patterns for the preservation of the degree of novelty' (Asplund 1967:105).

At the same time, unmasking oneself publicly and expressing hatred against individuals – any individual – is easier today than it used to be because of technological developments. It is no longer necessary to be a member of the elite in order to have one's reputation publicly besmirched. One no longer has to have a special position in society in order to keep a well-polished personal apologia at hand, because anybody, no matter who they are, may come to need one. As a consequence of this, a bright future is predicted for the growing companies that offer the digital services 'reputation management' and 'reputation control', and who target ordinary people. There will not be fewer scapegoats who embody guilt and apologise in the glare of publicity. There will be more. Next time it may be you or I who stand there, the blush of shame on our faces.

Appendix

Summaries of the media scandals[1]

Håkan Juholt, *politician, Social Democratic Member of the Swedish Parliament (October 2011–January 2012)*

The media scandal surrounding Håkan Juholt, who was party chair of the Social Democrats at the time of the scandal, mainly revolved around the revelation in the tabloid *Aftonbladet* that he had for several years applied for and received state compensation for a second home, in spite of his having shared his home in Stockholm with his partner, Åsa Lindgren, all this time. According to regulations, the couple should have covered Ms Lindgren's share of the rent themselves. The rules were examined but found not to be clearly formulated; consequently, a preliminary judicial investigation for fraud was discontinued. After intense and critical publicity, above all in the tabloids, Juholt nevertheless decided to refund the money. Before this, in connection with his being appointed party chair, newspaper billboards publicised the fact that his partner had once been convicted of fraud, which formed a kind of background for the revelations that followed later. That he continually made jokes in front of TV cameras, dropped a brick on a couple of occasions, and provided erroneous information in public speeches did not improve matters. As time went by, it became increasingly common for the media to describe Juholt as a charlatan, cheater, fiddler, and fraudster. The support of Social Democrats for their leader wavered and diminished along with the more and more intensified reporting in the media. However, it is not true that he was attacked by the

---

1 Two of the cases, those involving Ingmar Ohlsson and Floorball Dad, are presented in detail in Chapters 2 and 3 and are therefore not part of this overview. Nor is the scandal involving Peter Karlsson (fictitious name) presented, for obvious reasons.

media from the very beginning, as has been claimed by some people. In an analysis of the representation of Juholt in four newspapers during his first week as party leader, Gunilla Jarlbro and I arrived at the conclusion that he was generally described in very favourable terms, regardless of the political affiliation of the newspaper (Hammarlin and Jarlbro 2014:75–80). This media scandal, and the profound problems within the Social Democratic party which it laid bare, are described in detail in, among other works, Fredrik Loberg's biography *Håkan Juholt: utmanaren* (2012), Tommy Möller and Margit Silberstein's *En marsch mot avgrunden* (2013), and Daniel Suhonen's *Partiledaren som klev in i kylan* (2014).

Hanne Kjöller, *journalist,* Dagens Nyheter *(September–October 2013)*

In 2013, the publisher Brombergs Bokförlag published Hanne Kjöller's book *En halv sanning är också en lögn* ('Half a truth is also a lie'), which is about so-called victim journalism and deficient source criticism. Her scrutiny of a number of cases that had come in for attention in the media led to the conclusion that some journalism where victims play the main role is deficient in respect of accuracy, because it omits or suppresses information that undermines the original thesis of the reporting. However, a serious factual error in the book led to its contents ending up in the background. It turned out that the information about the home of a well-known restaurateur in Stockholm was not correct. The book claimed that the restaurateur owned a spacious apartment worth many millions of Swedish crowns, whereas he actually lived in a rented flat. Kjöller quickly issued a public apology, but she had been hoist with her own petard. Criticising prize-winning Swedish journalists for being deficient in their fact-checking and then committing exactly that same mistake herself was asking for harsh criticism. Among other things, this led to a large number of journalists going through the book with a fine-tooth comb and discovering one 'factual error' after the other, in a sort of personal vendetta where an outsider could not possibly judge the credibility in each case. At times the reporting can be described as vicious, and it increasingly targeted Kjöller as a person, something that commonly occurs in the context of media scandals. 'We have experienced media houndings many times before, but rarely have so many people simultaneously thrown themselves over one and the same person as when it comes to Hanne Kjöller of *Dagens Nyheter* and her book', wrote Erica Treijs in *Svenska Dagbladet* in a summary analysis (Treijs 2013). For a detailed description of this case the Swedish Wikipedia page 'En halv sanning är också en lögn' is recommended, not so much for the description of the course of events – Wikipedia should be considered an unreliable source – but for the wealth of links to other articles that is provided there.

Sven Otto Littorin, *consultant, former politician for the Moderate Party (July 2010)*

Right in the middle of Almedalen week,[2] on 7 July 2010, the then Minister for Employment, Sven Otto Littorin, announced his resignation following questions from *Aftonbladet* which contained accusations about the purchase of sexual services (which is a criminal act in Sweden). Littorin was also supposed to have sex-chatted while in the Government offices. At that time Littorin was going through a custody battle, covered in detail by the tabloids, and he came directly from a hearing in the District Court of Stockholm to Gotland. Already at the airport he was met by *Aftonbladet*'s reporter, who ran alongside the Minister and pantingly asked his questions, an example of what media researchers Mats Ekström and Bengt Johansson have called 'attack journalism' (Ekström and Johansson 2011). The Minister defended himself against the accusations with the words, 'No, no, please stop!' and 'No comment.' During the press conference at his resignation, Littorin used emotional language and, among other things, referred to his three children by name – for which he was later criticised – claiming that it was the heavy scrutiny of his private life and the price his children had had to pay for their father being a public figure that caused him to hand in his resignation, effective immediately. This became an intensely covered news item in all the Swedish media and led to a physical hunt for Littorin, which is described in Chapter 1. The soundness of *Aftonbladet*'s sources was weak. The paper had information from an anonymous woman who claimed that she had sold sex to Littorin a few years before. In an email interview in *Dagens Nyheter* a week later, Littorin's disclaimer was published, a disclaimer in which the accusations according to which he had committed a crime were firmly rejected. Analyses of this affair have since been conducted by the periodical *Fokus* (Agerman 2010) and

---

2 Every summer, 'Almedalen week' on the island of Gotland features public speeches by senior representatives of the Swedish political parties as well as a number of events arranged by various public bodies as well as private companies. Almedalen week has served as a source of inspiration for 'democracy festivals' in neighbouring countries.

in student essays, among others the readable 'Efter avgången: En studie av affären Littorin' ('After the Resignation: A Study of the Littorin affaire' [sic]) (Hovne et al. 2010).

Maja Lundgren, *author (August 2007)*

Literature professor Sara Danius called the debate surrounding the novel *Myggor och tigrar* ('Mosquitoes and tigers'), published by Bonniers, the literary scandal of the year 2007. In an analysis of the course of events, Danius writes that 'Lundgren was accused of lying, indeed, even of not being right in the head' (Danius 2010). The book is a kind of feminist settling of scores with a certain type of male chauvinism, and it was an early contribution to bringing to public attention the both explicit and implicit oppressive acts against women perpetrated by the so-called *kulturman* ('culture-man', a designation for a man of high standing in the intellectual-cum-artistic world who poses as a major authority on cultural issues and whose ego is typically expressed in the kind of speech known as 'mansplaining'). A number of named male cultural workers are criticised in the novel, men who mainly worked in the culture-and-arts editorial office of the tabloid *Aftonbladet*. There was much publicity about the book even before it appeared, and as it came out the media reporting about it, and about its author, was intense. Initially, attention focused on the way the book moved in a controversial borderland between fiction and reality; but soon the main interest of journalists came to be directed at Lundgren's personality. When the debate was at its most intense, the novel was called a 'scandal book', and a considerable amount of journalism was devoted to discussions of Lundgren's mental health. She was described as being unstable, a woman on the verge of a nervous breakdown. That caused other writers to react: when men with an exalted standing in the realm of literature write about their lives in confessional mode, it is considered a noble art; but when a female author does the same thing, it is condemned as tasteless, unintellectual, and even pathological. The publisher felt that there was a real threat against Lundgren and deployed private security guards at a few of her public appearances. Sara Danius again:

> Nowadays it's acceptable for books to portray hard-core pornography, sadism, and masochism, even rapes. But there is one thing you mustn't do. You mustn't attack cultural workers in the royal capital, especially if they are in positions of power. Then all hell breaks loose. (Danius 2010)

An analysis of this case has been conducted in the unpublished Master's thesis 'Kulturmaffians myggor och tigrar: en litteratursociologisk studie av litteraturkritik och härskartekniker i en tidningsdebatt' ('The mosquitoes and tigers of the cultural mafia: a literature-sociological study of literary criticism and domination techniques in a newspaper debate') (Mattisson 2011).

Anders Pihlblad, *political reporter and commentator, TV4 (October–November 2007)*

Late one evening in October 2007, TV4 reporter Anders Pihlblad sat in the restaurant Judit & Bertil in Stockholm together with Ulrica Schenström, then Under-Secretary of State and right-hand woman of Prime Minister Fredrik Reinfeldt. They drank wine, talked, and were merry, possibly inebriated. After a tip to the tabloid *Aftonbladet*, a team consisting of a photographer and a reporter went there. A number of compromising pictures were taken of the couple from the newspaper's car through the windows of the restaurant, which gave the photos a paparazzi character. One of the photos captures the two kissing and embracing. The newspaper made a big thing of the photo, splashing the image across its pages; but at that point no major affair was made of it – that is to say, relatively few news media followed up on the news. A few days later Håkan Juholt, who was at that time a Social Democratic Member of the Swedish Parliament working for the Swedish Defence Commission, raised the question of whether Schenström had been 'on call' at the time: had she been responsible for the national crisis management in the event of a possible disaster on that particular evening? Reinfeldt did not want to reveal this information and for a long time referred to secrecy concerns, but the pressure became too great. In connection with the Prime Minister's confirming that Schenström had indeed been on call during the much-publicised evening at the restaurant, she handed in her resignation. At the same time, a preliminary judicial investigation was initiated. Schenström was suspected of corruption and Pihlblad of bribery. Both crimes were committed as the TV4 reporter paid the restaurant bill, claimed the director of public prosecution, Christer van der Kwast. However, the investigation was dropped because of a lack of evidence. Pihlblad was deeply shaken by the scandal, which led to a severe personal crisis. He later wrote a book on the topic, *Drevet går: Om mediernas hetsjakt* ('The hunt is on: On being hounded by the media') (Pihlblad 2010).

Tiina Rosenberg, *professor, former non-professional politician (Feminist Initiative) (September-October 2005)*

Tiina Rosenberg has been in hot water with the media on a number of occasions. In 2005, political scientist Johan Tralau accused her of plagiarism in her research, which led to newspaper-billboard publicity and big headlines. In a debate article in the tabloid *Expressen* in connection with these events, historian Dick Harrison wrote a kind of apologia for Rosenberg. 'Gender witch Tiina, that queer professor who drives heteronormative patriarchy up the wall, is actually a big bluff. Her books are pieces of plagiarism. Her opinions are crazy', he wrote in a few ironic introductory lines which exactly captured the image that the media had already established of Rosenberg, an image that was later reinforced (Harrison 2005). My interview with Rosenberg mainly revolved around how news journalism portrayed her during her period as a non-professional politician in Feminist Initiative (Fi). Among other things, she was then accused by Fi's Ebba Witt Brattström of having made scandalous statements, such as 'women who sleep with men are gender traitors', which resulted in intense media attention. Political scientists Maria Wendt and Maud Eduards later conducted an analysis of the portrayal of Fi in the press (Wendt and Eduards 2010). They write that while they were working on the piece, it was difficult not to be troubled by the emotional, scornful tone of voice that many journalists used. This aggressive tone was mainly directed at Rosenberg who was, taken altogether, more or less explicitly portrayed as an extremist, militant, lesbian academic who hated men. When Rosenberg resigned from the party executive committee, the reporting in many instances came to be about her physical appearance. She was, among other things, described under the headline 'Problemet med Fi-Tiina' ('The problem with Fi-Tiina') as a loud-mouthed, middle-aged woman who dresses like a man and deliberately conceals her beauty (Marteus 2005). The excitedly hostile publicity about her appearance, which took on the proportions of a scandal from time to time, and the threats that ensued, contributed to Rosenberg leaving her post within the party, a development outlined in Chapter 1 above.

Gudrun Schyman, *politician (Feminist Initiative, former party leader of the Left Party) (September 1996, November 2001, January 2003)*

Like Tiina Rosenberg, Gudrun Schyman has been under attack in the media many times. Among other things, there was a good deal of publicity about her alcoholism, and about the scandalous situations she found herself in because of it, during the 1990s. After she admitted her addiction and publicly chose sobriety, criticism was checked and she could continue working as the leader of the Left Party. During my interview with Schyman, she was asked many open questions about media scrutiny during her long career as a politician. In her answers, she dwelt particularly on the *Expressen* affair. On 27 November 2001, the tabloid published an article about a film which party leader Schyman's former husband, Lars Westman, had made and which was partly based on conversations between himself and his ex-wife. The newspaper billboards on the same day read, 'GUDRUN SCHYMAN records EROTIC FILM with her ex-husband'. Under this headline, there was a quotation from Westman: 'YOU'RE SUPPOSED TO GET HORNY'. In my interview with Schyman she emphasised how completely exposed she felt when she saw the newspaper billboard, and she realised that it was pasted all over Sweden. There was nothing she could do to defend or explain herself. She experienced it as an assault and burst into tears. During the legal proceedings against the newspaper that followed, she argued that the billboard gave the impression that she was starring in a porn film, which was an offence both against her personally and against the party of which she was a representative. In 2003 the newspaper and its publisher, Joachim Berner, were convicted of defamation in the Swedish Supreme Court. The same year Schyman left her post as chair of the Left Party in connection with an affair that had to do with erroneous tax deductions, a more traditional media scandal by Swedish standards.

Cecilia Stegö Chilò, *professional board member, former journalist, and former politician for the Moderate Party (October 2006)*

The scandal surrounding Cecilia Stegö Chilò was part of the so-called minister affair that took place in October 2006, when the non-socialist Alliance government was being assembled for the first time. In the article 'Extra Extra. Hon sågas – hon avgår' (Extra Extra: 'She is denounced – she's resigning') (Pollack 2009:99–120), whose title is taken from a spread in *Aftonbladet* (15 October 2006), media researcher Ester Pollack investigates the dramaturgy of this scandal. Minister for Trade Maria Borelius and Minister for Culture Cecilia Stegö Chilò had to leave their posts after only a few days because of revelations about nannies paid under the table and advanced tax-avoidance schemes in the case of the former and a continual failure to pay the TV licence fee in the case of the latter. In her analysis, Pollack takes newspaper opinion pieces as her point of departure and shows how the reporting stripped both ministers of their competences in favour of a one-sided, negative focus on their characters. In one column and analysis after the other, Stegö Chilò and Borelius were portrayed as greedy, elitist people with dubious private morals, who believed they were above the law and who acted for their own benefit. Pollack calls it character assassination (Pollack 2009:116). She describes the chain of events as a play in three acts, where the final act is when the female protagonist of the drama, like the diva in innumerable operas, must die. She calls this the peripeteia of the scandal, its turning-point, when 'the sacrificial lamb is placed on the altar, the guilty party is punished, balance is restored, and the social body is purified' (Pollack 2009:116).[3] Pollack finds a few counter-voices in her material, one of which came from the left. Gudrun Schyman, who was then leader of Feminist Initiative, noted that of course she condemned both a failure to pay the licence fee and the use of undeclared labour, but that neither offence deserved these unanimous calls for resignation that echoed through the public sphere.

Ireen von Wachenfeldt, *former Chair of ROKS, the National Organisation for Women's Shelters and Young Women's Shelters in Sweden (May–July 2005)*

'Könskriget' ('The gender wars') was the name of a TV documentary by journalist Evin Rubar which was broadcast in two parts as a component of the programme *Dokument inifrån* ('Documents from inside [the country]'), Sveriges Television, in May 2005. The documentary was about the influence of so-called radical feminism on politics in Sweden. It came in for a very great deal of attention and was given a Golden Spade award; however, the Swedish Broadcasting Commission found it to be in breach of the regulations regarding partiality, and it was criticised for heavily biased interviews. Rubar's interview with Ireen von Wachenfeldt was found to be particularly noteworthy. The latter described the course of events to me as follows: During the interview Evin Rubar had the ROKS periodical *Kvinnotryck* ('Women's pressure/print') in her lap and referred to a review in that particular issue, which was two years old, of Valerie Solanas's feminist classic *SCUM Manifesto*, where men are described

---

3 This quotation has been translated from Norwegian into Swedish and then into English.

as animals. 'Do you think men are animals?' asked the reporter. 'No, I never even thought about it', chuckled von Wachenfeldt, whereupon the question was asked again and again with the justification that the reviewer in the periodical thought so. Because von Wachenfeldt was the chair of ROKS and the publisher of the periodical, she should support what was written in it, argued Rubar. This irritated von Wachenfeldt, and she eventually, under obvious pressure, fell into the trap and said, 'Men are animals, don't you think, don't you think so.' This interview technique, which may be described as a technique of exhaustion, can be seen in a long, unedited sequence on YouTube.[4] The statement caused a huge outcry. Condemnations were numerous, pleas in defence few. The 'men are animals' statement turned out to have considerable staying-power and is still alluded to. In time it has become a rhetorical figure, an example of *pars pro toto* (that is, where a part is made to represent the whole). It is customarily used in contexts where gender studies or so-called radical feminism are debated and criticised. To Ireen von Wachenfeldt the statement, and the subsequent media scandal, brought an abrupt end to her career; she also became the victim of numerous death threats, which led to her developing a social phobia, as described in Chapter 1.

Source-critical reflections

Discussions are ongoing within this research field about what should be referred to as a 'media scandal' and how that concept should be defined. For example, political scientist Tobias Bromander uses a wide-ranging method when selecting his scandal material (Bromander 2012:26–35), while media scholar Sigurd Allern and others choose a more precise method (Allern et al. 2012:30ff). Selecting scandals for my study, I sometimes collated the degree of intensity in the media coverage with media scholar Ester Pollack who, together with Sigurd Allern and other researchers, created a list of political scandals in the Nordic countries from 1980 to 2010 (Allern et al. 2012:29–51).

As a result of my desire to broaden the analysis, I included three people whose experiences might be characterised as something other than regular media scandals: the cases of Maja Lundgren and Hanne Kjöller could be designated as 'heated cultural debates', while the writings about Floorball Dad might be categorised as belonging to

---

4 https://www.youtube.com/watch?v=pBtKxYKQI_8 (accessed 7 March 2019).

the 'public shaming' phenomenon. In the latter case, this is precisely how I analyse it, public shaming being a kind of variant or extension of the media scandal. At the same time, these three informants have experienced the same things as the others, namely how the story about their actions – actions that were judged to constitute a severe violation of norms – multiplied through reporting in the media and reached a strength which is characteristic of the concept of media scandals, where harsh condemnations in public have been prevalent. As was the case with the rest of the informants, the scandal writings transformed them into embodied examples of morally reprehensible behaviour.

Because the book is built on interviews, I have been dependent on finding people who have had these experiences, but who were also prepared to talk about them and be part of a research study, which of course not everybody was. As one potential informant told me when declining my request for an interview, 'there are experiences in life which you would prefer to put behind you'.

I contacted the informants via email or telephone and then made an appointment for an interview in offices, in homes, and, in one case, in a café. Each informant was interviewed with a tape recorder for one to three hours, except for Gudrun Schyman, whom I met briefly before she was due to participate in a debate. That interview was short, about forty minutes, and was written down in a field diary; consequently, it is considered to be secondary material. Schyman invited me to her home for a longer session, but a lack of time unfortunately put paid to those plans. Hanne Kjöller agreed to be interviewed on condition that she could talk about journalism in particular and about personal experiences of scandal reporting only as an exception. For this reason I mainly refer to the interview with her in the final part of the book, which is based on journalists' perspectives on media scandals.

The interviews were conducted from time to time over the course of the project, spread out over several years, a circumstance which is likely to have affected the end result. If all interviews had been conducted in rapid succession, I would have had a different overview over the material from the outset and would have found patterns more quickly. The main reason why they were spread out in this manner is that different interviews were linked to different part-studies and that other tasks – I am also a senior lecturer – have sometimes had a disruptive effect on my research time. The unexpected advantage with this is that my knowledge of the subject grew before each interview, and that, I would argue, gradually increased the quality of the interviews. If I had done all the interviews at the beginning of the project, I would probably have missed some important questions that turned out to be crucial along the way.

The interview method I am using is tried and tested in ethnological and anthropological contexts and is best described as conversational, the researcher being the listening party. The ethnological interview is similar to a personal meeting between two individuals. It is more like an informal conversation than an interrogation on the basis of a previously prepared form (Fägerborg 1999, Ehn and Löfgren 1996). Before each occasion, I did research about the course of events of the pertinent media scandal and wrote down a number of questions; but during the meeting I put these aside in order to concentrate on listening to the informant with an open mind. I reacted spontaneously to what I was told, just like in a normal conversation, and interjected comments and follow-up questions as we went along. Afterwards, when we had reached some sort of concluding point, I returned to my prepared questions in order to check if we had missed anything.

The interviews were then transcribed by a transcription agency. I have thus missed out on the advantages of spending a lot of time with and being close to the material by personally transcribing the interviews. However, this was a very conscious decision on my part – it takes an unjustifiably long time to type out interviews, and it can be physically unhealthy for people who are not in possession of the correct technique. In return I have both listened to the recordings and read the transcriptions repeatedly, sometimes simultaneously, in order not to miss out on moods, nuances, and dimensions that are implicit in the material.

Sometimes the interviews with the informants are almost unreadable in their transcribed form while other people speak in whole sentences and are hence easier to quote. Some people are given greater space in the book because they possess a linguistic talent which means that they succeed in appropriately expressing what several of the informants only reflect and reason about. This is common in studies that are based on interview material. However, it is themes – mainly categorised on the basis of emotions expressed by the informants – that have governed the reproduction of the quotations, especially in Chapters 1 and 4.

A question that should be asked regarding the interviews in this publication is how feelings affect memory. A number of studies show that there is a positive correlation between memory and emotions, insofar as events that arouse strong emotions promote the ability to remember them afterwards. However, some studies indicate that very powerful emotional reactions sometimes seem to have the opposite effect – trauma, for instance, can cause the memory of an event to fade (see Reisberg & Heuer 2004), although the opposite has also been argued (Thurén 2005:32f). I have assumed a position with respect to the inherent unreliability of memory by focusing on the significance of the personal experiences and incidents described by the informants, rather than foregrounding details – for example times and persons – in the depicted events.

The fact that I am myself a trained journalist and have worked within the profession for many years may have had an effect on the interviews, primarily those with the journalists. There is a risk that I might have identified with them, although several years have passed since I was last active in the profession. On all interview occasions, I told the interviewees about my professional background; with some of the journalist informants I was extra clear about it, especially at times when I felt that they were becoming defensive. I would like to add that a general point of departure for me as a researcher has been an aspiration to understand the experiences, emotions, thoughts, and circumstances of the informants, rather than criticising them.

Many studies contain source-critical discussions about the advantages and disadvantages of qualitative interviews, and I recommend those who are interested in this method and in reflexive discussions about it to read, for instance, ethnologist Bo Nilsson's doctoral dissertation *Maskulinitet* ('Masculinity') (1999), the anthology *Perspektiv på intervjuer* ('Perspectives on interviews') (Lövgren 2002), consumption researcher Sofia Ulver's doctoral dissertation *Status Spotting* (2008:63–98), and communication researcher Stephen Coleman's book *How Voters Feel* (2013:34–76).

I could have included more of myself in the text, trying to imitate the reflexive style which some of my role models within anthropology employ in an impressively assured manner (see Miller 2011b). As matters stand, though, I remain in the background. When all is said and done, that is where the ethnologist belongs.

I have attempted to conduct an open work process. For instance, before publication I allowed the informants to read the entire manuscript and was attentive to suggestions for changes, which were ultimately few in number. Some of the informants expressly asked not to have to read the text beforehand, a request I respected.

Appendix

It is my hope that this serves as a guarantee regarding the ethical considerations which every study that starts out from the lives of real people must face and deal with.

One weakness inherent in the media material that is included in this study is that I have studied considerably more text than sound and image material, a shortcoming that is, embarrassingly enough, common in media research. At the same time, I have tried to listen for auralities in the text and develop a technique for examining how informal speech can be studied in writing (Hammarlin & Jönsson 2017). Even though I have been focusing on texts, I have been more interested in their motions and their modes of transfer, not least between speech and written text, than in the content itself. Regarding the Flashback threads that are included in the study, I have not kept statistics or drawn up lists of how often certain statements occur. Even so, there is a systematic element in my approach to this extensive material: I have subjected it to a kind of intermittent checking by studying every twentieth page, thereby forming a perception regarding the tone of voice and the changes over time among the posts. The relationship between traditional journalism and Flashback's citizen journalism has been at the centre of my searches in this area.

Google searches are, for obvious reasons, not mentioned in the bibliography; but the search engine has been a self-evident, indispensable, and daily part of my work. Media scandals have a wide impact, and it is impossible to account in writing for the vast quantity of interviews, articles, news items, commentaries, columns, analyses, and images that I have studied over the years and that form part of the secondary material of the book. As is customary, the media material mentioned in the bibliography is restricted to what has explicitly been part of the analysis and is directly mentioned or quoted.

Bibliography

Field materials

Taped interviews with 19 informants, 1–3 hours per person, and transcripts of these. In addition, a shorter interview documented by notes in a field diary. Several informants have agreed to the interviews being archived at the Folklife Archives in Lund, serial number M27092–M27102. A telephone interview of 19 September 2013 with the present Press Ombudsman, Ola Sigvardsson, is also part of the material. In addition, telephone conversations in May 2015 with the Chair of the Ängsbacken sports club (fictitious name), email correspondence, and telephone lists are part of the material for Chapter 3.

Archival sources

Mediearkivet (Retriever Research), free text search in all sources. 98 articles from 2 December 2005–3 March 2009 with regard to the 'Ingmar Ohlsson' scandal – as a fictitious name has been used for this person, as well as for the other person who became involved in the scandal, the search terms for both are not stated here; 151 articles 31 October 2007–6 November 2007, search terms: 'Anders Pihlblad' AND 'Ulrica Schenström'; 102 articles 7 January 2012–7 February 2012, search terms: 'innebandy' AND 'pappan' AND 'pojken', and 'innebandypappan' AND 'innebandypojken' (doubles have been removed manually).

Press and broadcast media sources

Agerman, Per. 2010. 'Rättshärvan bakom Littorins fall', *Fokus*, 35, 6 September

Avellan, Heidi. 2013. 'Tro och tycka är skilda saker', *Sydsvenskan*, 20 April, comment

Danius, Sara. 2010. 'Maja Lundgren: "Mäktig tussilago"', *Dagens Nyheter*, 13 March, book review

Harrison, Dick. 2005. 'Vi professorer gör alla som Fi-Tiina', *Expressen*, 7 October, debate article

Bibliography

Hedlund, Ingvar and Niklas Svensson. 2006a. 'Nu tvivlar Göran Persson på Lars Danielsson', *Expressen*, 10 May, news article
— 2006b. 'Persson-beviset. Här avslöjar statsministern tvivlet på Danielsson', *Expressen*, 10 May
Helin, Jan. 2010. 'Rätten att sätta en felaktig rubrik', *Aftonbladet*, 2 June, editorial
Jönsson, Fredrik. 2012. '"Spelade dåligt" – dumpad av pappa', *Aftonbladet* (Sportbladet), 12 January, news article
Lagercrantz, Leo and Linda Skugge. 2007. 'Duellen: Linda & Leo om veckans hetaste samtalsämnen', *Expressen*, 2 September, comment
Marteus, Ann-Charlotte. 2005. 'Problemet med Fi-Tiina', *Expressen*, 14 October, analysis
Nilsson, Torbjörn. 2006. 'Bloggarna bakom Danielssons drama', *Fokus*, 18, 19 May
Röstlund, Lisa. 2012. 'Fallet innebandypojken granskas av åklagare', *Aftonbladet*, 9 January, news article
Ström Melin, Annika. 2006. 'Ingen pressetik utan en gnutta trolöshet', *Svenska Dagbladet*, 19 October, review
Sveriges Radio. 2006. *Dagens eko*, 18 May, 4.45pm, telegram
Sveriges Radio. 2012. 'Vi kollar storyn om innebandypappan', *Medierna*, P1 (Radio 1), 14 January
Treijs, Erica. 2013. 'Kultursvepet', *Svenska Dagbladet*, 30 September
TT. 2012. 'Utredning om lämnad pojke', 9 January, news article

Electronic sources

Harper, Douglas. 2012. *Online Etymology Dictionary*, http://www.etymonline.com/
Hellquist, Elof. 1922. *Svensk etymologisk ordbok* (Lund: Gleerups), in *Projekt Runeberg*, http://runeberg.org/svetym/
Ingerö, Johan. 2006. *Right Online*. http://rightonline.blogspot.se/2006_05_01_archive.html (accessed 7 March 2019)
Josefsson, Jessica. 2012. 'Klubben hotas efter ryktet om 10-åring', Expressen. se, 9 January
OED Online, Oxford University Press, http://www.oed.com/
On the Media. 2015. 'Jon Ronson and Public Shaming', 24 July
SAOB. 1893–. *Ordbok över svenska språket* (*The Swedish Academy Dictionary*) (Lund, Svenska Akademien), https://www.saob.se/
Sveriges Radio. 2004. Text on consequence neutrality, on https://sverigesradio.se/sida/gruppsida.aspx?programid=3113&grupp=20752&artikel=5789843 (accessed 7 March 2019)
Söderlund, Henrik. 2012. 'Pojke "spelade dåligt" – lämnades kvar av förälder', Unt.se, 12 January
YouTube. 2009. 'ROKS: – Män är djur!', https://www.youtube.com/watch?v=pBtKxYKQI_8 (accessed 7 March 2019)

Flashback threads

'Skvaller om en viss statssekreterares närvaro på Regeringskansliet' ('Gossip about the presence of a certain Under-Secretary of State at the Government Offices'), 2,142 posts, https://www.flashback.org/t299276 (accessed 7 March 2019)

'10-åring lämnades utomhus av pappan pga dålig sportinsats' ('Ten-year-old left outside by dad because of bad sports performance'), 1,744 posts, https://www.flashback.org/t1762135 (accessed 7 March 2019)

Reports and material from public authorities

Ministry of Finance. 2007. *Tsunamibanden*, Official Government Reports Series, 2007:44

Prime Minister's Office. 2006. Press release regarding the resignation of Cecilia Stegö Chilò, 16 October

Standing Committee on the Constitution (KU8). 2005. *Regeringens krisberedskap och krishantering i samband med flodvågskatastrofen 2004*, Government Committee Report 2005/06:KU8

Statistics Sweden (SCB). 2010. *Tema: Utbildning – Könsstruktur per utbildning och yrke 1990–2030 (Theme: Education – Distribution of Sexes by Education and Profession 1990–2030)*, theme report 2010:1

Swedish Broadcasting Commission. 2012. Decision of 11 June 2012, ref. no. 12/00116

Swedish National Council for Crime Prevention (Brå). 2013. *Den anmälda korruptionen i Sverige: Struktur, riskfaktorer och motåtgärder*, report 2013:15

Swedish Police Authority. 2012. 'Utredningen om den övergivna pojken läggs ned', press release, 18 January

Swedish Prosecution Authority. 2012. Case no. AM-3575–12, 17 January

Literature

Ahmed, Sara. (2004). *The Cultural Politics of Emotion* (New York: Routledge)

Allan, Stuart. 2006. *Online News: Journalism and the Internet* (Maidenhead: Open University Press)

Allern, Sigurd, and Ester Pollack. 2009. *Skandalens markedsplass: Politikk, moral og mediedrev* (Bergen: Fagbokforlaget)

— 2012a. 'The Marketplace of Scandals', in *Scandalous! The Mediated Construction of Political Scandals in Four Nordic Countries*, ed. by Sigurd Allern and Ester Pollack (Gothenburg: NORDICOM), pp. 181–90

— 2012b. 'Mediated Scandals', in *Scandalous! The Mediated Construction of Political Scandals in Four Nordic Countries*, ed. by Sigurd Allern and Ester Pollack (Gothenburg: NORDICOM), pp. 9–28

Allern, Sigurd, and Ester Pollack (ed.). 2012c. *Scandalous! The Mediated Construction of Political Scandals in Four Nordic Countries* (Gothenburg: NORDICOM)
Allern, Sigurd et al. 2012. 'Increased Scandalization: Nordic Political Scandals 1980–2010', in *Scandalous! The Mediated Construction of Political Scandals in Four Nordic Countries*, ed. by Sigurd Allern and Ester Pollack (Gothenburg: NORDICOM), pp. 29–50
Alvesson, Mats, and Kaj Sköldberg. 2008. *Tolkning och reflektion: Vetenskapsfilosofi och kvalitativ metod*, 2nd edn (Lund: Studentlitteratur)
Anderson, Ben. 2009. 'Affective Atmospheres', *Emotion, Space and Society*, 2:77–81
Anderson, Benedict. 1991. *Imagined Communities: Reflections on the Origin and Spread of Nationalism* (London: Verso)
Asplund, Johan. 1967. *Om mättnadsprocesser* (Uppsala: Argos)
— 1987. *Om hälsningsceremonier, mikromakt och asocial pratsamhet* (Gothenburg: Korpen)
Baron, Naomi S. 2010. 'Discourse Structures in Instant Messaging: The Case of Utterance Breaks', *Language@Internet*, 7, article 4
Beckett, Charlie. 2010. 'The Value of Networked Journalism', Value of Networked Journalism conference, London School of Economics and Political Science, 11 June
Beckett, Charlie, and Mark Deuze. 2016. 'On the Role of Emotion in the Future of Journalism', *Social Media + Society*, 2(3):1–6
Berggren, Henrik, and Lars Trägårdh. 2015 [2006]. *Är svensken människa? Gemenskap och oberoende i det moderna Sverige* (Stockholm: Norstedt). Second edn.
Bird, S. Elizabeth. 1997. 'What a Story! Understanding the Audience for Scandal', in *Media Scandals: Morality and Desire in the Popular Culture Marketplace*, ed. by James Lull and Stephen Hinerman (Oxford: Polity Press), pp. 99–121
— 2003. *The Audience in Everyday Life: Living in a Media World* (London: Routledge)
Bjerke, Paul. 2012. 'Media Victims and Media Morals', in *Scandalous! The Mediated Construction of Political Scandals in Four Nordic Countries*, ed. by Sigurd Allern and Ester Pollack (Gothenburg: NORDICOM), pp. 165–79
Bourdieu, Pierre. 2005. 'The Political Field, the Social Science Field and the Journalistic Field', in *Bourdieu and the Journalistic Field*, ed. by Rodney Benson and Erik Neveu (Cambridge: Polity Press), pp. 29–48
Boydstun, Amber E., Anne Hardy, and Stefaan Walgrave. 2014. 'Two Faces of Media Attention: Media Storms versus Non-Storm Coverage', *Political Communication*, 31(4):509–31
Brewer, John. 2005. 'Personal Scandal and Politics in Eighteenth-Century England: Secrecy, Intimacy and the Interior Self in the Public Sphere', in *Media and Political Culture in the Eighteenth Century*, ed. by

Marie-Christine Skuncke (Stockholm: Royal Academy of Letters, History and Antiquities), pp. 85–106
Broady, Donald. 1988. 'Kulturens fält: Om Pierre Bourdieus sociologi', in *Masskommunikation och kultur*, ed. by Ulla Carlsson, NORDICOM-Nytt/Sverige, 1–2 (Gothenburg: NORDICOM), pp. 59–88
Broberg, Gunnar et al. 1993. *Tänka, tycka, tro: Svensk historia underifrån* (Stockholm: Ordfront)
Bromander, Tobias. 2012. *Politiska skandaler! Behandlas kvinnor och män olika i massmedia?*, Linnaeus University dissertations, 107 (Växjö: Linnaeus University Press)
Brunvand, Jan Harold. 1981. *The Vanishing Hitchhiker: American Urban Legends and Their Meanings* (New York: W.W. Norton)
Brurås, Svein. 2004. *Uthengt: Subjektive opplevelser av negativ pressomtale*, Working Report no. 166 (Volda: Volda University College)
Brurås, Svein, Guri Hjeltnes, and Henrik Syse. 2003. *3 uker i desember: En kritisk gjennomgang av medienes rolle i den såkalte Tønne-saken* (Oslo: Norsk presseforbund)
Burke, Kenneth. 1945. *A Grammar of Motives* (New York: Prentice-Hall)
Böll, Heinrich. 2009. *The Lost Honor of Katharina Blum, or: How, [sic] Violence Develops and Where It Can Lead*, trans. Leila Vennewitz (New York: Penguin). First published in German in 1974 as *Die verlorene Ehre der Katharina Blum oder Wie Gewalt entstehen und wohin sie führen kann*
— 2011. *Katharina Blums förlorade heder, eller: Hur våld kan uppstå och vart det kan leda*, trans. Karin Löfdahl (Gothenburg: Lindelöw). First published in German in 1974 as *Die verlorene Ehre der Katharina Blum oder Wie Gewalt entstehen und wohin sie führen kann*
Calvino, Italo. 1997. *Invisible Cities*, trans. William Weaver (London: Vintage). First published in Italian in 1972 as *Le città invisibili*
Carey, James W. 1992. *Communication as Culture: Essays on Media and Society* (New York: Routledge)
— 1998. 'Political Ritual on Television: Episodes in the History of Shame, Degradation and Excommunication', in *Media, Ritual and Identity*, ed. by James Curran and Tamar Liebes (London and New York: Routledge), pp. 42–70
Carlsson, Anita. 2008. 'Klick, klick, klart', in *Nyhetsfabriken: Journalistiska yrkesroller i en förändrad medievärld*, ed. by Gunnar Nygren (Lund: Studentlitteratur)
Carlsson, Ingemar. 1967. *Frihetstidens handskrivna litteratur: En bibliografi*, Acta Bibliothecae Universitatis Gothoburgensis, 9 (Gothenburg: Gothenburg University Library)
Casetti, Francesco. 1998. *Inside the Gaze: The Fiction Film and Its Spectator* (Bloomington and Indianapolis: Indiana University Press)
Clough, Patricia Ticineto, and Jean O'Malley Halley. 2007. *The Affective Turn: Theorizing the Social* (Durham, NC: Duke University Press)

Coleman, Stephen. 2013. *How Voters Feel* (Cambridge: Cambridge University Press)
Corner, John. 2000. 'Mediated Persona and Political Culture: Dimensions of Structure and Process', *European Journal of Cultural Studies*, 3(3):386–402
Corner, John, and Dick Pels. 2003. *Media and the Restyling of Politics: Consumerism, Celebrity and Cynicism* (London: Sage)
Darnton, Robert. 1997. 'Best-Sellers and Gossip-Mongers in 18th-Century France', *Unesco Courier*, 50(6):14–18
— 2000. 'An Early Information Society: News and the Media in the Eighteenth-Century Paris', *American Historical Review*, 105(1):1–35
— 2004. 'All the News that's Fit to Sing', *Smithsonian*, 35(7):110–19
— 2005. 'Mademoiselle Bonafon and the Private Life of Louis XV: Communication Circuits in Eighteenth-Century France', in *Media and Political Culture in the Eighteenth Century*, ed. by Marie-Christine Skuncke (Stockholm: Royal Academy of Letters, History and Antiquities), pp. 21–54
— 2010. *Poetry and the Police: Communication Networks in Eighteenth-century Paris* (Cambridge, MA: Belknap Press of Harvard University Press)
Daun, Åke. 1996. *Swedish Mentality* (University Park: Pennsylvania State University Press)
Dayan, Daniel, and Elihu Katz. 1992. *Media Events: The Live Broadcasting of History* (Cambridge MA: Harvard University Press)
Dégh, Linda. 1994. *American Folklore and the Mass Media* (Bloomington: Indiana University Press)
— 2001. *Legend and Belief: Dialectics of a Folklore Genre* (Bloomington: Indiana University Press)
Deuze, Mark. 2005. 'What Is Journalism? Professional Identity and Ideology of Journalists Reconsidered', *Journalism* 6(4):443–65
— 2014. 'Journalism, Media Life, and the Entrepreneurial Society', *Australian Journalism Review* 36(2):119–30
— 2016. 'Considering a Possible Future for Digital Journalism', *Mediterranean Journal of Communication* 8(1): pp. 9–18.
— 2017. 'Considering a Possible Future for Digital Journalism', *Mediterranean Journal of Communication*, 8(1):9–18
Djerf-Pierre, Monika, and Lennart Weibull. 2008. 'From Public Educator to Interpreting Ombudsman: Regimes of Political Journalism in Swedish Public Service Broadcasting 1925–2005', in *Communicating Politics: Political Communication in the Nordic Countries*, ed. by Jesper Strömbäck et al (Gothenburg: NORDICOM), pp. 195–214
— 2011. 'From Idealist-Entrepreneur to Corporate Executive: Provincial Newspaper Editors' and Publishers' Ways of Thinking from the Mid-1800s to the Present', *Journalism Studies*, 12(3):294–310
Djerf-Pierre, Monika, et al. 2013. 'Policy Failure or Moral Scandal? Political Accountability, Journalism and New Public Management', *Media, Culture & Society*, 35(8):960–76

Dresner, Eli. 2005. 'The Topology of Auditory and Visual Perception, Linguistic Communication, and Interactive Written Discourse', *Language@ Internet*, 2, article 2

Döveling, Katrin et al. 2011. *The Routledge Handbook of Emotions and Mass Media* (Abingdon: Routledge)

Eduards, Maud. 2007. *Kroppspolitik: Om Moder Svea och andra kvinnor* (Stockholm: Atlas akademi)

Ehn, Billy, and Orvar Löfgren. 1996. *Vardagslivets etnologi: Reflektioner kring en kulturvetenskap* (Stockholm: Natur & Kultur)

— 2004. *Hur blir man klok på universitetet?* (Lund: Studentlitteratur)

— 2010. *The Secret World of Doing Nothing* (Berkeley: University of California Press)

— 2012. *Kulturanalytiska verktyg* (Malmö: Gleerup)

Ekecrantz, Jan. 1996. 'Mediernas demimonde', in *Medierummet*, ed. by Karin Becker et al. (Stockholm: Carlsson bokförlag), pp. 292–316

Ekström, Mats, and Bengt Johansson. 2008. 'Talk Scandals', *Media, Culture & Society*, 30(1):61–79.

— 2011. 'When the Scandal Hits the Messenger', unpublished conference paper, *The Mediation of Scandal and Moral Outrage* conference, ECREA, LSE, 16–17 December

Elmelund-Præstekær, Christian, and Charlotte Wien. 2008. 'What's the Fuss About? The Interplay of Media Hypes and Politics', *International Journal of Press/Politics*, 13(3):247–66

— 2009. 'An Anatomy of Media Hypes: Developing a Model for the Dynamics and Structure of Intense Media Coverage of Single Issues', *European Journal of Communication*, 24(2):183–201

Engman, Jonas. 2014. 'Den skrattande löjtnanten: Parad, karneval och humor', in *Kulturella perspektiv på skratt och humor*, ed. by Lars-Eric Jönsson and Fredrik Nilsson, Lund Studies in Arts and Cultural Sciences, 5 (Lund: Lund University), pp. 19–37

Frank, Russell. 2011. *Newslore: Contemporary Folklore on the Internet* (Jackson: University Press of Mississippi)

— 2015. '*Caveat Lector*: Fake News as Folklore', *Journal of American Folklore*, 128(509):315–32

Frykman, Jonas. 1977. *Horan i bondesamhället* (Lund: Liber)

— 2012. *Berörd: Plats, kropp och ting i fenomenologisk kulturanalys* (Stockholm: Carlsson bokförlag)

Frykman, Jonas, and Orvar Löfgren. 1979. *Den kultiverade människan* (Lund: Liber)

— 1987. *Culture Builders: A Historical Anthropology of Middle-Class Life*, trans. Alan Crozier (New Brunswick, NJ: Rutgers University Press)

— 2005. 'Kultur och känsla', *Sosiologi i dag*, 35(1):7–34

Frykman, Jonas, and Maja Povrzanović Frykman. 2016. 'Affect and Material Culture', in *Sensitive Objects: Affect and Material Culture*, ed. by Jonas Frykman and Maja Povrzanović Frykman (Lund: Nordic Academic Press), pp. 9–28

Fägerborg, Eva. 1999. 'Intervjuer', in *Etnologiskt fältarbete*, ed. by Lars Kaijser and Magnus Öhlander (Lund: Studentlitteratur)
Gans, Herbert J. 2007. 'Everyday News, Newsworkers, and Professional Journalism', *Political Communication*, 24(2):161–6
Gerbner, George, and Larry Gross. 1976. 'Living with Television: The Violence Profile', *Journal of Communication*, 26(2):172–94
Gilje, N. (2016). 'Moods and Emotions: Some Philosophical Reflections on the "Affective Turn"', in *Sensitive Objects: Affect and Material Culture*, ed. by Jonas Frykman and Maja Povrzanovic Frykman (Lund: Nordic Academic Press)
Girard, René. 1986. *The Scapegoat* (London: Athlone)
Gluckman, Max. 1963. 'Gossip and Scandal', *Current Anthropology*, 4(3):307–16
Goffman, Erving. 1990a [1963]. *Stigma: Notes on the Management of Spoiled Identity* (New Jersey: Penguin Books)
— 1990b [1956]. *The Presentation of Self in Everyday Life* (London: Penguin)
— 2008 [1972]. *Interaction Ritual: Essays in Face-to-Face Behavior* (Brunswick, NJ: Transaction Publishers)
Gregg, Melissa, and Gregory J. Seigworth. 2010. 'An Inventory of Shimmers', in *The Affect Theory Reader*, ed. by Melissa Gregg and Gregory J. Seigworth (Durham, NC: Duke University Press)
Guerin, Bernard, and Yoshihiko Miyazaki. 2006. 'Analyzing Rumors, Gossip, and Urban Legends through Their Conversational Properties', *Psychological Record*, 56:23–34
Guerini, Marco, and Carlo Strapparava. 2016. 'Why Do Urban Legends Go Viral?', *Information Processing and Management*, 52(1):163–72
Guillou, Jan. 2010. *Ordets makt och vanmakt: Mitt skrivande liv* (Stockholm: Pocketförlaget)
Hall, Stuart (ed.). 1997. *Representation: Cultural Representations and Signifying Practices* (London: Sage)
Hammarlin, Mia-Marie. 2013a. '"Va? Är det sant?" En studie av medieskandalers förankring i vardagligt skvaller', *RIG: Kulturhistorisk tidskrift*, 96(1):11–28
— 2013b. 'Media Scandals and Emotional Expression', unpublished conference paper, *Media and Passion conference*, Department of Communication and Media, Lund University, 21 March
Hammarlin, Mia-Marie, and Gunilla Jarlbro. 2012. 'From Tiara to Toblerone: The Rise and Fall of Mona Sahlin', in *Scandalous! The Mediated Construction of Political Scandals in Four Nordic Countries*, ed. by Sigurd Allern and Ester Pollack (Gothenburg: NORDICOM), pp. 113–32
— 2014. *Kvinnor och män i offentlighetens ljus* (Lund: Studentlitteratur)
Hammarlin, Mia-Marie, and Lars-Eric Jönsson. 2017. 'Prat i text: Om skvaller som journalistisk metod', in *Celebritetsskapande från Strindberg till Asllani*, ed. by Torbjörn Forslid et al., Mediehistoriskt arkiv, 35 (Lund: Media History, Lund University), pp. 93–115

Hartley, Jannie Møller. 2011. 'Radikalisering av kampzonen: En analyse av netjournalistisk praksis og selvforståelse i spændingsfeltet mellem idealer og publikum', unpublished doctoral dissertation (Roskilde: Roskilde University)
Hartley, John. 2008. 'The Supremacy of Ignorance over Instruction and of Numbers over Knowledge', *Journalism Studies*, 9(5):679–91
Harvard, Jonas, and Patrik Lundell. 2010. *1800-talets mediesystem*, Mediehistoriskt arkiv, 16 (Stockholm: Royal Library)
Heidegger, Martin. 1974. *Teknikens väsen och andra uppsatser* (Stockholm: Rabén & Sjögren). Originally delivered in 1953 as a lecture, 'Die Frage nach der Technik', first published in 1954
Herring, Susan C. 2011. 'Computer-Mediated Conversation, Part I: Introduction and Overview', *Language@Internet*, 8, article 2
Herzfeld, Michael. 2005. *Cultural Intimacy: Social Poetics in the Nation-State* (New York: Routledge)
Hildeman, Karl-Ivar. 1974. *Visan som vapen i gammal tid: Om nidet i Östnorden* (Helsinki: n.p.)
Hirdman, Anja. 2001. *Tilltalande bilder: Genus, sexualitet och publiksyn i Veckorevyn och Fib aktuellt* (Stockholm: Atlas)
Holmberg, Claes-Göran et al. 1983. *En svensk presshistoria* (Solna: Esselte Studium)
Hovne, Anders et al. 2010. 'Efter avgången: En studie av affären Littorin', unpublished student essay (Gothenburg: University of Gothenburg Department of Journalism, Media and Communication (JMG))
Hultén, Lars J. 1999. *Ordet och pengarna: Om kamp och kapitulation inom journalistiken* (Stockholm: Natur & Kultur)
Häger, Björn. 2014. *Reporter: En grundbok i journalistik*, 2nd edn (Lund: Studentlitteratur)
Jansen, Stef. 2016. 'Ethnography and the Choices Posed by the "Affective Turn"', in *Sensitive Objects: Affect and Material Culture*, ed. by Jonas Frykman and Maja Povrzanović Frykman (Lund: Nordic Academic Press), pp. 55–77
Jarlbrink, Johan. 2006. 'Hjältereportern: Målet för reporterns resa', *RIG: Kulturhistorisk tidskrift*, 89(2):85–94
— 2009. *Det våras för journalisten: Symboler och handlingsmönster för den svenska pressens medarbetare från 1870-tal till 1930-tal*, Mediehistoriskt arkiv, 11 (Stockholm: Royal Library)
Jenssen, Todal Anders, and Audun Fladmoe. 2012. 'Ten Commandments for the Scandalization of Political Opponents', in *Scandalous! The Mediated Construction of Political Scandals in Four Nordic Countries*, ed. by Sigurd Allern and Ester Pollack (Gothenburg: NORDICOM), pp. 51–71
Johansson, Bengt. 2006. *Efter valstugorna: Skandalstrategier och mediemakt* (Gothenburg: University of Gothenburg)
Journal of American Folklore. 2018. Special Issue, 'Fake News: Definitions and Approaches', 131(522)

Jönsson, Lars-Eric, and Fredrik Nilsson. 2014. 'Skratt som fastnar', in *Kulturella perspektiv på skratt och humor*, ed. by Lars-Eric Jönsson and Fredrik Nilsson, Lund Studies in Arts and Cultural Sciences, 5 (Lund: Lund University), pp. 7–18

Kafka, Franz. 2009. *The Trial* (Oxford: Oxford University Press). First published in German in 1925 as *Der Prozess*

Kapferer, Jean-Noël. 1988. *Rykten: Världens äldsta nyhetsmedium* (Stockholm: Norstedts)

Karlsen, Kim Edgar, and Fanny Duckert. 2018. 'Powerful and Powerless: Psychological Reactions of Norwegian Politicians Exposed in Media Scandals', *International Journal of Communication*, 12:3134–52

Katz, Jack. 1999. *How Emotions Work* (Chicago: University of Chicago Press)

Kepplinger, Hans Mathias. 2007. 'Reciprocal Effects: Toward a Theory of Mass Media Effects on Decision Makers', *Harvard International Journal of Press/Politics*, 12(2):3–23

— 2016. 'Warum fühlen sich die Skandalisierten auch dann als Opfer der Medien, wenn sie zugeben, was man ihnen vorwirft?', in *Mediated Scandals*, ed. by M. Ludwig, T. Schierl, and C. von Sikorski (Cologne: Herbert von Halem Verlag), pp. 58–76

Kindeberg, Tina. 2011. *Pedagogisk retorik: Den muntliga relationen i undervisningen* (Stockholm: Natur & Kultur)

Kitta, Andrea. 2012. *Vaccinations and Public Concern in History: Legend, Rumor, and Risk Perception* (New York: Routledge)

Kitta, Andrea, and Daniel S. Goldberg. 2017. 'The Significance of Folklore for Vaccine Policy: Discarding the Deficit Model', *Critical Public Health*, 27(4):506–14

Kjöller, Hanne. 2013. *En halv sanning är också en lögn* (Stockholm: Brombergs förlag)

Klintberg, Bengt af, and Ulf Palmenfelt. 2008. *Vår tids folkkultur* (Stockholm: Carlsson bokförlag)

Kress, Gunther, and Theo van Leeuwen. 1996. *Reading Images: The Grammar of Visual Design* (London: Routledge)

Kroon Lundell, Åsa. 2010. 'The Fragility of Visuals: How Politicians Manage their Mediated Visibility in the Press', *Journal of Language and Politics*, 9(2):219–36

Kumlin, Staffan and Peter Esaiasson. 2012. 'Scandal Fatigue? Scandal Elections and Satisfaction with Democracy in Western Europe, 1977–2007', *British Journal of Political Science*, 42(2):263–82

Lagerkvist, Amanda. 2017. 'Existential Media: Toward a Theorization of Digital Thrownness', *New Media & Society*, 19(1):96–110

Laine, Tarja. 2010. 'SMS Scandals: Sex, Media and Politics in Finland', *Media, Culture & Society*, 32(1):151–60

Levinas, Emmanuel. 1985. *Ethics and Infinity: Conversations with Philippe Nemo*, trans. Richard A. Cohen (Pittsburgh, PA: Duquesne University Press)

— 1989. 'Ethics as First Philosophy', in *The Levinas Reader*, ed. by Sean Hand (Oxford: Basil Blackwell)
— 1998. *Entre nous: On Thinking-of-the-Other* (London: Athlone Press). First published in French in 1991 as *Entre nous: essais sur le penser-à-l'-autre*
LeVine, Robert A. 2007. 'Afterword', in *The Emotions: A Cultural Reader*, ed. by Helena Wulff (Oxford: Berg)
Loberg, Fredrik. 2012. *Håkan Juholt, utmanaren: Vad var det som hände?* (Stockholm: ETC förlag)
Lull, James, and Stephen Hinerman. 1997. 'The Search for Scandal', in *Media Scandals. Morality and Desire in the Popular Culture Marketplace*, ed. by James Lull and Stephen Hinerman (Oxford: Polity Press)
Lundell, Patrik. 2010. 'Nykterhetsfrågans mediala förutsättningar och karaktär', in *1800-talets mediesystem*, ed. by Jonas Harvard and Patrik Lundell, Mediehistoriskt arkiv, 16 (Stockholm: Royal Library)
Lundgren, Maja. 2007. *Myggor och tigrar* (Stockholm: Bonniers)
Lövgren, Karin (ed.). 2002. *Perspektiv på intervjuer: Genus, generation och kulturmöten* (Stockholm: SAMDOK/Nordiska museet)
Marcus, George E. 1995. 'Ethnography in/of the World System: The Emergence of Multi-Sited Ethnography', *Annual Review of Anthropology*, 24:95–116
Martín-Barbero, Jesús. 1993. *Communication, Culture and Hegemony: From the Media to Mediations* (London: Sage)
Massumi, Brian. 2002. *Parables for the Virtual: Movement, Affect, Sensation* (Durham, NC, Duke University Press)
Mattisson, Ramona. 2011. 'Kulturmaffians myggor och tigrar: En litteratursociologisk studie av litteraturkritik och härskartekniker i en tidningsdebatt', unpublished Master's thesis in Library and Information Science, 2011:25 (Borås: Swedish School of Library and Information Science)
Melin-Higgins, Margareta. 2004. 'Coping with Journalism: Gendered Newsroom Culture', in *Gender and Newsroom Cultures: Identities at Work*, ed. by Marjan De Bruin and Karen Ross, Hampton Press Communication Series: Women, Culture and Mass Communication (Cresskill, NJ: Hampton)
Midtbø, Tor. 2007. *Skandaler i norsk politikk* (Oslo: Universitetsforlaget)
Miller, Daniel. 2008. *The Comfort of Things* (Malden, MA: Polity Press)
— 2011a. *Stuff* (Cambridge: Polity Press)
— 2011b. *Tales from Facebook* (Cambridge: Polity Press)
Morley, David. 2007. *Media, Modernity and Technology: The Geography of the New* (New York: Routledge)
Mulvey, Laura. 1975. 'Visual Pleasure and Narrative Cinema', *Screen*, 16(3):6–18
Möller, Tommy, and Margit Silberstein. 2013. *En marsch mot avgrunden: Socialdemokratins svarta år* (Stockholm: Bonniers)
Nilsson, Bo. 1999. *Maskulinitet: Representation, ideologi och retorik* (Umeå: Boréa)

Noppari, Elina et al. 2014. 'Critical but Co-operative: Netizens Evaluating Journalists in Social Media', *Observatorio Journal*, 4:1–16

Nord, Lars. 2001. *Statsråden och dreven: Rainer-affären 1983 och Freivalds-affären 2000*, report no. 1:2001 (Stockholm: Stiftelsen Institutet för Mediestudier)

Nord, Lars et al. 2012. 'Pundits and Political Scandals: A Study of Political Commentators in Norway and Sweden', in *Scandalous! The Mediated Construction of Political Scandals in Four Nordic Countries*, ed. by Sigurd Allern and Ester Pollack (Gothenburg: NORDICOM), pp. 87–102

Nygren, Gunnar. 2008. *Yrke på glid: Om journalistrollens de-professionalisering* (Stockholm: Sim(o))

Nygren, Gunnar et al. 2005. *Bloggtider* (Stockholm: Sellin & Partner)

Orbach, Susie. 2001. *Towards Emotional Literacy* (London: Virago)

Petersson, Olof. 1994. 'Journalistene som klass, journalismen som ideologi', in *Media og samfunnsstyring*, ed. by Terje Steen Edvardsen (Bergen: Fagbokforlaget)

Petersson, Olof et al. 2006. *Mediernas valmakt*, SNS Democracy Policy Council report 2006 (Stockholm: SNS förlag)

Petley, Julian (ed.). 2013. *Media and Public Shaming: Drawing the Boundaries of Disclosure* (London: Tauris, in association with the Reuters Institute for the Study of Journalism, University of Oxford)

Pihlblad, Anders. 2010. *Drevet går: Om mediernas hetsjakt* (Stockholm: Natur & Kultur)

Pitt-Rivers, Julian. 2011. 'The Place of Grace in Anthropology', *HAU: Journal of Ethnographic Theory*, 1(1):423–50

Pollack, Ester. 2009. 'Extra Extra: Hon sågas – hon avgår', in *Skandalens markedsplass: Politikk, moral og mediedrev*, ed. by Sigurd Allern and Ester Pollack (Bergen: Fagbokforlaget)

Putnam, Robert D. 1995. 'Bowling Alone: America's Declining Social Capital', *Journal of Democracy*, 6(1):65–78

— 2000. *Bowling Alone: The Collapse and Revival of American Community* (New York: Simon & Schuster)

Reisberg, Daniel, and Friderike Heuer. 2004. 'Memory for Emotional Events', in *Memory and Emotion*, ed. by Daniel Reisberg and Paula Hertel (Oxford and New York: Oxford University Press), pp. 3–41

Richards, Barry. 2009. 'Explosive Humiliation and News Media', in *Emotion: New Psychosocial Perspectives*, ed. by Shelley Sclater Day et al. (New York: Palgrave Macmillan), pp. 59–71

— 2012. 'News and the Emotional Public Sphere', in *The Routledge Companion to News and Journalism*, ed. by Stuart Allan (London and New York: Routledge)

Richards, Barry, and Gavin Rees. 2011. 'The Management of Emotion in British Journalism', *Media, Culture & Society*, 33(6):851–67

Ricœur, Paul. 1988. *Från text till handling: En antologi om hermeneutik*, trans. by. Margareta Fatton, ed. by Peter Kemp and Bengt Kristensson (Stockholm: Brutus Östlings Bokförlag Symposion)

Ronson, Jon. 2015. *So You've Been Publicly Shamed* (London: Picador)
Rosenberg, Göran. 2000. *Tankar om journalistik* (Stockholm: Prisma)
Rothstein, Bo. 2007. 'Anti-Corruption: A Big Bang Theory', QoG Working Paper Series 2007:3 (Gothenburg: Quality of Government, University of Gothenburg)
— 2013. 'Corruption and Social Trust: Why the Fish Rots from the Head Down', *Social Research*, 80(4):1009–32
Rowbottom, Jacob. 2013. 'To Punish, Inform, and Criticise: The Goals of Naming and Shaming', in *Media and Public Shaming: Drawing the Boundaries of Disclosure*, ed. by Julian Petley (London: Tauris, in Association with the Reuters Institute for the Study of Journalism, University of Oxford), pp. 1–18
Sabato, Larry J. 1993. *Feeding Frenzy: How Attack Journalism Has Transformed American Politics* (New York: Free Press)
Sartre, Jean-Paul. 1956. *Being and Nothingness: An Essay of Phenomenological Ontology*, trans. Hazel E. Barnes (New York: Philosophical Library). First published in French in 1943 as *L'Être et le néant*
— 2002. *Sketch for a Theory of the Emotions*, trans. Philip Mairet (Abingdon: Routledge Classics). First published in French in 1938 as *Esquisse d'une théorie des émotions*
Scanlon, Larry. 2007. *Narrative, Authority, and Power: The Medieval Exemplum and the Chaucerian Tradition* (Cambridge: Cambridge University Press)
Schutz, Alfred. 1970. *On Phenomenology and Social Relations* (Chicago: University of Chicago Press)
— 1973. *The Structures of the Life-World*, vol. 1, ed. by Thomas Luckmann (Evanston, IL: Northwestern University Press)
— 1989. *The Structures of the Life-World*, vol. 2, ed. by Thomas Luckmann (Evanston, IL: Northwestern University Press)
Scott, Marvin B., and Stanford M. Lyman. 1968. 'Accounts', *American Sociological Review*, 33(1):46–62
Silverstone, Roger. 2007. *Media and Morality: On the Rise of the Mediapolis* (Cambridge: Polity Press)
Stephens, Mitchell. 2007. *A History of News*, 3rd edn (New York: Oxford University Press)
Suhonen, Daniel. 2014. *Partiledaren som klev in i kylan: Berättelsen om Juholts fall och den nya politiken* (Stockholm: Leopard)
Tangyin, Kajornpat. 2008. 'Reading Levinas on Ethical Responsibility', in *Responsibility and Commitment. Eighteen Essays in Honor of Gerhold K. Becker*, ed. by Tze-wan Kwan (Waldkirch: Edition Gorz)
Thompson, John B. 2005. 'The New Visibility', *Theory, Culture & Society*, 22(6):31–51
— 2008. *Political Scandal: Power and Visibility in the Media Age* (Cambridge: Polity Press)
Thurén, Torsten. 2005. *Källkritik*, 2nd edn (Stockholm: Liber)

Todal Jenssen, Anders. 2014. 'Medierte politiske skandaler: Sårbare politikere – usårbare partier?', *Norsk medietidskrift*, 21(2):100–18
Tunstall, Jeremy. 1971. *Journalists at Work: Specialist Correspondents, their News Organizations, News Sources, and Competitor-Colleagues* (London: Constable)
Uhnoo, Sara, and Hans Ekbrand. 2017. 'Flashback för kriminologer', in *Kriminologiska metoder och internet*, ed. by Agneta Mallén (Lund: Liber)
Ulver, Sofia Sneistrup. 2008. *Status Spotting: A Consumer Cultural Exploration into Ordinary Status Consumption of 'Home' and Home Aesthetics*, Lund Studies in Economics and Management, 102 (Lund: Lund Business Press)
van Heerde-Hudson, Jennifer, and Orlanda Ward. 2014. 'The 2009 British MPs' Expenses Scandal: Origins, Evolution and Consequences', in *The Political Costs of the 2009 British MPs' Expenses Scandal*, ed. by Jennifer van Heerde-Hudson (London: Palgrave Macmillan)
Vermeule, Blakey. 2006. 'Gossip and Literary Narrative', *Philosophy and Literature*, 30(1):102–17
Vogel, Joachim. `. 'Welfare Production Models and Income Structure: A Comparative and Longitudinal Perspective, the European Union and Sweden 1963–1998', in Statistics Sweden (SCB), *Levnadsförhållanden, report no. 100: Välfärd och ofärd på 90-talet* ('Living Conditions, report no. 100: Good Times and Hard Times in Sweden during the 1990s'), pp. 43–79
Vogel, Joachim, and Göran Råbäck. 2003. 'Materiell ojämlikhet i tids- och internationellt perspektiv', in Statistics Sweden (SCB), *Levnadsförhållanden, report no. 100: Välfärd och ofärd på 90-talet* ('Living Conditions, report no. 100: Good Times and Hard Times in Sweden during the 1990s'), pp. 81–101
Wachenfeldt, Ireen von. 2007. *Den Goda, den Onda i media*, in cooperation with Svante T. Stenebakk (Örebro: Bokverkstan)
Wendt, Maria, and Maud Eduards. 2010. 'Fienden mitt ibland oss: Kön och nation i pressbevakningen av Feministiskt initiativ', in Maria Jansson et al., *Den nationella väven: Feministiska analyser* (Lund: Studentlitteratur)
White, Melissa Autumn. 2007. 'Critical Compulsions: On the Affective Turn', *Topia, Canadian Journal of Cultural Studies*, 19:181–8
Wien, Charlotte, and Christian Elmelund-Præstekær. 2007. *Om mediestormens magt: Om mediestorme på ældreområdet og deres inflydelse på ældrepolitikken* (Odense: Syddansk Universitetsforlag)
— 2009. 'An Anatomy of Media Hypes: Developing a Model for the Dynamics and Structure of Intense Media Coverage of Single Issues', *European Journal of Communication*, 24:183–201
Wiik, Jenny, and Ulrika Andersson. 2016. 'Managing the Newsroom: Perceptions of Influence and Control among Swedish Newspaper Professionals', *Journal of Applied Journalism & Media Studies*, 5(3):465–84

Wigorts Yngvesson, Susanne. 2006. '*Den moraliska journalisten: En analys av yrkesetik, ideal och dygder*' ('The Moral Journalist: An Analysis of Professional Ethics, Ideals and Virtues'), unpublished doctoral dissertation, Uppsala Studies in Social Ethics, 32 (Uppsala: Uppsala University)
— 2008. *Drabbad av journalistik: Moral och värderingar bakom rubrikerna*, PMJ (Visby: eddy.se)
Wilkinson, Richard G., and Kate Pickett. 2010. *The Spirit Level: Why Equality Is Better for Everyone* (London: Penguin)
Williams, Kipling D. 2001. *Ostracism: The Power of Silence* (New York: The Guilford Press)
Willim, Robert. 2010. 'När nätet växer: Om algoritmiska och irreguljära metoder', *Nätverket: Etnologisk tidskrift*, 17:34–8
Wirth, Werner, and Holger Schramm. 2005. *Media and Emotions*. Special Issue of *Communication Research Trends*, 24(3)
Wolfsfeld, Gadi, and Tamir Schaefer. 2006. 'Competing Actors and the Construction of Political News: The Contest over Waves in Israel', *Political Communication*, 23:333–54
Wästerfors, David. 2005. 'Skandalresponser', in *Fiffel-Sverige: Sociologiska perspektiv på skandaler och fusk*, ed. by Glenn Sjöstrand (Malmö: Liber)
— 2008. 'Skandalen och publiken', in *Medier, brott och den aktiva publiken*, ed. by Malin Åkerström (Malmö: Bokbox)
Ziel, Paul. 2005. 'Eighteenth Century Public Humiliation Penalties in Twenty-First Century America: The "Shameful" Return of "Scarlet Letter" Punishments in U.S. v. Gementera', *Brigham Young University Journal of Public Law*, 19(2):499–522
van Zoonen, Liesbet. 1994. *Feminist Media Studies* (London: Sage)
Åhlén, Bengt et al. 1986. *Ord mot ordningen: Farliga skrifter, bokbål och kättarprocesser i svensk censurhistoria* (Stockholm: Ordfront)

Index

accounts
 the term as used by Scott and Lyman 144
affective turn 9, 10, 11, 132
affects, the concept 8
Aftonbladet 30, 43, 93, 95, 112, 113, 117, 142, 158, 171, 172, 175
Ahmed, Sarah 10
Allern, Sigurd 6, 7, 22, 27, 42, 58, 71, 139, 150, 151, 177
Alvesson, Mats 126
Anderson, Benedict 56, 57
Andersson, Ulrika 143
asocial responselessness 37, 39, 49
Asplund, Johan 37, 46, 168

ballads
 vehicles for scandal dissemination 82, 85
 see also songs
Baron, Naomi S. 88
Beckett, Charlie 162
Berger, Peter L. 14
Berggren, Henrik 17, 18, 20, 21
bias, among media actors 152, 159, 163, 176
Bild-Zeitung 2
Bird, Elizabeth 7, 15, 78, 79, 82, 100, 105
Bjerke, Paul 12, 46, 58, 60, 62
blog(s) 23, 91, 93, 95, 111, 112, 123, 128, 151
 bloggers 91, 93, 95, 108, 123
Bourdieu, Pierre 147
Boydstun, Amber E. 7
Brewer, John 84, 92, 98
Broady, Donald 147

Bromander, Tobias 27, 177
bruit public 82
Brurås, Svein 12, 42, 46
Burke, Kenneth 145
Böll, Heinrich 1, 2
 Lost Honour of Katharina Blum, The 1

Calvino, Italo 165
Carey, James W. 14, 54, 55, 56, 57
Carlsson, Anita 60
Carlsson, Ingemar 85
censorship 85
chronique scandaleuse 81, 84
Clough, Patricia Ticineto 9, 11
coffee-houses 82, 85
Coleman, Stephen 180
commonness 54
communication 3, 5, 7, 8, 13, 14, 15, 25, 26, 37, 38, 54, 55, 75, 76, 77, 78, 82, 86, 88, 101, 102, 106, 123, 124, 125, 128, 167
communion 54
community 54, 55, 66, 79, 100, 115, 125, 154, 165
 see also imagined community
Computer Mediated Communication (CMC) 88
consequence neutrality 133, 134
Corner, John 71, 72
corruption 16, 17, 18, 19, 20, 21, 100, 173
cultural intimacy 103

Dagens Nyheter 22, 29, 63, 113, 137, 153, 170, 171

Darnton, Robert 7, 25, 26, 81–5, 91, 92, 98, 99, 166
Poetry and the Police 26
Daun, Åke 21
Dayan, Daniel 7, 8, 57
dehumanisation 41
Dégh, Linda 124, 127, 130
Deuze, Mark 6, 149, 162, 163, 167
digital town squares 87, 88, 101
disgrace 21, 50, 104
see also falling from grace
Djerf-Pierre, Monika 7, 149, 150
Dresner, Eli 88
du Barry, Marie Jean, la comtesse 98
Duckert, Fanny 12

echo archives 166
Eduards, Maud 60, 174
egalitarian attitudes 18, 20, 21
see also equality
Ehn, Billy 10, 23, 24, 179
Ekbrand, Hans 26
Ekecrantz, Jan 147
Ekot (formal term *Dagens Eko*) 31, 94, 113, 133, 137, 141, 153
Ekström, Mats 7, 171
Elmelund-Præstekær, Christian 7
emotional literacy 160
emotions, the concept 8–12
Engman, Jonas 50
Enlightenment 18, 81, 86
equality 18
see also egalitarian attitudes
Esaiasson, Peter 17
l'esprit publique 83
ethics 42, 88, 99, 127
ethnography 109, 110
see also multisited ethnography
everyday life 1, 3, 8, 10, 12, 13, 24, 31, 34, 35, 38, 48, 57, 61, 67, 72, 73, 74, 76, 89, 144, 165, 166
everyday talk 25, 78, 79, 81, 87, 88, 89, 99
excommunication 39, 55, 108
exemplum 104
Expressen 30, 43, 66, 94, 99, 113, 123, 146, 147, 148, 152, 157, 158, 161, 162, 174, 175

face-to-face communication 5, 37, 78, 88
fake news 128
falling from grace 104
see also disgrace
feelings, the concept 8–12
fellowship-of-the-hounded letters 68, 69
Fladmoe, Audun 6, 7, 63
Flashback Forum 26, 87, 114, 115
Flashback 23, 27, 91, 92, 93, 94, 95, 103, 114, 115, 121–5, 127, 181
folklore 85, 124, 127, 128, 129
folkloristic elements 5, 107
Frank, Russell 127, 128
French Revolution 84
Frykman, Jonas 9–13, 18, 73, 109
Fägerborg, Eva 179

Gans, Herbert J. 79
gaze, the concept 50, 51, 52
Girard, René 145
Gluckman, Max 79–81, 100
Goffman, Erving 38, 41, 44, 45, 59–70, 168
gossip, the concept 22, 25, 77–81, 84, 93, 101, 166
gossipmongers 81
Gregg, Melissa 11
Guerini, Marco 128
Guillou, Jan 58, 59, 62, 97, 146, 147

Hammarlin, Mia-Marie 4, 16, 25, 27, 77, 91, 152, 181
Hartley, Jannie Møller 60, 151, 152
Hartley, John 25, 105, 106, 166
Harvard, Jonas 86, 87, 101, 102
Heidegger, Martin 13, 73, 74
Herring, Susan C. 88
Herzfeld, Michael 104
Heuer, Friderike 180
Hinerman, Stephen 7, 53, 54
Holmberg, Claes-Göran 82–5
home, the concept 72–5
honour 42, 52, 55, 58, 61, 104, 149
hounding 4, 15, 23, 29, 42, 59, 62, 63, 69, 97, 136–9, 153–9, 164, 170
humiliation 2, 54, 58, 109

Index

hunt, as metaphor 5, 22–3, 33, 41, 43, 55, 56, 63, 93, 116, 139, 148, 149, 153, 154, 157, 163, 164, 171, 173
Häger, Björn 25

imagined community 57, 103
  see also community
impartiality 133, 135, 163
intermedial connections 101, 125

Jansen, Stef 10, 11
Jantelagen 21
Jarlbrink, Johan 135, 150
Jarlbro, Gunilla 4, 16, 27, 152, 170
Jenssen, Todal Anders 6, 7, 63
Johansson, Bengt 7, 12, 171
journalism 2, 6, 25, 60, 62, 63, 69, 82–5, 88, 99, 105, 106, 121–68
journalistic institution 147
Jönsson, Lars-Eric 4, 25, 50, 91, 152, 181

Kafka, Franz 36
Kapferer, Jean-Noël 94
Karlsen, Kim Edgar 12
Katz, Elihu 7, 8, 57
Katz, Jack 9
Kitta, Andrea 128, 129
Klintberg, Bengt af 124, 125
Kumlin, Staffan 17

Lagerkvist, Amanda 13, 73, 130
Lehrer, Jonah 107–9
Levinas, Emmanuel 155–158
LeVine, Robert A. 12
libellers 150
  libellous writing 85, 92
libertines, historical 83, 84
lifeworld 4, 12, 38, 73, 166
limit-situations 73
loneliness 2, 31, 35, 40, 42, 59, 70, 71, 75
Luckmann, Thomas 14
Lull, James 7, 53, 54
Lundell, Patrik 86, 87, 101, 102
Lyman, Stanford M. 144–7, 154–6
Löfgren, Orvar 10, 11, 18, 23, 24

magical behaviour 45, 46
Marcus, George E. 23
Martín-Barbero, Jesús 82, 100
Massumi, Brian 11
mauvais discours 83
mauvais propos 26, 83
media circuit 5, 21
media event 55–7
media scandal, the concept 21–3, 27, 28, 100, 131, 136, 168,
media system, the concept 85–9, 101–5
mediated orality 77, 167
mediedrev 22
  drev 136, 153
melodrama 82, 99
Midtbø, Tor 7
Miller, Daniel 72, 74, 109, 180
mobile phones 73–5, 108, 113, 116, 123, 162
Moderate Party 29, 33, 69, 90, 96, 138, 171, 175
moral conduct (and its opposite) 27, 28, 41, 53–6, 71, 79, 80, 84, 93, 100, 104, 105, 122, 127, 129, 139, 147, 155–64
Morley, David 8
MPs' Expenses Scandal, UK 16, 21
multisited ethnography 23, 24

naming and shaming 71, 115
narrative contagion 126, 127
news books 82, 83
news legends, the concept 123–8
newslore 125
newsmonger 80, 82
newsroom/s 25, 81, 82, 88–91, 95, 96, 101, 113, 117, 127, 133, 139–43, 148, 151–8, 162, 163, 166
Nilsson, Bo 180
Noppari, Elina 122
Nord, Lars 62, 78, 81, 105,
norms 15, 27, 55, 56, 85, 100, 104, 124, 129, 145, 149, 158, 178
nouvellistes à la main 84
nouvellistes de bouche 81, 88
Nygren, Gunnar 95, 143

objectivity, the concept 132–5, 160–3
O'Malley Halley, Jean 9

On the Media (podcast) 109
oral communication 5, 25, 26, 77–83, 85, 86, 88–93, 98–102, 105, 124, 127, 128, 166, 167
Orbach, Susie 160
ostracism 39, 40, 44, 49, 104
Other, the 39, 46, 51, 156

Petley, Julian 70, 71, 117
Pickett, Kate 18
poems
   as vehicles of scandal reporting 26, 81, 85
political scandal 7, 16, 22, 23, 27, 28, 69, 78, 83–5, 92, 99, 105, 131, 137–42, 150, 158, 168
Pollack, Ester 6, 22, 27, 42, 58, 62, 139, 150, 151, 175–7
popular culture 105, 106, 129, 166
postulated legend 130
Povrzanović Frykman, Maja 9, 10, 73
Press Ombudsman 139
public opinion 7, 55, 57, 83, 100,
public service 30, 65, 94, 113, 116, 133, 153
public shaming 107–9, 115, 165, 168, 178

Rees, Gavin 132–5, 160, 161
Reisberg, Daniel 180
reputation 55, 68, 84, 98, 116
   reputation management 168
Richards, Barry 54, 132–5, 160, 161
Ricoeur, Paul 88
rituals 55–7
Ronson, Jon 107–9
   So You've Been Publicly Shamed 107
Rosenberg, Göran 5, 153, 157, 164
Rothstein, Bo 19, 20
routines 16, 21, 24, 31, 48, 72, 131
Rowbottom, Jacob 71, 116
rumour, the concept 77, 79–89
rumourmonger 82
Råbäck, Göran 18

Sabato, Larry 7
Sacco, Justine 108

Sartre, Jean-Paul 10, 45, 46, 50, 51, 52, 74
   Being and Nothingness 50
   Esquisse d'une théorie des emotions 45
satire 85, 92, 100
scandal fatigue 17
scandalmonger 82
Scanlon, Larry 104
scapegoat 40, 49, 104, 145, 168
   scapegoating 145
Schadenfreude 104
Schutz, Alfred 12, 13, 34–9, 72, 73
   'social, natural attitude, the' 13, 73
Scott, Marvin B. 144–7, 154–6
Seigworth, Gregory 11
Senior, Jennifer 108
sentiment 9
shame, the concept 48–59
   see also public shaming
Silverstone, Roger 161
Sköldberg, Kaj 126
slander 22, 79, 80
social capital 18–20
Social Democrats 31, 69, 74, 131, 132, 136, 141, 169
social media 13, 70, 78, 87, 88, 95, 107, 114, 117, 122, 126, 127, 129
'social, natural attitude, the'
   see Schutz
songs
   as vehicles of scandal dissemination 26, 81, 84
   see also ballads
source-critical elements in scandal reporting 30, 62, 121, 123, 126, 127, 167, 177, 180
source criticism 121, 126, 133, 170
Stephens, Mitchell 82, 86–88, 104
stigma 41, 44, 45, 48, 67, 70
   stigmatisation 42, 45, 104
Stockholm 31, 65, 96, 141, 169, 170, 171, 173
Stockholms Sqwallerbytta 84
Strapparava, Carlo 128
Ström Melin, Annika 154
suicide 42, 46
Svenska Dagbladet 30, 90, 113, 137, 170

Index

tabloids 2, 28, 30, 61, 84, 91, 93–96, 102, 105, 112, 113, 115, 116, 142, 146, 148, 157, 169, 171–175
talk-text hybrids 126, 129, 167
Tangyin, Kajornpat 156
technology 14, 70, 74, 75, 86, 87, 89, 109, 148, 162
Thompson, John B. 6, 7, 27, 71, 76–78, 81, 105
  Political Scandal: Power and Visibility in the Media Age 77
Thurén, Torsten 126, 180
Trägårdh, Lars 17, 18, 20, 21
Tunstall, Jeremy 151
Turner, Victor 100
Twitter 27, 87, 107, 108, 114
Tønne, Tore 42

Uhnoo, Sara 26
Ulver, Sofia 180
urban legend 124–8
  see also news legends

values 24, 45, 55, 57, 60, 87, 100, 135, 145, 151, 154, 155

van Heerde-Hudson, Jennifer 16
Vermeule, Blakey 84
visibility
  of scandal protagonists 35, 39, 70, 71, 76
Vogel, Joachim 18

Ward, Orlanda 16
Wendt, Maria 60, 174
White, Melissa Autumn 11
Wien, Charlotte 7
Wigorts Yngvesson, Susanne 155, 157, 164
Wiik, Jenny 143
Wilkes, John 84
Wilkinson, Richard G. 18
Williams, Kipling D. 40, 49, 59
Willim, Robert 23
Wästerfors, David 7, 63, 102, 104

Ziel, Paul 108

Åhlén, Bengt 85

EU authorised representative for GPSR:
Easy Access System Europe, Mustamäe tee 50,
10621 Tallinn, Estonia
gpsr.requests@easproject.com

www.ingramcontent.com/pod-product-compliance
Ingram Content Group UK Ltd.
Pitfield, Milton Keynes, MK11 3LW, UK
UKHW021127160426
5217IPUK00046B/65